SOLITARY COURAGE

Mona Winberg and the Triumph Over Disability

J. Patrick Boyer & Mona Winberg

Blue Butterfly Books

THINK FREE, BE FREE

Blue Butterfly Book Publishing Inc.
2583 Lakeshore Boulevard West, Toronto, Ontario, Canada M8V 1G3
Tel 416-255-3930   Fax 416-252-8291   www.bluebutterflybooks.ca

Complete ordering information for Blue Butterfly titles can be found at:
www.bluebutterflybooks.ca

First edition, soft cover: 2010

LIBRARY AND ARCHIVES CANADA CATALOGUING IN PUBLICATIONS

Boyer, J. Patrick
Solitary courage : Mona Winberg and the triumph over disability /
J. Patrick Boyer & Mona Winberg.

ISBN 978-0-9781600-5-0

1. Winberg, Mona, 1932-. 2. Cerebral palsied--Canada--
Biography. 3. People with disabilities--Canada--Biography.
4. Journalists--Canada--Biography. I. Winberg, Mona, 1932-2009 II. Title.

RC388.B69 2010   362.196'8360092   C2010-905841-0

Cover design by Heidi Hopper /
Interior design and typeset by Evolution Ltd.
Printed in Canada by Transcontinental-Métrolitho
Text paper contains 100 percent post-consumer recycled fibre.

Mixed Sources
Product group from well-managed forests,
controlled sources and recycled wood or fiber
www.fsc.org Cert no. SW-COC-000952
© 1996 Forest Stewardship Council
FSC

How wrong can a doc be?

EW SUN COLUMNIST

child, Mona Winberg was declared a "human table" and her mother was told by the doctor nd her away and forget about her. She didn't. er daughter is now an accomplished profes- al writer.

"Mother, this child will never walk and she'll never talk. She'll be nothing but a human vegetable. The best thing that you can do is put her in an institution and forget you ever had her."

So spoke a leading Toronto pediatrician more than 40 years ago. The child whom he was calling a "human vegetable" was myself and it was my mother who heard his devastating words.

After a minute or so, she drew herself up to all of her 4 feet, 10 inches and said:

"Doctor, I suggest that you try doing that to one of your children." And she stalked out of his office.

I did not walk till I was four and did not talk till I was six — my family claims I have been making up for it ever since! I have cerebral palsy, a condition caused by an injury to the brain before, during or after birth.

Encouraged to be independent

No two cases of cerebral palsy (CP) are alike.

In my case, it has left me with little hand co-ordination (I type with one finger), slow, halting speech and a hearing impairment for which I wear an unusual hearing aid.

One of the main causes of cerebral palsy is deprivation of oxygen to the brain. Brain hemorrhages sometimes suffered by premature babies can be another cause. Lead poisoning and trauma caused by child abuse are others. Some causes, however, are still unknown.

Though there are no Canadian statistics, estimates have been made that cerebral palsy occurs in 1.5 to 3 cases in each 1,000 births. An interesting fact to keep in mind is that up to 60% of CP births could be *prevented* under optimal conditions.

My childhood recollections are of a warm, close family where the conversation ranged from politics to whether we should keep a stray cat my sister had found.

In our home lived my mother, grandmother, two brothers and a sister — all older than myself. My father died when I was a child.

Throughout this time, my mother constantly urged me to be independent so that I would not be a "burden" to anyone when she died.

My schooling included a special public school, some classes at Central Commerce (some of whose teachers I still keep in contact with) and an extension course in journalism at the University of Toronto. I then spent some time at Corbrook Sheltered Workshop, where I did the payroll of the disabled workers.

MONA WINBERG

Disabled Today

My mother died several years ago. A brother and my sister have died in recent years. Without the love, support and encouragement of my family and friends, I would never have managed.

I am also a grateful recipient of the excellent services provided by the Victorian Order of Nurses and Coordinated Services to Jewish Elderly (they serve adults of all ages).

This new column will bring you short, topical items of news as well as express opinions on subjects of interest to both able-bodied and disabled readers.

You'll learn about the joys versus the difficulties for the disabled living alone (independent living); sexuality — with an explanation and definition that may surprise you; and marriage and parenting when one or both partners are disabled.

We'll also get involved in political issues. We'll question whether the Ontario government's so-called WIN (Work Incentive) Program for disabled people actually *discourages* them from finding jobs and becoming financially independent.

And we'll shoot down some myths. Example: People with disabilities are *not* always happier in each other's company!

Personalities introduced

You will also meet such remarkable people as:

Gary Zemlak, of Don Mills, owner of a business, TYKRIS, that provides "Technical Services for the Differently Abled."

Sara Binns, a resident of Scarboro's Providence Villa, whom I can only describe as "84, going on sweet 16!"

Eric Wilson, of Vancouver, who has written the first Canadian novel to feature disabled children as central characters.

This column is an opportunity to show that disabled people are neither larger-than-life heroes nor pathetic objects of pity. We possess strengths and weaknesses, hopes and fears, capabilities and limitations.

Just like everyone else.

When Mona Winberg, against all odds, became a major newspaper columnist for Toronto's Sunday Sun *in 1986, she led off with the story of her mother's solitary courage. Mona told readers how Sarah Winberg in the 1930s vowed not to place her child, as a doctor recommended, in an institution because she would "never walk and never talk," but to instead raise her to be self-reliant and as independent as possible.*

DEDICATION

To Vim Kochhar ...

*whose ideas and actions
show that in Canada
dreams can become realities*

Mona's Resolute Courage

Mona Winberg stood out for me as one of the brightest stars. She personified what an individual's resolute courage could accomplish, both for herself and as "role model" to those overcoming disabilities. I was inspired by the freshness with which she articulated issues, and how she relentlessly advocated improvements for people too long left at the margins of Canada's comfort-seeking mainstream.

I first met Mona in 1987. I was chairing the new Parliamentary Committee on the Status of Disabled Persons, Canada's first on-going parliamentary committee whose only business was the status of citizens with disabilities. Our all-party committee of MPs was grappling in a major way with the disabilities agenda, and making far-reaching recommendations that were being implemented.

When I organized a conference on new opportunities for disabled people, Mona, who was leading the charge in her "Disabled Today" newspaper column, was a natural to invite. The Saturday event was an emotion-filled day and Mona was an exceptional panelist. Her message reached a wide audience through television broadcast of the proceedings and follow-up newspaper reports. She topped off that media coverage with one of her own columns, reporting on the event to her *Sunday Sun* readers. She never missed a beat.

I often raised Mona's concerns, or mentioned her ideas, in our parliamentary proceedings. That became part of parliament's *Hansard*

MONA WINBERG

Disabled Today

Parents of disabled air beefs

"We are expected to be therapists, psychologists, teachers and medical experts," panelist Mark Jones said in describing the many demands made upon parents of disabled children.

He was on the first panel, "Youngsters: Special Needs and Existing Services," at a recent public forum sponsored by Patrick Boyer, Conservative MP for Etobicoke-Lakeshore. Boyer is also chairman of the parliamentary committee on the disabled and handicapped. His forum was entitled, "Finding the Mainstream — New Opportunities for Disabled People." It drew almost 200 people from Metro and outlying areas.

Jones's comments were expanded upon by other angry parents in the audience who vividly described their frustrations in coping with professionals who made them feel that they had no rights or knowledge regarding their children. There was emphatic agreement that parents should question the decisions made by professionals if they felt uneasy about them.

**PATRICK BOYER
MP sponsors forum**

The next panel dealt with transportation issues. We were reminded that accessible transportation, like accessible housing, was far more economical if it was constructed that way at the beginning instead of having to be renovated later.

Alan Hewson, manager of Wheel Trans, Metro's transportation system for disabled people, warned that with an increasing aging population the demands upon Wheel Trans are going to grow.

Before lunch, we were treated to a live theatre production of "Given Half A Chance," a gentle spoof of attitude barriers faced by disabled people in finding employment. It was performed by Rolling Thunder, an integrated theatre group. If any of our readers are interested in booking this enjoyable

Mona reviews "Finding the Mainstream" conference

record. She wrote about initiatives our parliamentary committee was taking on behalf of citizens with mental and physical disabilities. That became part of the published *Toronto Sun* record. Our interaction of personal commitment, which first drew us together, continues now, though in a decidedly different time and context, with this book.

Mona Winberg and I had been working on this book for some time. She was encouraged that something more might be done to revivify the sagging agenda on disability issues, in the enduring form of a book. The *Toronto Sun*, which long believed a collection of her best columns needed to be published, provided consolidated copies of them all and a green light to proceed. The people at the Sun knew as much as Mona how urgent it was to tell Canadians what should be happening.

Yet *Solitary Courage* is more than a collection of yellowed newspaper columns. It is the story of human willpower. It tells of Mona's defiant mother,

Sarah Winberg, who called herself "the last angry woman" because she felt alone standing up against injustices to disabled people like her daughter. Sarah's maternal love combined with her outrage to challenge conventional wisdom in 1930s and 1940s Canada about severely disabled people, the "retards," as they commonly were called. She saved her infant daughter Mona, "the human vegetable," from the common fate of being institutionalized and forgotten. Instead, the two women together determined to make the best of life and pioneered the revolutionary concept and practice of "independent living."

This book reveals the solitary nature of their courage, and documents their sense of humour, irony, and outrage over injustice. It focuses on issues that Mona, the talented writer and articulate advocate, defined in print and battled to win in the arenas of national, provincial and municipal public affairs. It is about the soaring hope of achieving real progress, and the incessant heartbreak of personal setbacks and governmental cutbacks.

Ultimately, Mona Winberg's life personifies Eleanor Roosevelt's insight that, "without action to uphold human rights close to home, we shall look in vain for progress in the larger world." Mona took action where she could, making a real difference in the lives of countless thousands in the larger community we inhabit.

From 1986 to 1999, Mona was the only disabled columnist regularly published in North America. After she stopped writing her column, issues she'd kept before political leaders and the general public for a dozen years seemed to slip lower on the radar screen, if not right off.

This book is both my account of Mona's personal story and Mona's public message as offered in her own words through her *Toronto Sun* columns. Together, I hope they kindle renewed resolve to overcome disability challenges and convey her optimistic realism to a new generation of policy-makers and citizens.

Mona Winberg went courageously where there was no path. *Solitary Courage* now marks the trail she blazed for us to follow.

J. Patrick Boyer, Q.C.
Toronto, Ontario

A stream of inspiration

My friend Mona Winberg was easy to love. I saw her in action. I enjoyed being with her on different occasions. I corresponded with her. She was a stream of inspiration. By her deeds and action she enriched the quality of life of thousands.

Mona was a woman who made a difference. She did this in a number of ways. First, by the way she lived her life, Mona gave leadership to others by her own example. Second, through her years of work in community organizations that serve the interests and meet the needs of people with disabilities – from Colbrook Sheltered Workshop to "Participation House" in Markham to Bellwoods Park House in Toronto, from the Cerebral Palsy Association to the United Way of Greater Toronto – she helped us see the power of teamwork and partnership in bringing about necessary change. Third, and perhaps most remarkably, Mona made a difference by becoming an informed, outspoken, and articulate advocate for disabled persons through the hundreds of columns she wrote over a dozen years for *The Toronto Sun*.

Mona Winberg could only accomplish what she did, however, and could only create awareness of the injustices she sought to overcome for herself and others, by confronting discrimination. There's no other way around it. Whether a citizen confronts racial discrimination or discrimination based on distinguishing attributes like their religion, gender, ethnic origin, or mental or physical disability, he or she

requires courage to overcome the obstacles and to rise above the fears and dangers.

Patrick Boyer could not have chosen a better title, in my view, to express this reality in the case of Mona – *"Solitary Courage"* is what it takes, and that is what Mona Winberg demonstrated in "her quest for equality."

I have known Patrick for more than 40 years, first meeting him as a university student working on Parliament Hill when I was an MP. Years later, when he himself was a Member of Parliament, he chaired the Parliamentary Committee on Equality Rights, and became first chair of the new Parliamentary Committee on the Status of Disabled Persons. That work is legendary, and is one of the reasons Douglas Fisher, a former NDP MP who became dean of the Parliamentary Press Gallery, ranked Patrick Boyer in his *Toronto Sun* column as "one of the top ten MPs" in the period following the Second World War.

A number of Mona's columns tracked the public work and parliamentary advocacy of Patrick's quest for justice for Canadians with disabilities. It always seemed to me the two were well matched – Mona Winberg the media advocate and Patrick Boyer her counterpart in Parliament. After Mona retired from writing her columns and now that Patrick is no longer in the House of Commons, this book tells her story and shares with new readers "the best of Mona Winberg." It is a natural extension of their mutual commitment to create justice by eliminating injustice.

From my own vantage point over the years – whether in the practice of law, as a Member of Parliament, as Minister of Labour in the Government of Canada, as Lieutenant-Governor of Ontario, as Chancellor of University of Guelph, and many other perspectives too numerous to mention – I have seen how individuals can make a difference. A single voice can become a chorus. The tide of conventional wisdom can be turned. When equality becomes a foundation for our society, diversity and difference are more than "celebrated" – they become the basis of justice for all. Yet it takes courage. This inspiring book not only tells us why. In a very personal way, it also shows us how.

Hon. Lincoln M. Alexander, P.C., C.C.
Hamilton, Ontario

CONTENTS

Part I

MONA WINBERG'S STORY

Part II

MONA IN HER OWN WORDS

Part III

THE LESSONS OF MONA WINBERG

PART I

Mona Winberg's Story

Forget you ever had her

It is hard to imagine how a person, so severely afflicted by cerebral palsy that a doctor said she'd never walk or talk, could become a leading advocate for disabled people, an award-winning newspaper columnist, and a member of the Order of Canada.

Mona Winberg's parents met and married at Toronto in 1920, mother Sarah from New York and father Max from Poland. After their August 22 wedding, the couple moved into a rented house at 605 Euclid Avenue in central Toronto and produced a succession of children, Wolfe, Barbara, Sydney and, on January 27, 1932, their fourth and last, Mona.

The Winberg family had been leading a fairly typical life until the 1929 stock market crash triggered an economic depression that began hollowing out everything it touched. As the "Dirty Thirties" dragged on, the Winbergs found it harder to make ends meet. Even when the economy had been buoyant, Max, working mostly in the city's produce trade, had difficulty keeping a substantial job for long. Now he really struggled to support his family, sometimes traveling great distances in search of paying work. To make matters worse, he was in poor health.

Several months after Mona was born, her mother saw her latest baby was not developing as rapidly as the others had. Even before Mona reached her first birthday, Sarah started making the rounds of doctors, asking why her daughter wasn't sitting up like most infants. Finally, after too many evasive diagnoses, she took her baby to Dr. Aaron Brown, Toronto's leading paediatrician. His diagnosis was cerebral palsy, a condition caused by damage to the brain around the time of birth.

No two cases of cerebral palsy were alike. A doctor such as Aaron Brown in Toronto in the early 1930s, recognizing the symptoms of cerebral palsy in an infant, would know the disease was not synonymous with mental deficiency. Yet he would also know that more than half the children afflicted would, to some extent, not develop mentally, a significant fact when trying to make his overall evaluation of the child's mental deficiency.

Once injured, the brain does not heal without scar tissue. Areas are destroyed and cannot function. While not fatal, this long-term disease of the central nervous system is crippling, with degrees of physical

1920: Mona's parents, Sarah Rose Keller from New York and Max Winberg from Poland, met in Toronto and married on August 22.

disability, impairment, and mental slowness varying from one victim to the next.

Because there was no cure for this condition, any path into the future would be hard. It would require great patience and extensive treatment – muscle training in mild cases, braces to support weak muscles and prevent muscle shortening in more severe ones. Speech therapy would be essential. In the case of Sarah Winberg's baby, the doctor's diagnosis was *severe* cerebral palsy, a type called athetosis, to be precise, which occurs in about ten percent of cases.

The attributes of athetoid cerebral palsy in particular are damage to the cerebellum or basal ganglia, the areas of the brain responsible for processing the signals that enable smooth, coordinated movements as well as maintaining body posture. Damage to these areas may cause a child to develop involuntary, purposeless movements, especially in the face, arms, and trunk. These involuntary movements often interfere with speaking, feeding, reaching, grasping, and other skills requiring coordinated movements. For example, involuntary grimacing and tongue thrusting may lead to swallowing problems, drooling, and slurred speech. The movements often increase during periods of emotional stress and disappear during sleep. In addition, children with athetoid cerebral palsy often have low muscle tone and problems maintaining posture for sitting and walking, one of the symptoms already manifesting in the Winberg baby.

Dr. Brown foresaw a bleak future for Mona and exasperating hardships for her mother. He counselled Sarah from across his desk:

"Mother, this child will never walk and she'll never talk. She'll be nothing but a human vegetable. The best thing that you can do is put her in an institution and forget you ever had her."

Sarah Winberg sat in stunned silence. Slowly, she rose from her chair, drew herself up to her full height of four feet, ten inches, and retorted:

"Doctor, I suggest that you try doing that to one of your own children."

Then she gathered her baby and stomped out.

The Winberg's three-generation household in 1929: Sarah's mother Fanny Keller (left) holds her granddaughter Barbara, while Max (right) has son Syd on his knee. In photo as in life, Sarah is the family's centre. First-born son Wolfe stands at left rear.

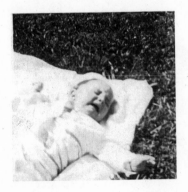

The summer of '32: Baby Mona Fleur Winberg, second daughter and fourth child of Sarah and Max, has now arrived and sunbathes on the grass.

The stars at night

So began a stubborn transformation to turn the "human vegetable" into a most exotic flower.

Mona's middle name was, indeed, "Fleur," which had been inspired when pregnant Sarah was reading a romantic novel with a heroine of this name, one that appealed to her since earlier encountering it in John Galsworthy's *Forsythe Saga*. Sarah lived in the imagination through books, and now she and her daughter Mona Fleur would live out the plight of their romantic tale by re-writing the plot.

Mother and daughter resolved to defy all odds with the support of mechanical braces, tough love, and a spunky spirit that over the years miraculously only grew stronger in the face of adversity.

Sarah Winberg rented a tricycle to strengthen the muscles in Mona's legs. "Every day, someone would accompany me as I peddled down the street." By age four, the child "who will never walk" started to walk. When she reached age six, the child who would "never talk" also began to talk, and talk, and talk. She certainly had lots to say.

1933: Mona is held by her mother on the back steps at 605 Euclid Avenue together with Barbara, Syd, and Wolfe. Sarah Winberg has just learned Mona has severe cerebral palsy.

Walking and talking were hardly the only challenges a child like Mona with severe cerebral palsy had to overcome, however. Hearing was difficult, control of hands very limited, and use of thumbs non-existent.

All the same, Mona was able to hear. She listened intently as her mother, judging her daughter now old enough to get an explanation for her questions about why she was different from her brothers and sister, told her the story of

Dr. Brown. She explained clearly and directly how her love for Mona had driven her to keep her out of an institution.

"Why didn't you believe what the doctor said?"

"I could see it in your eyes. You were alert to what was going on."

The three other Winberg children had fun playing with their little sister. Wolfe (ten years older than Mona), Sydney (seven and a-half years older) and Barbara (five and a-half years older) found it easy and natural to be with her, kids fooling around together in the back yard or playing childhood games along the street.

Mona felt the safety of family. Her grandmother, Fanny Keller, had moved in to live with her daughter's family after her husband died, and helped Sarah with the children. For their part, Mona's brothers and sister learned, with their mother's guidance, the delicate balance between being supportive of Mona but not becoming overly protective of her.

As well, Sarah resolved to continue the family's summer practice, begun in the 1920s, of going to a rented cottage for a few weeks. It had been easier before the Depression, when money could be saved and Sarah's father contributed toward the family cottage they'd take turns using. Now, with little money and no financial help from her deceased father, Sarah struggled desperately every year to scrape together funds for their escape to a lakeside cottage. She enjoyed it, and had fun, as did her children. She thought it might be good

1934, early summer: Two-year-old Mona is supported by brother Wolfe and flanked by Syd and Barbara.

1934, late summer: Mona and her mother.

for Max's health; certainly it was beneficial for Mona's. "My mother looked upon this as a form of therapy for me. It was much easier to walk on sand than cement. Also, she encouraged me to do things with my hands, like building sand castles and just playing in the sand."

1935: Wolfe and Mona, the family's two curly-heads, with Barbara, Syd, and mother Sarah. The children called their mother "Bubie."

1935: Three-year-old Mona, with leg weights above ankles to strengthen muscles, supported by maternal grandmother Fanny Keller and Barbara.

Playing at ground level, whether in the Erie's shoreline sand or the backyard at Euclid Avenue, kept Mona dirty enough for her chummy brother Syd to nickname her "Schmutz," German for dirt. The moniker others in the family had for her was "Topsy," deriving somehow from an amalgamation of her curly head of hair, her seemingly large head by age two, and her pigtails. Nobody even remembered her middle name "Fleur," except the woman who saw her daughter as a flower even before she was born.

Despite Mona's severe disability of speech, mobility, and hearing, her mother encouraged her to be as independent as possible. Sarah seized every opportunity to give Mona the experience of doing things for herself, and started sending her each summer to a camp for disabled kids at Lake Erie where she could play with other children in a new setting.

Once one of Sarah's friends asked, "Aren't you sorry you had Mona? How can she ever accomplish anything in her life?"

"She's able to look up at the stars at night and see their beauty," answered Mona's mother evenly. "Isn't that better than if she had never existed?"

— 3 —
Schooling and death

In 1938, when she was six, Mona began attending Wellesley Orthopaedic School, predecessor of Toronto's Sunnyview School for pupils with disabilities. Wellesley Orthopaedic was located on the same grounds as another elementary school for non-disabled children near the intersection of Wellesley Avenue and Bay Street, a dozen blocks east of the Winberg home.

1936: Mona in her mother's strong arms, at Van Wagner's Beach, Lake Erie, near Hamilton.

1937: The Winberg's happy annual summer holiday at Van Wagner's Beach, with Sarah holding five-year-old Mona, surrounded by Syd, Wolfe and Barbara.

Years later Mona would say one of her greatest regrets was that she never had the opportunity to attend a regular elementary school. "If I had," she explained, "I might have been spared the nightmare of being harassed on the street by a group of little boys, all laughing and calling me names. Children don't torment anyone they are familiar with and understand."

But segregated schooling for children with disabilities was the order of the day, and at least Mona was in school and supported by a loving family, not vegetating in an institution as Dr. Brown had proposed.

In much the same way the doctor had seen the sensibility of segregating a severely disabled child in an institution, the school authorities thought they were doing the right thing with their two-stream approach. Teachers were not trained to work with disabled children. The school buildings were not accessible, and lacked proper facilities for those with special needs. Segregation was the best way to cope, moreover, because in truth they believed it was impossible to teach these children, openly called "retards."

Part of their education included field trips by streetcar to city parks, which were little more than supervised excursions to fill time. In place of a teacher to instruct them, a clown might be engaged for a day of "fun," adults not understanding how universally youngsters fear and dislike clowns. In the case of the Wellesley Orthopaedic students, they felt apprehensive and perplexed by the featured presence of this human caricature.

In 1939, while Mona was in her second year at her elementary school, world events again touched the Winbergs. Just as the 1929 onset of the Great Depression had made its dire impacts felt on the family, Nazi Germany and Imperial Japan began their conquests of other countries that triggered worldwide warfare, which in the process began resuscitating Canada's economy through wartime production. The Winbergs still managed to rent a summer place, keeping alive one of their best and most important family traditions.

As the months passed, Max Winberg, who had been feeling more poorly than ever, left for British Columbia to see if its climate would make a difference. His health may have improved, but for sure his income did. Before long he had successfully landed war work on the west coast.

With money Max sent from B.C., frugal Sarah did her best to make ends meet for her family. Now in effect a single parent, she ran the household and looked after her four children. Her hope was that, if

1938 and another holiday: Barbara and Syd at water's edge, with vindicated mother Sarah supporting six-year-old Mona, who has just begun to talk.

Mona was three when her mother rented a tricycle to strengthen her leg muscles so she could walk. In this 1940 photo she is eight and able to walk, but still loves her trike, and her frail legs need exercise.

1940: Mona, now eight years old, is attending Wellesley Orthopaedic School in Toronto, segregated from schools for "normal" children. The pupils with disabilities get an outing to High Park, where a clown holds a dissatisfied Mona.

1940: The Winberg family again gathers in summer, with a friend named Evelyn in the picture (right) and Max Winberg, too, about to leave for British Columbia in hopes of better health and paying work. Syd, supine photographer, is represented only by his foot. Wolfe is working.

Max's health improved, she and the rest of the Winberg family would move to British Columbia to join him.

By early June 1944, with Max still in the west but not enjoying much improvement in his health, he went into hospital in Prince George for an operation. A few days later on June 15, 1944 Sarah was handed a telegram at the door of their Euclid Avenue home, send by the hospital to his "next of kin." Max had died in the operating room during a botched surgery.

With Max Winberg's death, the family's plans for a new life in British Columbia died as well. Sarah went to work in the business office of the YMHA to earn money. Of these times, Mona recalled that she "was left quite a bit on my own."

Mona was not, however, entirely abandoned. A stray kitten her sister Barbara had brought home became, after supper table debate, a new member of the family and a steady companion for Mona.

Certainly more important than a kitten was the caring companionship of Mona's grandmother Fanny Keller, who had taken up residence under the Euclid Avenue roof following the death in 1935

Mona (Topsy) 1940

Mona by age eight, as seen at left, was called "Topsy" by the Winbergs. Her brother Syd had another nickname for her, "Schmutz," German for dirt, because Mona was often dirty from playing on the ground.

2 sweet girls (mine)

At right, 14-year old Barbara holds her sister Mona, now eight, the "two sweet girls" of Sarah whose writing appears on these photographs.

of her husband Benjamin. "She lived with us and took care of the house while my mother went out to work." Fanny had originally come from Czechoslovakia, and Mona considered her "a visionary." Clearly the old woman and her granddaughter had time for important conversations. "She liked the fact we didn't call her 'Grandma,' but 'Ma.'"

In June 1934 Sarah had begun keeping a diary she would maintain for the next dozen years. She poured out her internal reflections on pressing themes in her life, including her marriage; their struggle with grinding poverty in the 1930s; her horror over the rise of Hitler, the war, and the world's abandonment of Jews; the cruelties, hypocrisies, and occasional beauty of life, as she saw it. She expressed contempt for most any type of social welfare agency, reflecting the lack of practical support she received for Mona. She frequently expressed her fears and aspirations for her children, especially Mona. Sarah's displayed her profound love of reading throughout the diary. She mentioned almost no one by name except immediate family and favourite authors. Reading was both solace and enlightenment for Sarah, with poverty no barrier because the public library offered free books. Scarce money was a bigger hurdle to Sarah's oft-diarized desire to take the children to "the country" in the summer. She recorded how these trips particularly benefited Mona.

By war's end in 1945, there were some good prospects. Mona's brother Syd started medical school. When that did not pan out, there was another good prospect: he started up a sod farm and landscaping business, borrowing money from others in the family to launch the enterprise. When that did not pan out either, he left. Mona was the only one at home as her brother threw a few items into a suitcase, but she could not stop him. Winberg men could be as determined as Winberg women. After Syd left for the west, nobody heard from him. For years Mona felt guilty about not having been able to talk her brother out of leaving home in shame.

On his own, Syd lived in El Passo, Texas, for a number of years until U.S. Immigration gave him the boot. He then made his way to Vancouver and was living at the Burrard Street YMCA when he met and married Emily MacLeod, a nurse working a few blocks away at St. Paul's Hospital.

4

Determined to integrate education

When Mona finished grade eight at the segregated Wellesley Orthopaedic School, she craved more education. But the school's principal believed she would not be able to cope in a regular high school. He refused, "for her own good," to help her.

Fortunately for Mona, her embattled mother, who referred to herself sometimes as "the last angry woman," still had fight left in her.

Sarah Winberg, in the vanguard of "independent living" for those like her daughter with disabilities, of necessity now extended the logic of this concept. She became a strong champion of school "integration" as well, as a corollary or necessary condition of living independently. Sarah's radical idea was that schools should have a place for *all* the neighbourhood's children – including those with disabilities.

When Mona was denied the right to attend Harbord Collegiate, a high school across the road from the Winberg's home and the obvious place for her to enrol, Sarah was disappointed but not daunted. She began canvassing all schools in the larger neighbourhood, going further and further afield, each time being denied the right for her daughter to attend. It was not easy being rebuffed, but although Sarah felt utterly alone, she would not give up. For "integration" to work, she had to find a school that would admit a girl with special needs.

The more Sarah pushed for a place in school for Mona, the more initial politeness faded into hostility and rudeness. What part of "No!" did Mrs. Winberg not understand? It was not simply an uncooperative individual whom Sarah confronted, but society's deeply entrenched attitude that children with disabilities probably belonged at home, and certainly *not* in a classroom with "normal" children.

While still not abandoning hope, Sarah and Mona attempted some alternatives, anything to keep her education going. For awhile there was special tutoring at the home of one of Mona's friends, who was a good student and also disabled, but this small scale private arrangement ended when the other girl, uninterested in any more schooling, gave up and the teacher stopped coming.

Dissatisfied with stopgap measures, Sarah Winberg kept looking. One evening, in conversation with a friend who was a guidance teacher at Central Commerce High School, a new idea emerged. The two women hatched a plan. When they proposed it to the principal of Central Commerce, this "most understanding and welcoming gentleman" was open to their idea of Mona monitoring classes at his school as a part-time student. His only proviso was that she not be listed officially as a student at the school.

So, under the radar, Mona Winberg would become pretty much the first child in Canada to pioneer her mother's idea of "integration." What this plan lacked in official status it made up for in value to Mona's education, and in planting a seed that would eventually radicalize the Canadian school system by making it inclusive of students with disabilities.

In 1947, when Mona started at Central Commerce, the sense that has since developed for integrating disabled students into the educational system simply did not exist – apart, that is, from its dominant place in plucky Sarah Winberg's value system. "I believe I was the first severely disabled person to be at the school," recalled Mona.

1945: Now beginning her teen years, city-girl Mona delights in mixing with ducks at the Winberg's rented summer cottage. Her legs are stronger and she is getting around better on her own.

Central Commerce was close enough that Mona could walk the distance of about half an hour. She found it "a huge help" that her mother assisted her to get dressed in time. When classes began that September it was not easy for Mona at first, mainly because she was shy. Her only prior schooling had taken place in a segregated special needs school, an experience that left her unaccustomed to interacting with "normal" students.

The school's guidance teacher, Sarah's friend, initially smoothed the way by explaining Mona's condition of cerebral palsy to students. In that initial year, Mona felt grateful to the students, teachers, and principal of Central Commerce for appreciating their struggling new student's great love of reading and writing, and encouraging it. "I really appreciated that they didn't treat me any differently than the other students.

If Mona needed extra help in the classroom, she got it. Because she had difficulty hearing, she was assigned a front row seat to hear the teacher better. Because of her inability to manage a locker, due to lack of control and strength in her hands, she was given an alternate place to leave her coat.

Because of the cerebral palsy, Mona had very limited use of her arms and hands, no use at all of her thumbs. Among other things, this meant she could not do up buttons, and could not write. She experienced difficulty hearing. Even though she had, against all odds, learned to talk, Mona's condition caused her to lose control of her muscles, which left her speech sometimes very difficult to understand. The problem of muscle control also made her body go into contortions at unpredictable times.

At this stage of her affliction Mona could still hold her head erect better than would be the case in later life, but even so, she never ate at school because she was very self-conscious. She did not have to be at school all day anyway, because she took just two subjects, English literature and English composition, the only ones she could get help with and was interested in.

With insufficient control over her fingers to hold a pen for writing, the only way Mona could write was by typewriter. Learning this, with her mother's expert help and "you can do it, you must do it" discipline, was the big breakthrough for Mona, one of the single-most important developments in her life after being kept out of an institution.

The typewriter was mechanical in those days, not the later electric typewriter, or the even easier light-touch computer keyboards of today. "So when I made a mistake it was not that easy to remedy, but we managed." At whatever stage Mona found herself in the rapid evolution of typing technology throughout her life, she herself remained constant: she could only use one finger to do the job.

Despite the apparently helpful atmosphere at Central Commerce, it was nevertheless a measure of the social distance experienced by this little pioneer in school integration that Mona didn't really feel she "belonged" until the fourth or fifth year. "I then made some friends. That may not sound like much, but I was and I still am very shy. It's

1951: Mona is near the end of her teens and the pigtails are long gone, but the need to hold onto a support remains. Seen here at her favourite Camp Woodeden, near London, Mona sang while riding these swings.

just that as you get older you learn to hide it better. I still am very shy." She smiled sheepishly and looked down while saying this.

Whatever the challenges, Mona remained "always thankful that I was given this opportunity to further my education." Countless thousands of others would be grateful too, in time, for her mother's initial insistence on integration, and Mona's own resolute dedication, in turn, to further advance the cause of integrated schooling as an advocate and influential columnist in her adult life.

Mona completed her high school education at Central Commerce in 1952 when she was 20. Her abiding love for writing led her to next enrol in journalism studies, through evening extension courses from the University of Toronto, which she continued to 1954.

Taking the evening extension courses, she acquired a boyfriend of sorts, which was so rare as to be close to a unique experience. She was open with him in describing the barriers created by her disabilities.

"This disease I have is not socially acceptable."

"It is better than having syphilis," he joked.

When the journalism courses came to an end, so did the brief connection with her fellow student.

Mona's journey through the offerings of Wellesley Orthopaedic public school, Central Commerce high school, and the University of Toronto had now brought her to the end of formal education. Yet for the rest of her life she would continue to avidly read books and follow events closely, remaining curious about everything and unquenchably thirsty for self-education.

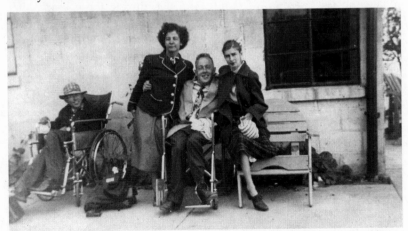

1954: Now in her twenties, Mona's stylishness is evident in her longer hair and tailored outfit. At Blue Mountain Camp near Collingwood, she stands with Russell Avery at left, while Jim Peterson has his arms around both Mona and Mary Lister.

5

Independent together

"I had a very remarkable mother," said Mona. "Looking back, I'd say she was a hundred years ahead of her time. She let me do things other parents were horrified to let their children do. Most of all, she was realistic."

Independent living was a concept both women worked to make real in their own lives and for others. "My mother believed people should be taught to help themselves long before 'empowerment' became the catch word of the 1990s." In Mona's growing-up years, "my mother instilled in me a desire to be as independent as I could, and to not become a burden to anyone."

Sarah Winberg certainly had the courage to raise Mona to be as independent as possible. It can be described many ways, but what she really gave her daughter was, as Mona put it, "a legacy of inner strength" that would enable Sarah's equally gutsy daughter to cope alone.

As ardent a practitioner and advocate for "independent living" as Mona herself would become in later decades, she was essentially applying and extending what she'd learned from her visionary mother a generation before. "My mother encouraged me," said Mona, "to work toward independent living on my own at a time when independent living was not believed possible for disabled people."

"Independent" became a special concept in this context, because it did not mean "apart from family" so much as it was about "self-reliance in the presence of family." In fact, during these years, after Sarah Winberg's father died and her widowed mother moved in with her family, the Winberg household had a second example of being with one's family even as one was making her own way.

Had Sarah called her program "self-reliant living" instead of "independent living," there may have been less ambiguity about what her concept really entailed. But rolling the phrase "self-reliant living" off one's tongue would not have been as easy, nor would it likely have caught on as readily, given Canadians' political views of the different implications for "independence" versus "self-reliance."

A loving family presence, with the backup of available community services such as an integrated school or accessible public transit, would be the optimal conditions for a child to develop this self-reliant or independent quality. While the larger community had not yet adapted, the family side of this equation was strong. Mona's recollections of her childhood were of "a warm, close family" where discussions ranged from world politics to whether the Winbergs should keep a stray cat Mona's sister, Barbara, had brought home. "Without the love, support, and encouragement of my family and friends, I would never have managed," she would one day tell readers in her very first *Sunday Sun* column.

Sarah let Mona deal with things herself, going as far as she could on her own even though it took more time and even when it required self-restraint from a mother whose first instinct would be to help out, or rescue, her daughter. Of course a "hands-off policy" was never a hard and fast rule because practical considerations of daily living intervened. But Sarah, Mona, and the rest of the Winberg family pursued "freedom" over "dependency" any way they could, understanding the risks of both. Perversely, the risk of freedom entailed a double standard. If an able-bodied child had an accident, he would likely be blamed for carelessness, but if a disabled child had an accident, it was her mother who would likely be blamed for not being protective enough.

During these growing-up years, Mona had a girlfriend with cerebral palsy, and their mothers became friends, too.

"How can you allow Mona to do so much? If she were my daughter, I'd worry about her dreadfully."

"I do worry about her," replied Sarah Winberg quietly. "But what good will that do? When I am gone, she will have to manage on her own."

– 6 –

Making payroll

By 1954, 22 year-old Mona had landed her first job as payroll clerk for Toronto's Corbrook Sheltered Workshop.

Corbrook, located at 581 Tretheway Drive in north Toronto, was a fresh experiment, just beginning. It had been established by a group of volunteers only four years earlier as a therapeutic and recreational centre, operating initially a half-day per week, for adults with cerebral palsy. It was no surprise to Sarah that this is where her daughter landed her first job. She had been one of the volunteers who'd supported the idea, knowing in advance that as part of Mona's independent living, something innovative like a supervised workplace would be needed once her schooling was over. "Another idea of my mother," said Mona in recalling these early days of community development, "was occupational therapy."

In its first four years the program expanded and, by the time Mona arrived, individuals with other disabilities were in the program as well. Participants were trained to do piecework of a simple, repetitive nature. The crafts they made were sold to contribute to the program's costs.

During Mona's years at Corbrook, light packaging and assembly contracts were added to enlarge the work opportunities for participants, and the operation became a full-time one, allowing individuals with varying degrees of ability a supportive environment in which to work, earning "incentive" money. Expansion continued as machinery was added to the facility and a variety of additional contract jobs taken on.

Financial administration was a long way from Mona's dream of being a journalist or writing for publication, but she was in the workforce and this was part of independent living. At Corbrook she did both payroll and banking. The former meant seeing how much the workshop's disabled workers earned and paying them. The latter included everything from collecting unused taxi money from the workers to recording other money that came in from workshop contracts and going to the bank to deposit it.

She went into the workshop four days a week, but also did some of the work at home, in order to manage. What she enjoyed most was going to the bank and putting through those transactions, because it meant interacting with others and accomplishing something. Although it took her a long time to do the payroll, that was part of her job too, and she liked it.

As a teenager, when monitoring the English Comp and English Lit classes at Central Commerce, Mona had become enthralled with the act of writing. The writer in her first found expression when attending the Easter Seal Society's summer camp and editing its newspaper, something she was still able to do for a few weeks each summer since she continued to attend adult camp. But mostly her all-consuming work at Corbrook drew her away from writing.

As for what she observed about the Corbrook Sheltered Workshop, Mona eventually concluded that such an operation had benefits, but was not a great long-term solution for most individuals working there. "Many people think all they have to do is establish a sheltered workshop and disabled people will be happy there for the rest of their lives. Maybe some are, but most people want change. Can you imagine yourself doing the same work for fifty years?"

In her own case, Mona would work fourteen years at Corbrook. "My mother would help, get me dressed in the morning, put the bus ticket in my mitten, and heaven help me if I dropped it." One winter, having dropped her ticket in the snow, Mona did not want to take off her mitten to retrieve it because she knew she would never be able to fit her mitten back on her hand. So she asked a young girl also waiting for the bus if she could please pick it up. "No!" shouted the girl. The hurt expression that must have formed on Mona's face was enough to bring a young man over.

"Anything I can do to help you?"

"Yes, can you pick up my ticket?" He did. She got her bus ride to work, wearing her mittens.

– 7 –

Touching the world beyond

As Mona entered her thirties, her cerebral palsy complications were making it more difficult to hold up her head. She travelled with her mother to Johns Hopkins Medical Clinic in Baltimore to see what could be done about the deteriorating condition. The tilting head could not be reversed, nor corrected, but simply offset by use of a neck brace.

In the 1960s there were other trips, ones that involved repair and healing in the Winberg family. British Columbia loomed large in the lives of the Winbergs. It was in B.C. where Max Winberg had found work, earned money for his family, and died. British Columbia was also where Syd Winberg had fled shame-faced after his Toronto gardening venture collapsed, taking with it the savings other family members had staked him. Because nobody back east heard from him for ten years, Syd was presumed to have died, too.

In fact he was alive, living with his wife, Emily, and their first two sons, David and Harold, having nightmares about the gap of silence, but believing he couldn't reconnect with the family in Toronto until he was finally successful. There was healing to be done. By 1960 Syd had turned his life and fortune around enough that he could repay the money and restore his honour. So he got in touch with his brother Wolfe.

A tentative, tender reunion ensued. Sarah went west to see her long-lost son and daughter-in-law Emily, and meet her two grandsons Harold and David for the first time.

1961, April: Sarah Winberg, standing with Mona at the open roadside in British Columbia, brought her to be reunited with her brother Syd and his family after a decade-long break.

For that trip, and for several others she made to visit Sydney's family, Sarah left Mona in Toronto on her own. She was resolute about preparing her daughter for "independent living," that inevitable day when she herself would no longer be alive. No doubt devoted Sarah even enjoyed some rare respite as she travelled west alone, freed for a while from the need to be directly attentive to her. Meanwhile, back in Toronto, these experiments tested independent living to its outer edges. "It was very difficult," recalled Mona later, "the first couple times she did this."

But by the spring of 1961 mother and daughter made the trip west together. The journey was a thrilling new adventure for Mona, and generated deep satisfaction for Sarah as she watched her daughter gaze in awe at the Prairies, thrill to the Rocky Mountains and, after a decade of separation, be reunited with her brother Syd with whom she'd had the most fun growing up and about whom she had felt guilty since last seeing him.

"I like this," slurred Mona as she sipped a Kahlua milkshake, enjoying the Mexican liqueur's not very powerful effect as well as its splendid strong coffee flavour. Her nephews, now in their mid-teens, delighted in getting Mona a little tipsy, for her own sake, as they saw it. "The family in Toronto," opined Mona's nephew Harold, "was too stuffy. We had fun, got ourselves happy, and enjoyed a lot of laughing."

One evening Wolfe's wife Norma, who'd come west with them on this trip, asked as the evening got late, "Where's Mona?"

"Out with friends," answered Sydney.

"But it's late!"

"So what?"

Mona was "getting educated," recalled Harold, "gaining her independence." She found real happiness with her family in B.C. Even her psoriasis cleared up, which her nephew attributed to "the carefree, relaxed, western Winberg influence."

Another relaxing place for Mona away from home was summer by a lake, which in some form or other was an annual highlight. Since she'd been a girl, she'd enjoyed summers with her family at rented cottages by Lake Erie, often at Van Wagner's Beach, not too far from Hamilton.

Then her mother began sending Mona to camp, so she could meet and play with new children and develop greater self-confidence. Over a couple of decades, Mona attended three different ones, Lakewood Camp on Lake Erie, Blue Mountain Camp near Collingwood, and Camp Woodeden at Byron near London – three of the five Ontario camps operated by the Society for Crippled Children (since renamed the Easter Seal Society). She found Blue Mountain "a bit cool" because of Georgian Bay's chilly waters, "but when you're young you don't really mind." Lakewood was "warmer because it was further south" on Lake Erie. Her clear favourite was

1955: This year Mona attended Lakewood Camp, run by the Society for Crippled Children on Lake Erie, joining these adult campers preparing for a stage presentation. Mona, whose pigtail is back, stands in centre rear, in a white blouse.

Woodeden, probably even more for its agreeable social temperature than its climate.

Through the late 1950s and early 1960s, well into her thirties, Mona continued going to Woodeden. A camp for adults, separate from the children's camp, it consisted of seven cabins, each holding two counsellors and eight campers who suffered a variety of disabilities. It was situated on a former estate, whose grounds included an exotic Japanese mansion.

"Mona was the most intelligent camper there," recalled Sheila Edgar, "and the one most with the world. She stood alone and walked on her own. Mona was friendly and outgoing. She went from camper to camper, making sure they were having a good day. She had gone to grade 12, and was very bright. She seemed to be intuitive and put me right at ease," added Sheila, who later married

1956: Mona, the pigtail gone for good, returned again to Lakewood Camp, enjoying the quieter company of a camper friend on the sands of Erie's shore.

another counsellor, Harry Edgar. Since it was Mona who had first introduced them, they called her "cupid" thereafter.

Mona seemed less shy, and made good friends. She edited the camp newspaper, which put her in the know about everyone, and which fed the flame of interest in writing first sparked in her English Composition classes at Central Commerce. She talked so much that her fellow campers, knowing nothing about "Schmutz" or "Topsy," gave her the new nickname "Windy."

Mona's Woodeden camp buddies included Dorothy Wilson from Willowdale, a polio victim who worked at North York city hall; Bill O'Neal from Windsor, an intense and fit young man with a rare spinal condition whose sense of humour kept people on their toes and sent Mona under the cover of a towel when he decided to photograph her in the bathtub; and especially, the handsome and friendly Floyd Martelle, who used a walker as he and Mona strolled the grounds together.

Mona loved the standing swing, singing "Shine On, Shine On Harvest Moon" as she moved back and forth on it. She then moved her performances from swing to stage, via the musicals performed by campers in Woodeden's recreation hall. In a 1962 performance of "Oklahoma," Mona not only sang the juicy number "I'm Just a Girl Who Can't Say No," but performed it, recalled Sheila, "with all the mannerisms, moving with good mobility, and in a wild costume." One summer, to Mona's delight and everyone's astonishment, a Woodeden innovation became a testament to determination: the counsellors and campers built a wheelchair-accessible tree house.

Mona enjoyed a friendship with Floyd Martelle at Woodeden Camp. He used a walker, partially in view in the left photo as the pair descends low-rise, long-run steps. Mona, in her mid-20s, is getting around without support at this time because her legs have become quite strong. In the right photo, the two enjoy getting together at a Woodeden reunion in March 1961.

Apart from these adventures and travels, mother and daughter had become largely wedded to their accustomed Toronto routines, which centred on Mona's life at home, her work at Corbrook, and riding TTC buses between the two. This habitual pattern was no longer a challenge to Mona who, beneath the veneer of normalcy resulting from these predictable rounds, had an independent streak as strong as her mother's.

In the 1960s, her heart condition causing Sarah to contemplate with anxiety what lay ahead, she began giving fervent instructions to her three oldest children that, upon her death, Mona must *not* be put in "an institution." She bolstered this edict by reminders that "charity begins at home" and that "blood is thicker than water." In counterpoint, Sarah wrote Mona a message on November 30, 1963, exhorting: "Carry on my dear, keep face with yourself, dear. It takes guts but you can have it, rather than be pitied." On August 22, 1968, a few months before her death and still seeking to stiffen Mona's courage, Sarah urged her daughter: "Stand up to life. Even if and when it deals you blows, *stand up to it*."

Camp Woodeden was Mona's favourite (ahead of Lakewood and Blue Mountain) and she kept returning for the adult camp well into her thirties. **Upper left:** Mona is with friend Dorothy Wilson, and Bill O'Neal of Windsor, a man with a rare spinal condition and a good sense of humor. It was O'Neal who took this photo, **upper right**, of Mona in her bath, with two counsellors, getting her hair washed. **Bottom left:** Mona poses with her Willowdale friend Dorothy Wilson (seated), a polio victim, who worked at North York city hall. **Bottom right:** For Camp Woodeden's 'Last Night Dress-Up Party,' Mona and Dorothy Wilson gathered by the fireplace "with a couple of long-forgotten dates."

8

Igniting the human spark

In late 1968 Sarah Winberg, despite health difficulties with her heart, had turned 70. When her 16-year old granddaughter Marla, daughter of Wolfe and Norma, died from leukemia on December 7, she was devastated. In her despair over Marla's death, Sarah's problem heart surrendered to a sudden, fatal seizure.

The day her mother had prepared Mona for had suddenly arrived. She was 36-years old.

Sarah Winberg had been a far-seeing woman, Mona understood, because of how she had openly talked with her daughter about death. "Mona, when I die I don't want you to fall to pieces," she had directed her. "There will be some friends who won't know that I have died, so I'll want you to phone them and tell them." Mona found doing exactly that, when the time came, gave her "a real sense of usefulness."

On the emotional level, as well as in countless practical ways, the absence of her mother created a void at the very centre of Mona's being. It would take years of getting used to.

As hard as these initial days were for Mona, she was not as traumatized as she might otherwise have been because mother and daughter, knowing this day would show up, had prepared for its arrival by their unrelenting emphasis on "independent living." Although Mona found it difficult the first times her mother left her alone – an adult with disabilities, she would later write, "I have always been grateful for that experience because, when my mother died suddenly some years later of a heart attack, it was not as shattering as it might have been."

Yet that was looking back. True, by being deliberately left alone for periods of time, by being sent away to summer camps, and by inculcating both a practical frame of mind and a deeply thought-out philosophy about independent living, Mona had been conditioned to cope. However, in the immediate moment, while she may not have been traumatized by her mother's death, not much else was happening. Just sitting at home in the aftermath, as she was doing, with nothing else changed or changing, was a state of stagnation. Independent living required the existence of necessary conditions, certainly, but their existence is never enough if the human spark itself is missing.

It required her older sister Barbara, as Mona remembered, "to throw down the gauntlet after mother died." Part of what shocked Mona about the insistent challenge her sister issued was sheer surprise. The sisters were five and a-half years apart in age. After early years playing together, and posing for photos, they grew apart. Barbara had her separate circle of older girlfriends, not to mention her own feelings about her younger sister, and into adulthood the two women increasingly developed different interests and outlooks. Mona therefore "was surprised that Barbara stepped forward and encouraged me so much." In fact, her elder sister's tone almost sounded like it was their late mother speaking:

"I would like you to try living on your own. Mind you, I don't know if you can do it."

That also shocked Mona: the sudden sharp challenge to prove that, yes, she really could live on her own. Was that real doubt on Barbara's part, or an astute challenge to prod Mona the way their mother might have once done? Like their mother, Barbara had a good supply of tough love to dish out:

"If you have a problem, I'm always here. But remember, Mona, everyone has difficulty and I'm not interested in hearing about your small concerns."

Brothers Wolfe and Sydney took their cue from Barbara, and encouraged their sister to live independently. All four of them knew their mother had wanted her to try.

Syd wrote from Vancouver: "Mona, our mother wrote letters and provided us news of the family regularly. We would like you to take over." His practical suggestion, based on what he had already learned about how disabled people need responsibilities, served everyone's family interests and gave Mona, as she noted, "another interesting job, another responsibility." Never mind that writing letters was not as easy, physically, as it had been for their mother.

The timing of Barbara's straight talk was perfect. "What my sister said taught me to be more self-reliant intellectually and emotionally," Mona herself acknowledged. The verbal challenge snapped Mona to action. It hit her with the realization that living independently meant she did not turn to somebody else, or wait for anybody else to decide what to do. It was up to her. It was now Mona Fleur Winberg who was in charge of her life. The human spark had been ignited.

How to begin? It was one thing to believe conceptually in independent living, but it would sure be of practical help to see how others were doing it. Yet Mona could find no model. "I really didn't know any other disabled person with my degree of disability living on their own." It dawned on her just how much of a pioneer she was really going to have to be, when a disabled friend told her:

"We will be watching you very carefully, Mona. If you can do it, we all can do it."

Unable to learn from the examples of others, she saw that she might potentially provide leadership for others – such as those watching friends – by her own example. In her solitary way, Mona set about to get it right.

Heading into these uncharted waters, there was something else Barbara had said that was valuable guidance, in large measure because her older sister had a fairly dispassionate view of Mona's circumstances. This was possible because the Winberg sisters were not alike. They had grown up with quite different views of the world and their places in it. Larger concerns involving the government which seized Mona left Barbara unfazed. Where one grew irate over public spending scandals, the other shrugged them off as inevitable. Unlike Mona, who was immersed in the work of organizations, Barbara was not, and had no interest in becoming so. Indeed, Barbara believed such activities demanded too much of her sister's time and energy. She told Mona so.

In this evaluation, Barbara was probably not far off the mark. Now completely on her own, Mona quickly became aware of just how much longer it was taking her to do even simple things – a half hour to put on her winter coat. Her mother, perhaps more than either of them realized, had oftentimes given Mona a helping hand, notwithstanding their concerns for accomplishing independence in living.

"I had to get up even earlier in the morning just to do the same few things," sighed Mona. Stealing hours from the night was certainly one way to get more time. Another would be reducing her obligations, especially those keeping Mona from what she really wanted to do with her life, which was writing. Accepting, as Barbara had pointed out, that "I was spreading myself too thin," Mona began taking charge.

9

Mona takes charge

Taking charge meant no longer working at her all-too familiar Corbrook Sheltered Workshop job. "When my mother died, I decided it would be very different, and difficult, for me to keep up my work there."

It also meant moving from the familiar little house on Gilgorm which she and her mother had shared for two decades. Finding an apartment of her own was not easy, though, because people discriminated. "They'd take one look at me and just say the apartment was rented, even though the vacancy sign was still hanging out. I can't blame them. I guess I looked pretty strange."

Winberg persistence, always a reliable factor when making such soul-crushing rounds, eventually paid off. Mona did not stop until she found and moved into an apartment at 65 Ellerslie Avenue, just west of Yonge Street in north Toronto's Willowdale district. Here she would live on her own, only switching twice to other apartments within the same building, for the rest of her life.

Naturally, support and services were needed, as they would be for anybody. Mona got these from her family, community organizations, and social service agencies, among them the Victorian Order of Nurses, homecare helpers, and Coordinated Services to Jewish Elderly which, despite its name, had an elastic concept of elderliness and served adults of all ages, including 36-year-old independent women. Mona booked rides on Wheel-Trans, signed up for the library's Outreach Program for books, and joined the Meals-on-Wheels program.

Mona received weekly visits from the Victorian Order of Nurses, the national organization administered and controlled by nurses in partnership with volunteers to provide care in a patient's own home. One VON nurse, Carol Spain, came regularly for long enough that the two women became close. "I consider Carol a friend as well as a nurse," Mona wrote, adding "the VON helps me live independently in the community."

As for the books, she intended to slake her thirst for continuing education by use of the public library. "I read a lot because I enjoy it," explained Mona who, like her mother, was never without a book close to hand. "It's a way of keeping abreast." That was why, shortly after relocating to her Ellerslie Avenue residence, she had joined the North York library's extension service, which selected and delivered books to shut-in readers. When asked her reading preferences, Mona replied with relish and glee that she liked mysteries, then added with seriousness that she enjoyed historical fiction, and, after a pause, said in a meek and reflective voice that she read books about disabled people.

1970: Mona lived on her own after her mother's death in 1968, supported by VON nurses who made calls to her apartment in Willowdale. Nurse Ruth Sinclair, seen with Mona in her bedroom, became "a friend as well as a nurse." The Victorian Order of Nurses, Wheel-Trans, Meals-on-Wheels, the public library's Outreach Service, and others, helped Mona live independently – her mother's goal from the day she rejected the doctor's advice to "put her in an institution and forget you ever had her."

Did she read for inspiration, or for information?

"A bit of both," she answered, "but I'm not crazy about inspiration. I like inspiration, but only in small doses. I don't care for books that promote people, saying 'Look at me! I've accomplished so much!' I want to learn, and get new ideas."

When the first shipment arrived, it consisted of seven books – all of which Mona had previously read. She phoned in good humour and the library promptly made another delivery. As winter came on, the library's outreach program was a real boon because Mona found it hard to get out and could, instead, curl up with a good mystery.

Beyond taking full advantage of these superb community support services in order to enjoy a full life, Mona also advanced "independent living" by adapting her residence with assistive devices and the latest communications equipment, improving accessibility into and within the apartment, and upgrading its facilities from bathroom to bedroom, kitchen counter to desk top. She had buttons to push and electronic devices standing by to perform tasks.

The money to pay for Mona's assistive devices, in the late 1960s and since, was largely provided by government under health programs and social service benefits, on the basis that she met the criteria and had applied. This period in Canada was unique because governments were able to afford such measures, the programs were fresh, and administrators were keen. Mona was venturing out into independent living on a rising tide, not in the ebbing era of cutbacks and clawbacks that came later.

Community services supported her, and operating systems rendered her apartment hospitable and functional, but Mona Winberg herself was in charge.

– 10 –

A compass of personal freedom

Although Mona lacked the physical freedom enjoyed by most, she had by her mid-thirties managed to carve out a large compass of personal freedom through the attentive love of her cherished family, her determination to be an independent thinker, her practice of "independent living," the employment she had been able to undertake, and her non-stop encounters with new worlds through the universe of books.

It wasn't all a breeze. In order to leave her apartment at 8 a.m., Mona got up at 5 a.m. to give herself time to wash, dress (buttons being "the bane of my existence"), make her bed, have breakfast, and allow for unexpected problems. One occurred shortly after she'd moved into her apartment: her zipper stuck. She asked her superintendent for help, "but wouldn't recommend it as the ideal way to meet your neighbours." The superintendent and his wife had wanted to help, Mona discovered, but were nervous about offering. "After all, it takes guts to offer help when you're not sure of the response."

Her new neighbourhood was not entirely without problems. Little boys lying in wait by Mona's Ellerslie Avenue apartment would jump out to startle, and then tease, her. She grew fearful that if she was badly scared she might slip on the winter ice. She decided to go to the neighbourhood school and talk about physical disabilities. She explained to the students that her thumb wouldn't work because it couldn't press an opposable finger. She had them try getting into their snowsuits not using their thumbs. Then she explained why there were no buttons on her coat, but Velcro. The teasing stopped.

There was obviously an emotional component to independent living. "Living on your own is not for everyone," she observed. "Even some able-bodied people don't like to do it." But Mona was up for it. As her nephew Michael observed, "Mona enjoyed being able to live alone."

At this stage, something deeper even than the major changes of living without her mother, giving up her job, changing her residence, or revamping her emotions was in the works. Mona now felt free to heed her long-denied desire to write. Her love of English classes at Central Commerce, her happiness working on the summer camp newspaper, the $2 she won in 1953 as second prize in an "Imaginative Prose Contest," her stimulating journalism courses from the University of Toronto, even the sweet poem about her mother she wrote for Sarah's birthday in 1957, all pointed her in all pointed her in the direction of self-expression.

At the same time, Mona's understanding of cerebral palsy, combined with her intelligence and friendly nature, suggested to her that her best immediate career opportunity awaited in the one organization dealing with the cluster of cerebral palsy issues and policies, programs and people – the Ontario Federation for Cerebral Palsy.

– 11 –

A player in her own right

There was good reason for her to think this way when hoping to expand her career as a writer. Mona had already joined into activities of the Ontario Federation for Cerebral Palsy while working at the Corbrook Sheltered Workshop, as an active volunteer helping out with the Federation's newsletter. After a while, she'd been given the title "associate editor," a recognition that both pleased and encouraged her toward her dream. Heeding her sister's admonition that she had spread herself too thinly over too many activities, Mona now concentrated on what she could do in the OFCP organization.

Working on the newsletter, Associate Editor Mona Winberg pegged away as a volunteer, increasingly coming into the orbit of others in the cerebral palsy community and at the Federation's offices. All organizations like to tap willing talent and the OFCP was no exception. In 1969, Mona Winberg was elected vice-president of the Ontario Federation.

This advancement of her career was further recognition of her abilities. But it was also a signal that the OFCP wanted someone directly knowledgeable about cerebral palsy near the organization's decision-making summit. Mona, earning respect in the disabled community for her demonstrated ability to live independently, was increasingly being seen as a player in her own right.

Meanwhile, just the year before, a decision had been made to form a national body, the Canadian Cerebral Palsy Association, so as to pool strength with similar cerebral palsy organizations in other provinces and make a bigger impact on national policies. Mona had been invited to join the Canadian Association's founding board in 1968. As a result, she was now directly involved in the operations of both cerebral palsy organizations, a board member of one and vice-president of the other.

One of the first items of business for the new Canadian Association had been establishing a newsletter to link and inform all interested parties. Mona, to no one's surprise and her delight, became its first editor. When she explained the forthcoming publication to her 12-year old nephew, Michael Winberg, the boy proposed *Contact* as a name and that is what the newsletter came to be called.

As editor of *Contact*, Mona felt herself increasingly confident that she was now on the right track. Writing much of the newsletter's contents she found an especially fulfilling task, because instead of haltingly speaking her opinions to her family or small circles of friends, she could address a much wider audience in succinct written form. Moreover, because everybody connected with cerebral palsy was reading *Contact*, Mona Winberg emerged as an authoritative voice of advocacy on behalf of cerebral palsy's victims, and one of the best resources for information for journalists wanting background and governments wanting consultations.

Given what she now saw as her main calling – writing about issues affecting people with disabilities, and evaluating the effectiveness of programs and services for disabled people in general and those with cerebral palsy in particular – Mona would volunteer in the 1970s to write the Canadian Sunshine Club's newsletter, thereby acquiring yet another readership audience. Her views on the news were influencing the perceptions and policies of others. Spreading oneself thin did, at least, extend coverage.

After some eight great years producing *Contact*, however, this perfect outlet for Mona's talents moved beyond her grasp when, in 1976, the Toronto-based Canadian Cerebral Palsy Association, being a national association, finally realized that relocating to Ottawa would enable more frequent and direct interaction with those running Canada's government. Moving to the nation's capital was not, however, an option for Mona. It was very frustrating to her that she'd have to surrender the editorship of *Contact*, but her support network and family were in Toronto, not Ottawa. "Independent living" was always constrained by reality.

– 12 –

The reluctant advocate about cerebral palsy

Forced by circumstances from the editorship of *Contact*, Mona was not dealt as hard a blow as she might have suffered if that had been all she was doing. Her decision, following Barbara's advice to stop doing too many things and to refrain from wearing herself ragged, had translated into a more exclusive focus on cerebral palsy activities. Yet the reality was that in this arena she found many roles to play. So, true to her inherent nature, Mona had gladly taken on a number of them, such as leadership of the organization itself.

In the early 1970s members of the Ontario Federation for Cerebral Palsy still consisted mainly of able-bodied individuals whose families included someone with cerebral palsy. But in 1969, as something of a departure, Mona had been elected vice-president of the OFCP, and, amid some controversy, in 1972 she became the first disabled person elected president of the Ontario Federation.

The controversy was over whether someone with difficulty getting around and having problems speaking could most effectively be the energetic and engaging spokesperson for the Ontario Federation for Cerebral Palsy. There was also the issue of whether the OFCP's president should be a harmony-seeking chief officer or an outspoken advocate for the interests and needs of people with cerebral palsy. "In what was then a very polite society," notes her nephew Sidney Troister, "she made her opinions known, and as everyone in her family knows, Mona always had opinions."

In fact, Mona Winberg had more than "opinions." She had informed beliefs. She had an abiding sense of justice. And now, as president of the OFCP, she had a platform.

The paradox was that Mona became a spokesperson reluctantly. Her hesitation was not for any lack of belief in the cause, but because speaking out was hard, moving around physically was tough, and getting to places on time was exhausting.

Hers were ground-breaking efforts. Those who spoke on disability issues were articulate individuals, highly presentable on television or public platforms, talking *on behalf of* others who actually were living with the disability. It required a radical move to break through this pastiche of proxy representation.

One of the first cracks to occur in this overlay came in 1968 – the year Mona had joined the board of the new Canadian Association for Cerebral Palsy, and a year before she was elected vice-president of the Ontario Federation for Cerebral Palsy – when television producer Elsa Franklin lined up Suzanne Moss, disabled by cerebral palsy, for an interview on the Pierre Berton Show. "Pierre was very good with her in the interview, because he treated her like any other person he would on camera. He did not pussyfoot around. He did not kow-tow to her." For her part, Suzanne Moss, despite badly shaking arms and the formation of saliva around her mouth, overcame her difficulties of speech and performance to give a touching and effective accounting of herself, recalled Franklin. "Still," she added, "most people at the time thought it was a crazy risk to interview someone on television who faced such a challenge speaking."

In Mona's case, shyness made it even harder. As with most people who are self-conscious about their appearance and performance, it took a huge act of daring to overcome her natural reluctance about exposing her disabilities. Ever since she had been a schoolgirl teased by boys who saw her awkward performance as something to berate, Mona's instinct had been to maintain her dignity by restricting her exposure.

Yet as shy and self-conscious as Mona was, she felt more deeply about disability issues. So she summoned her courage and began, as head of the Ontario Federation for Cerebral Palsy, to speak out as someone who lived the reality 24-hours a day.

— 13 —

The thrill that this is really me

Mona thus emerged as one of the first spokespersons for disabled persons who was herself seriously thwarted by disabilities that included, ironically yet magically, speech. She spoke softly, haltingly, in a way that was painful for many to listen to because they felt sympathy for her and wanted to complete what they imagined the sentences eventually would be.

The magic was that, in the sense Marshall McLuhan explained how "the medium is the message," Mona Winberg at once changed the message by her very presence and performance. She was a different medium; not a proxy, but the real deal.

One had to be patient listening to her, and pay close attention to every word spoken. Regardless of what she said, it was a new day for people with disabilities. Unlike the proxy spokespersons, Mona represented what she herself presented. What people saw was what they got.

No longer by others, but by an individual with disabilities herself, would the concerns of the disabled community be expressed. Those who had been on the margins were, thanks to Mona's solitary courage and that of valiant others like Suzanne Moss, now becoming players themselves.

Mona lobbied for Wheel-Trans, and for improvements in accessibility by disabled people to public buildings. She lectured architects about accommodating people with disabilities in their designs for buildings and public spaces. Her increasing contributions as an intelligent and inspiring advocate began to make a difference to Canada and the place of disabled people in it, a contribution even more significant because what she accomplished could only have been done by a disabled person.

Through the 1970s and into the 1980s, as an increasingly sought-after speaker, Mona accepted so many engagements that the Winberg family began to jest that she came home only long enough to change her clothes before she was off again.

As Mona picked up the pace of her advocacy, "she had no fear of talking to important people to advance a cause she held dear," recalled Harry Edgar, her friend since Woodeden Camp days in the early Sixties. On one occasion in the late 1970s, Edgar drove her to address the Preston-Hespler Rotary Club about building a facility for physically disabled people. "Mona spoke eloquently about the need for such a residence," he remembered, "and how to integrate it into the community. She received a standing ovation at the end." Although Rotary Clubs enjoy high success rates with their projects, this one never got off the ground, despite Mona having sent the Cambridge-area Rotarians themselves into orbit for the cause.

Not all of Mona's trips were for work. Several years after that speech to the Rotarians, Mona was again being driven by Harry, this time from Toronto to Stratford to see the Festival's production of "Macbeth," then returning late that night. Mona was the one who had to keep Harry awake at the wheel, as tired as she was herself.

These pleasure trips also found Mona going further afield. She enjoyed travel and several times stayed with friends in St. Petersburg, Florida. Some years later, when sent to Florida by the *Toronto Sun* newspaper to write about travel, restaurants, and accommodation for people with disabilities – a topic of interest for many *Sun* readers because so many Canadians trek to the sunshine state – it was another matter. She found the trip "a different kind of holiday when I knew I was going to have to write about it."

Such "working holidays" would in due course find Mona making over-night stays at Toronto and Montreal hotels to report on them in her *Sun* column. There was always something to write about. One hotel was proud to offer rooms "specially designed for the handicapped" but its then-innovative key, a magnetically coded plastic card that replaced the traditional metal key, was impossible for her to use. Even where so much of value had been created to accommodate citizens with disabilities, none of it counted if it was inaccessible, the big point Mona made with the small example of a door that could not be opened by someone with problem hands.

Then there were working holidays of another sort, such as Mona's trip to England as a delegate representing the Canadian Cerebral Palsy Association for a 1960s international conference on the issues of disabled people.

Whatever the purpose of travel, whether to enjoy a play or advance issues for people with disabilities, Mona took satisfaction every time, even discounting the frustrations and fatigue, because she was living independently – outside an institution and making decisions for herself.

"Every time I walk into my apartment," Mona said, "I can't get over the thrill that this is really me, Mona Winberg, living on my own. I'll keep on going as long as I can and as long as I am needed."

– 14 –

Restless leadership

By 1976, though four years into her presidency of the Ontario Federation for Cerebral Palsy, Mona continued to hold onto her very first volunteer position as associate editor of the Federation's newsletter, *Partici-Paper*. She was reluctant to give up any outlet for her views, especially one that involved writing on her part. It was convenient and efficient for communication from a small organization that the president keep a hand in the publication. Its odd name *Partici-Paper* derived from the "Participation Houses" operated by member groups of the OFCP for residents with cerebral palsy.

In this same year, Mona was elected to the board of the Markham Participation House, one of five such facilities in Ontario, and became chair of its admissions committee. As a gesture to sister Barbara's admonition to not spread herself too thin, and to her own emerging view that one should not stay in the same position too long as routine kills the spark of innovation, Mona relinquished her long-time role as a board member at Bellwoods Park House as she joined the Participation House board.

Mona enjoyed working with Johnny Wayne, renowned as half of the Wayne & Schuster comedy team, in the early development of

Markham's Participation House, for which he raised money. They also shared in the work of the Ontario Federation for Cerebral Palsy, of which he was a board member. "Although we did not become close friends, Johnny and his wife Bea always treated me nicely," said Mona. When she discussed the challenges of her public speaking role, Wayne drew on his experience with audiences to confidently reassure her, "Unless you get nervous before you make a speech you will not do a good job."

The year 1976 was bringing changes for Mona: leaving the board of Bellwoods in Toronto, joining the Participation House board in Markham, and surrendering her editor's role with *Contact* because of the Canadian Cerebral Palsy Association's move to Ottawa. Then, just when she was finishing up her last edition of *Contact*, the editor of the provincial cerebral palsy newsletter *Partici-Paper* died. Mona was then, almost automatically, elevated from associate editor, her very first volunteer job with the OFCP, to fill the vacant editorship of the Federation's newsletter.

To some it seemed only logical that, because Mona Winberg had emerged as the Federation's principal spokesperson, as its president, and now was also editor of its main publication, she might just as well be hired as the organization's information officer, too. She was, and this was a paid position.

Thus despite initial controversy about her role, by 1976 Mona's position had become consolidated as pretty much *the* voice of the Ontario Federation for Cerebral Palsy. For the next decade, her bundled roles would be Mona's main focus and, "depending on good ol' Wheel-Trans," she went to the OFCP offices on Toronto's Lawrence Avenue West two or three times a week to deal with her duties and advance the cause.

Mona's work at the office of the Ontario Federation for Cerebral Palsy involved a lot of reading. As information officer/editor she still turned out the newsletter once a month, telling the membership about anything new in the disability area. In addition, there was a little newspaper that came out three or four times a year, but to produce it Mona needed extra help because her typing was still based on using only one finger "and that finger didn't move very fast."

Writing provided Mona's single best platform for advocacy. Through it she addressed issues from financial concerns to human rights. It was her vehicle to make both government and the general public aware of the needs, achievements, problems, and capabilities of disabled people.

There was more, however, than newsletter advocacy. By now it had dawned on Mona that the doctrine of Spread-Too-Thin was glib nonsense, that everything is connected and all open channels should be filled by who you are, what you believe, and whatever your mission is to accomplish, seamlessly and totally. Thus Mona became personally involved in current issues in more ways, appearing before the Social Assistance Review Committee in its appraisal of financial entitlements and benefits and their impacts on the predicaments of citizens with disabilities, and before both the Toronto Transit Commission and the Metro Toronto Transportation Committee in their deliberations about Wheel-Trans. "I will continue to fight," Mona was quoted in the book *Canadian Legacies*, "for the right of all disabled people to have lives of dignity, privacy, and self-determination."

By 1981 Mona's life had evolved nicely along the trajectory she'd plotted after her mother died – a direction that involved ideas, issues, and self-expression. It was hard to imagine there could be anything more. She was editor of the *Partici-Paper* newspaper of the Ontario Federation for Cerebral Palsy. She was a board member of the Ontario Social Development Council, the North York Advisory Committee on Services to the Disabled, the New Directions Committee, and Participation House in Markham. She found time for B'nai B'rith Women. She was now in her late forties and living in sweet "independence," alone in her own apartment with the support of a range of services from Meals-on-Wheels to a VON nurse, regular bundles of fresh books, and a weekly homemaker to do the heavy cleaning.

Yet five years later, in 1986, although still liking what she was doing at the Ontario Federation for Cerebral Palsy, she "began to get weary of it. You know that old syndrome." Mona Winberg was ready for something new.

How to become a star columnist

Mona had been dismayed for years by the way newspapers treated her and millions of others as if they did not exist. Chronic failure of news organizations to report serious developments about Canadians with disabilities profoundly upset her.

In 1986, when Mona was stirring restlessly to turn her reflections on this injustice into action, some 3,800,000 Canadians had varying degrees of mental and physical disabilities, a number multiplied many times over by the families they lived with, the friends they had, and the uncounted thousands of care-givers across the country who worked for and with them, not to mention the people in hundreds of organizations dealing with disabilities and in the many sections of national, provincial and municipal governments who addressed issues affecting the status of disabled people. All told, a significant community of Canadians connected with disability issues was excluded from the news columns and broadcasts of mainline media organizations, in effect condemned to the status of second-class citizens.

Mona was ready to do something about it. Though physically small and frail, like her mother before her, Mona never shied away from taking up battle. The harder the contest, the more courageous she became.

"I've been writing the newsletter for the cerebral palsy association," Mona told Jill Keenleyside, a close friend. "But I have thoughts and feelings about so much of the disabled world that I'm wondering about a column for a wider audience. What do you think?"

Keenleyside, who was handling CBC publicity for a 1981 cerebral palsy benefit telethon when they'd first met five years earlier, not only encouraged Mona but offered to help. She knew someone at the *Toronto Daily Star* from her CBC days. Jill urged Mona to write him about her proposed column "because the *Star* claims to be for the underdog and the paper has columns for everything else but the disabled."

The *Star* was certainly the logical newspaper. It was a reform-minded publication. It cared about the social welfare of citizens. It was the country's biggest daily. And it published in Mona's hometown. Mona had already ruled out Toronto's *Globe and Mail* because much of what she wanted to write about arose from the local scene, a perspective she knew best but which she understood would not interest a national newspaper.

They broached the subject with Jill's CBC contact, Denis Harvey, now the paper's managing editor. Their pitch challenged the *Star* to increase its coverage of disability issues by adding a regular column, possibly to be written by Mona, about issues and important developments for disabled people. Harvey seemed openly sympathetic to the idea and suggested Mona send a sample column. She did. He next suggested Mona send outlines for additional story ideas. She in fact wrote two or three more columns.

"It was quite a big package she put together for the *Star*," recalled Keenleyside, who also remembered editor Harvey "being so impressed with Mona and the idea. I got the sense he really would have liked to hire her. She is a good writer. It went quite far. Her columns were about the underdog, and had real human interest, both important criteria for the *Star*."

But the *Star* declined to take her on. At the time, two people with disabilities were already on staff at the newspaper. The decision was made internally to go with them rather than hire an outsider over their heads. At least Mona's prodding led to more articles appearing in the *Star* about people with disabilities, written by these two staffers.

Mona had not got this far in life by giving up. Her secret-dream column also met criteria suited for another local daily, the *Toronto Sun*. Mona's letter to the *Sun* pointed out, again, how the paper had a column on everything except disabled people's concerns. Already an experienced writer, and a person with cerebral palsy, she again suggested herself as a potential columnist, this time more directly. Along with the letter she sent samples of her writing.

This letter of chastisement over inadequate coverage for disabled people, and a proffered solution, had been directed specifically to Michael Burke-Gaffney, features editor of the *Sunday Sun*. It turned out that, as the parent of Jesse, a three year-old child with Down Syndrome, he was delighted to get such a proposal because he personally believed greater attention was needed for the disabilities agenda. But Burke-Gaffney also knew not everybody at the paper felt the same way, anymore than did most people running other North American dailies which conspicuously published no columns by or about people with disabilities.

Burke-Gaffney invited Mona to submit six columns and ten ideas for future columns, to better understand what she had in mind, but especially to help him persuade others who did not feel the way he did, provided her columns really were up to scratch.

Immediately upon receiving his letter, Mona closeted herself in her apartment and wrote non-stop through the 1986 Labour Day holiday weekend and beyond. She was not as disabled then as she became later in her typing, so managed to get the columns done. She sent Burke-Gaffney not the six columns he'd asked for, but ten, and not the ten ideas for future columns he'd wanted, but twelve.

Mona understood the format and appeal of the *Toronto Sun*. Her savvy reply to Burke-Gaffney, along with her samples of writing, suggested her column could bring readers brief topical items of news and express opinions on subjects of interest to both able-bodied and disabled readers. She also knew enough about the *Sun* to explicitly propose that future columns could cover such topics as sexuality and human relationships, marriage and parenting when one or both partners are disabled, and the joys versus the difficulties for disabled people living alone, which she identified as "independent living."

She also said the column ought to get involved in political issues, and offered a sampler that questioned whether the Ontario government's so-called WIN (Work Incentive) Program for disabled persons didn't actually *discourage* them from finding jobs and *prevent* them from becoming financially independent. Also appealing was Mona's promise to use the column to "shoot down some myths" about disabled people. Finally, hitting still another hot button at the *Sun* (one that would have been just as hot at the *Star*, too), Mona said her column could introduce readers to "remarkable people" and gave three examples: Torontonian Gary Zemlak, whose business provided technical services for the "differently abled," legendary Toronto activist Sarah Binns, whose 1920s and 1930s militancy for women and welfare rights as a union organizer came to include agitation for disabled people after she herself became a wheelchair user in the 1930s, and Vancouver novelist Eric Wilson, whose books featured disabled children as central characters. Clearly, she had a handle on the situation.

Given this prompt and fulsome response, Burke-Gaffney sent word he wanted to meet her in person. Mona was "suddenly overwhelmed with a big fear that when he met me he wouldn't give me the job. When you have a conspicuous disability," Mona explained, "especially if it affects your face, many people feel uncomfortable with it."

But summoning up her courage she did meet Burke-Gaffney, who had meanwhile shown her columns around to others on the paper's editorial board. They had been impressed and gave him the green light. Throughout the interview he was remarkably understanding, and very keen on Mona doing the column.

"I want you to write for us because you are known as a fighter."

"That," replied Mona with a huge smile, "suits me perfectly."

– 16 –

The adventure begins

A couple of weeks later, Mona Winberg's inaugural "Disabled Today" column appeared in the November 2, 1986 *Sunday Sun*. The adventure was underway.

"This column is an opportunity to show that disabled people are neither larger than life heroes nor pathetic objects of pity," she opened. "We possess strengths and weaknesses, hopes and fears, capabilities and limitations, just like everyone else."

In that same edition, *Sunday Sun* editor Burke-Gaffney introduced Mona and the issues of disability in an extensive separate feature under his own by-line.

"Mona Winberg was born and raised with cerebral palsy. Now in her 40s, she was raised in a loving family and today lives on her own in a Willowdale apartment.

"She's a writer and editor for the Ontario and Canadian cerebral palsy associations. She's on the boards of Participation House and Three Trilliums Community Place, a member of the North York Advisory Committee on Services for Physically Disabled, and an honorary member of the North York chapter of B'nai B'rith Women.

"Read her inaugural – and eloquent – *Sunday Sun* column and you'll see the disabled are able to handle it. The question is: Are we?"

The day Mona's column premiered, with a front page announcement "New Sunday Column on the Disabled," the rest of the front page was filled with a dramatic photo of Rick Hansen, taken the day before, rolling ahead in his wheelchair on Highway 2 east of Cobourg, heading to Toronto, a young man who'd lost the use of his legs due to a spinal cord injury. The paper hyped his Man in Motion World Tour, which was raising awareness of the abilities of disabled individuals and raising millions of dollars for spinal chord research. On Sunday morning Hansen propelled his wheelchair into the city as thousands lining the route cheered him, many along the streets holding their copies of the *Sunday Sun*. If you cared about people with disabilities, it was a morning to take your breath away.

The first interview Mona did for her column "Disabled Today" was with Rick Hansen, who paused his tour to spend time with the city's news media. It was not easy. Most questions, after her struggle to get the words out, elicited brief Yes or No answers. In the curious inner workings of disabled community politics, it was as if Rick would have preferred an interview by someone without such disabilities as Mona evinced, or at least that was her feeling.

All the same, she was consistent in putting the cause ahead of her emotions, and gave the handsome athlete full support in her columns, even rising to defend him in print thereafter from detractors in the disabled community. Rick Hansen, whose 40,000 kilometer Man in Motion World Tour heightened global awareness of the abilities of people with disabilities, focused attention on barriers they faced in reaching their full potential, and raised some $90 million for spinal cord research in the process, would go on to become a co-founder of National Access Awareness Week, with Mona's support all the way.

– 17 –

Sunrise for Mona

Her *Sunday Sun* column, a breakthrough for disabled citizens, found Mona basking in happiness.

Not only had her coveted newspaper column for a wider audience become a reality, but behind the scenes she was treated like a real person, as someone able to do this herself. When Burke-Gaffney made her re-write columns, she did not grumble but was delighted, interpreting the extra work as a further dimension of independent living because "that told me he was treating me equally to all his other writers and columnists, not as a disabled person."

He was supportive of Mona, but also a responsible editor for his newspaper. "The effort was deplorable," she remembered, shaking her head in recalling the perseverance required by the re-writes. Then she smiled.

In the opening days Mona felt slightly uncomfortable while she adjusted to the *Sun* and while its personnel adapted to her. "At first some of the people looked at me as if wondering, 'Is she animal, vegetable, or mineral?' But she gave them her great smile, and "soon everyone began greeting me warmly."

In fact, Mona's weekly visits to the *Sun* newsroom increasingly became celebrated events. She would book Wheel-Trans and go downtown from North York every week to deliver her column in person rather than sending it, which would have been much easier. She did not send it because she wanted human contact, wanted to feel part of this newspaper family she now belonged to. Her anticipated appearance was, recalled one reporter, "a major tour."

Upon her arrival at the *Sun*'s King Street door, security guards cleared Mona's way. Assistants accompanied her entourage. The time was filled with lots of hellos, chatting, and hugs. "I felt I got an extra bonus being hired by the *Sun*. I didn't expect how nice and friendly everyone would be."

"Her weekly visit touched everyone," recalled editor Burke-Gaffney, "from the security guards, to the receptionist with whom she'd exchange conversation, to reporters and editors with whom she'd discuss 'news' and story ideas for her columns or their pieces. There was no one else like her, with her appearance, her wheelchair, her perspective, and intelligent friendliness, coming to the *Sun*."

What Mona entered was a real newsroom of the era: the vast space crammed with desks, people, telephones, hanging ferns, typewriters, notice boards, and stacks of papers harvested wherever a flat surface presented itself. Just above this cohesive commotion hung a low-lying cloud of noise – phones ringing, typewriter keys pounding, metal desk drawers opening, metal filing cabinet drawers slamming shut, motors humming, quick shouts across desks from one reporter to another, laughter, declamations. The smell of paper, of upward swirling smoke from idling cigarettes as deadlines loomed or a crucial phone interview trumped another drag, all mingled pleasingly with the heady mixture of peoples' aromas and machinery's heat. Why would anyone just send a column down here from across town when she could rightly be part of the party? Mona grinned uncontrollably when remembering her first job in the sheltered Corbrook workshop and now witnessing in contrast the *Toronto Sun's* beehive of a newsroom. Hadn't she come a long way!

Mona would stop at desk after desk. She was interested in her colleagues, got to know them individually, and chatted about their families and their problems. She had the capacity to make them feel good because they realized their problems were nothing in comparison to hers.

Some told her of news and ideas that might help for her column. Others came up to her, just wanting to make contact. One reporter described her visit as "the high point of the week in the newsroom." They all saw her column each week, with her smiling face and her punchy topics, in their paper and welcomed her as a distinctive, and distinguished, member of the *Sun* tribe.

After delivering her column, Mona picked up her mail from Pauline Mason, the *Sunday Sun* secretary, who'd opened the letters in advance, knowing Mona had trouble doing so. Pauline would also help her off, and on, with her overcoat in winter. In the larger picture, Pauline supported Mona with various forms of public relations, sometimes explaining to strangers what "the disabled woman" was doing at the *Sun* offices, sometimes helping Mona prepare and send out covering letters with copies of her columns.

Mona was proud of her columns. She wanted to share information. She was the disabled community's unrelenting advocate and activist, sending copies of "Disabled Today" to officials she wanted to ensure were informed about an issue, especially if they were outside the *Toronto Sun's* circulation area. As an MP in Toronto I could get the *Sun*, but that did not mean I did not also receive clipped columns from Mona about issues important for our parliamentary committee on the status of disabled persons.

Columns also went out to her friends, sometimes to update them as Mona's simplest way of sharing an experience, sometimes reporting on a program or system that was, or wasn't, working well. After Mona's friend Jill Keenleyside moved from Toronto to Ottawa, she began receiving columns in the mail. When they were ones to conveniently share a personal experience, Jill found that moving. When they addressed a public issue Mona felt strongly about, Jill knew she'd better keep a closer eye on the issue herself.

Like a full orchestra, her columns played many notes: informative, inspirational, trenchant, tender, pithy, witty, and critical. "Disabled Today" began receiving tremendous endorsement from organizations working with disabled people. Mona Winberg was becoming a household name, and her reach extended far beyond readers with disabilities themselves.

Issues Mona raised that dealt with the federal government were clipped and included in the daily compilation of politically relevant news and views from across Canada prepared for parliamentarians in Ottawa, on our desks in the Commons and the Senate on Monday morning.

Her columns were not only interesting to disabled individuals who needed her information and insights, but to others who became intrigued by these human issues and the frank honesty with which Mona wrote about them. Her nephew Harold Winberg, then working at Pennzoil's Canadian head office in Oakville, learned that amongst a staff of 30, five or six able-bodied people who had no connection whatsoever with disability issues read Mona's "Disabled Today" column every week, even before they connected that he was related to the columnist, because they were simply fascinated by what she had to say. Some such readers seemed truly exceptional. Her former camp counsellor and driving companion, Harry Edgar, wrote Mona: "I read your column even before looking at the Sunshine Girl. How's that for loyalty?"

"Disabled Today" had become an important vehicle for raising wide community consciousness. Her column was often at the forefront, opening topics nobody else was addressing, frequently opening a way for others to follow, its well-honed edge helping advance a period of far-reaching transition for Canadian policies and programs to upgrade the rights and respect the needs of people with mental and physical disabilities.

Mona's writing necessarily offered more than just a continuing critique of public policy. Because mainstream news media continued to under-report the disabled community, her column also doubled, just as she had initially envisaged, as a newsy forum about events and developments in schooling, arts, and social intercourse as they touched the lives of people with disabilities. That information, of course, was a further part of her column's draw, just as it showed non-disabled readers the activity and range of vital interests engaging their fellow citizens.

"I hired Mona Winberg because there was a need for the column and because she had the talent to be a columnist," said Burke-Gaffney. "She knew how to write and had a sense of what needed to be written, doing what every good columnist does by writing well and touching on issues that are important to her readers in a very personal way."

For her part, Mona enjoyed teasing Mike. "By hiring me, you covered all the minorities: I'm a woman, I'm hearing impaired, I have trouble with my speech."

Mona would continue writing "Disabled Today" every week for the next dozen years, leaving a legacy of well over six hundred columns, emerging as one of Canada's best-known and consistent advocates for people with disabilities.

– 18 –

The transformations of Mona

Behind the scenes all the while Mona had been undergoing transformations, some relating to how she connected with others through her column and some to how she actually wrote it, all part and parcel of writing for a newspaper.

One magic of writing was the portal it offered through which she now connected with others. When Mona first emerged as a public-speaking advocate for the disabled, she had changed the "message" by virtue of her own appearance and speaking difficulty. Now, as a columnist, the opposite phenomenon occurred. Her message was conveyed in a medium, the neat printed page, which caused no difficulty whatsoever for those she was addressing.

Gone was the slow, painstaking speech. The writer herself still faced the daunting challenges of her disabilities, but none of that now showed. Reading her columns did not require waiting out her hesitations, feeling awkwardness at her struggles to speak. Behind the scenes Mona spent the entire week typing a single column, but on Sunday morning her readers got only a crisp report on some issue of the day, one that, by looking like all the other stories and features running through the columns of the newspaper, offered a quick and engaging read. It was a familiar, and therefore comfortable, format.

The difference between writing and a cerebral palsied person's face-to-face speech or telephone voice was how the orderly typeset words cancelled out hindrances and hesitations. In the same way being on the Internet equalizes everyone's beauty or ugliness by an interposed screen common to all, or the way wearing uniforms or academic gowns camouflages individuals' differences of wealth or poverty, the format of published writing lets someone be seen for who he or she is, or projects themselves to be, not for any differences they have when compared with others around them. Through her newspaper column, the people Mona now communicated with could no longer be distracted from her message by her slow speaking and her unframed appearance.

"My disability is not really socially acceptable because it upsets my speech and what is the first thing anybody notices about you? It is your speech. But in writing, I can get around that, and become eloquent in print. So I become socially acceptable."

Did that give her notoriety?

"Fame!" she beamed.

In Mona's back-stage transformation, a second barrier that disappeared was her shyness. Precisely because Mona was a shy woman, it seemed natural her private life would be something she would want to safeguard. However, her columns revealed details about her family and private life. She unhesitatingly shared them through her column, paralleling how the Internet's anonymity is conducive for people to say things they would never express to someone face-to-face.

A third transformation touched Mona as a writer. To be a columnist for a major city newspaper demanded a different effort by her on a professional level, which required altering the way she thought about her column and worked to create it.

Burke-Gaffney, who had hired Mona to draw attention to disability issues because she was already a proven writer with valuable things to say, went to work polishing her like a jeweller might a rough diamond. "First, get the facts right," instructed the editor, "then distil them through your own eyes." To "get the facts right" Mona began working closely with the *Sun*'s librarians, who were keen to help. Glenna Tapscott recalled, "We had the pleasure of Mona's company when she came to the library for research. I liked and admired her very much. She was a wonderful and brave person."

As important as getting the facts right, Burke-Gaffney emphasized, now working to bring out Mona's lustre on another plane, is to show the other side. "You must be balanced and fair." That hallmark of good journalism for news stories Mona resisted for herself; she expected more freedom as a columnist.

"You can criticize all you want," said the seasoned diamond polisher, "but you must get the other side of the story, too."

She found it an emotional and logical challenge to present explanations for "the other side." But she had overcome other disabilities and, to be transformed into a polished newspaper columnist, Burke-Gaffney was determined she clear this hurdle, too. The reality Mona had to accept was that she was no longer talking to her family about her opinions, or dispatching a cerebral palsy newsletter into the disabled community's shared consensus of biases, but addressing a major newspaper's column to the widest spectrum imaginable.

In the past, she had just forged ahead. But a newspaper column is for everyone. A paper is read by people who trust it, as much as like it. And trust demanded, as Burke-Gaffney stressed, while taking another polishing pass over Mona's rough edges, verified facts, balance, and fairness. He then handed back one of her early columns for a complete rewrite.

Not all aspects of her transition were easy. Perhaps she did not appreciate that in pushing her to be even-handed, even while she remained critical, Burke-Gaffney knew this would make her a more credible columnist and, just as important, protect her column. The *Sun*'s editorial board was not interested in publishing a rant.

In struggling to "be fair," it might have appeared that Mona's biggest hurdle was her genetic stubbornness. Three years into the writing of "Disabled Today" she would still be telling Ryerson journalism student Wendy Purves, "I prefer column-writing to reporting because it lets me express opinions." However, a dozen years later she was actually proud when a government official told her, "Mona, you always criticized us enough, but you were always very fair."

In fact, Mona's awkward handling of this aspect of her transition issued less from an inaccurate balance on her part between "subjectivity" and "objectivity," and more from the fact she rightly understood there was no such dichotomy to begin with. A more realistic state, and certainly one with more practical benefits, would be to achieve a clear and dispassionate view of one's present circumstances. Mona, highly intelligent and widely read, understood this almost instinctively.

The whole thing was curious, a journalistic conundrum. The *Toronto Sun*, whose editorial standards she was now being groomed to fit, had itself struggled with its "voice." Born like a phoenix out of the funeral ashes of the *Toronto Telegram* by bleary-eyed mourners, the *Sun* had staggered for balance since first wobbling into print with its own precocious testing of objectivity, subjectivity, and truth. Its initial handling of stories established the *Sun* as an attention-grabbing paper of sensation and titillation. One of its early front pages dripped with a graphic photo of a man standing stunned and helpless beside a mail box in Northern Ireland, his hands and remnant lower arms blasted into bloody pulps by an IRA bomb, under the alarmist headline for Toronto readers, "Could This Happen Here Next?" The *Sun* loved controversy and carried columnists who pushed the political and ideological edges as much as its photographers tested limits of prurience and prudence, and in so doing, "The Little Paper that Grew" spawned a multi-city publishing empire. The problem Mona faced about objectivity or balance in 1986 issued, too, from this larger context of the *Toronto Sun*'s own quest for balance.

Mona never backed down, but over time she did learn to fully and accurately back up what she was saying.

"You've got to fight for what you believe in and try to get people involved in the cause," were her articles of faith. And Burke-Gaffney, while still making her do rewrites, check facts, and present the other side, loved best of all that she was fighting for people with disabilities and getting others involved.

There was another important element of transition for Mona in these days. To Burke-Gaffney, as important as it was for Mona to get her facts right and be fair, "plunging right into the heart" of her subject was essential. She might even try shocking readers, he said, according to true *Sun* orthodoxy, to get their attention.

"Unless you grab the reader in the very first sentence," instructed Burke-Gaffney, "you won't be read. You have to get right to the point." While he favoured Mona's subject matter and liked its general treatment, he made her rewrite the opening of columns whenever they failed to achieve dramatic attention-getting effect.

This lesson Mona did not resist in any way, but eagerly embraced. From then on, she gleefully wrote provocative opening sentences with the zeal of a convert:

"*I never thought I could read too much about sex.*" began one attention-grabber that critically reviewed an American book on sexual activities between people with disabilities.

"*Last week I had a one night stand at the Royal York Hotel.*" started another that reported on Mona's overnight stays at a number of Toronto hotels to test their accessibility and services for disabled people.

A variant on this technique was to start off with a bold statement by a person in the know (*"People are being abused there. They're being raped. They're being drugged. They're being beaten."*), or an unacknowledged fact (*"People with impaired hearing make good workers because they aren't distracted by noises around them in the office."*), or sometimes, just juxtaposition of improbable or unfamiliar elements (*"Art and athletics make an unusual combination."*). With that, Mona would then proceed to explain, as in that last reference from a 1994 column, the beneficial connection between sport, art, and kids with special needs at a unique summer camp.

As a good advocate is also an educator, this edgier pattern of writing became a hallmark of the way Mona taught lessons. It suited her purpose of breaking through conventional wisdom, perhaps inspiring others by an example she then presented of some pioneering initiative along the disabilities frontier. It was certainly a natural fit for her own temperament, once she saw the educational advantage of catching attention by tricking people's expectations.

Mildly provocative humour became a Mona specialty simply because it appealed to her intelligent sense of fun, even as it jolted folks awake from their sleepwalking attitudes about disabled people. She discovered how using words to break apart commonplace perspectives, and to introduce concepts that radically challenged habitual practices or comfortable assumptions, worked the same way good art could disturb or inspire a person to see a familiar thing in a new way.

"Mona clamped down on a story and gave it a good shake," summed up Orville Endicott, the lawyer for the Community Living Association in Ontario who followed disability issues closely.

– 19 –

Making every word count

Her lifetime of making every word count, when it was hard to be heard and difficult to speak, paid off royally now in the pithy brevity that became, of necessity, her style.

Before she could do any writing, of course, Mona had to prepare. This behind-the-scenes activity was painstaking and slow. She spent quite a bit of effort getting ready to interview someone for the column, doing background research, sorting out her questions, and arranging the time, all of which she enjoyed. Extra work was needed if she was going to be asking questions of someone unfamiliar with her.

Face-to-face interviews required a great deal of orchestration to mesh her Wheel-Trans itinerary with the schedules of busy public figures, but personal contact had its own value. Mona and those she met invariably established a friendly bond. Sometimes the person she went to see was shocked to discover that "Disability Today" was actually written by a disabled person, which in itself, Mona thought, taught them a good lesson. Of the three Ontario premiers Mona interviewed, she felt Bob Rae had the most thorough grasp of the issues and problems confronting disabled people. He also, more than David Peterson or Mike Harris, "felt at ease in my presence."

Most often, however, she preferred to conduct her interviews by telephone. This not only leapfrogged the inconvenience of travelling around but allowed use of both an adaptive hearing device to amplify the other person's voice and a connected recording machine.

Sometimes in making a cold call, slowly trying to say her piece as clearly as she could, the person at the other end would get impatient or not understand what the situation was and, mistaking her for a prankster, a child, or a friendly drunk, would hang up on her. Every journalist faces a range of problems calling those they want to interview, but in Mona's case there was this extra hurdle to clear.

Often "Disabled Today" gave the people she interviewed their full say. Rather than paraphrasing or selecting just a few snippets, Mona might include fairly extended passages of direct quotation. This was no shortcut to her weekly deadline, but the very opposite. She wanted knowledgeable people to have a reasonable say through her column, and knew that if her readers were at all like her, they enjoyed the rarity of getting a fairly full story from an interesting person at the centre of some action. The result was that "Disabled Today" became a column of record, and because of this serves today as an invaluable source of solid information and perspective.

About once a month Mona telephoned lawyer Orville Endicott at the Toronto offices of the Association for Community Living. He was one of a number of leading people immersed in disability issues on her regular call-list.

"Orville, what is going on? What do you want me to write about?"

Nobody else in the media, Endicott noted, "was so proactive." Obviously the lawyer appreciated this opportunity to advance the agenda for Canadians with mental disabilities. "Orville," Mona later said, "gave me some of my best interviews."

Most of Mona's columns dealt with disability topics in Ontario, and particularly the greater Toronto community. There were good reasons. This large area of millions of people contained many disabled individuals and programs intended for them. This was where she lived so she would be able to write with authority about what she experienced directly. And this was where most of her *Sunday Sun* readers lived.

Yet scattered throughout "Disabled Today" columns was evidence that Mona was keeping an eye on the larger picture, too. Sometimes this entailed a reference to developments across Canada or in the United States. Other times she devoted entire columns to important developments, whether positive or negative, in different parts of the country.

Mona's issues were informed by her own raw experiences over a lifetime of confronting the twin restraints of disability and the discrimination it engenders in others. Indeed, the *Sun* columns continued to emphasize themes and echo concepts Mona had already been dealing with for some time in her efforts to reach out and raise awareness. Ideas and material from articles she had previously written for *Contact* and *Partici-Paper* Mona, especially in her early months at the *Sun*, revised and updated for "Disabled Today."

No one could have written what Mona did, nor have emerged the advocate she became, without surmounting deep frustrations and challenging episodes. Just as the strongest steel comes from the hottest part of the blast furnace, the result strengthened Mona and she became an inspiration to all who met her – high public officials, hardened journalists, co-workers, care-givers, her cherished relatives, children, and just about anyone else whose path ever crossed her own, or who caught one of her smiles.

"Nobody," enthused Michael Burke-Gaffney, looking proudly at the polished diamond, "could write a column the way Mona did."

Finding a family

Back when Mona was still a teenager, Sarah Winberg had starkly informed her, "You'll never have dates, never get married, never be a wife or a mother. Get used to it."

Without knowing the context or hearing Sarah's tone of voice, it is impossible to say whether that was Jewish humour, tough love, or something else. Whatever its genre, it was certainly plain talk. Mona, as her mother foretold, never did marry or have children of her own, although she did have one or two modest relationships and was interested, in theory if not for practical application, in sexual dalliances between individuals with disabilities.

Without husband or children, Mona embraced her extended family and its members embraced her. Whatever she was up to over the years, Mona's family was vital to her in both emotional and practical ways.

Brother Wolfe's wife, Norma, brother Syd's wife, Emily, and sister Barbara's husband, Bill Baltman, all treated Mona "as if I were their own sister." Her nieces and nephews, and their families, further filled her own familial vacuum, and Mona delighted in the accomplishments of this niece or that great-nephew.

Mona's pivotal place in this extended Winberg family was held together through a careful balance of unbounded affection and respectful distance. Her nephews and nieces adored her, and found her a source of inspiration. Yet they also felt trepidation about making a misstep on some important issue Auntie Mona felt strongly about, and had been instilled with the Winberg family's mission to foster "independent living," which required knowing where helpful support ended and undue protection began.

The family record is replete with evaluations of Mona by her in-laws:

"Smart and clever," is how Sidney Troister described his aunt, even as he cautioned that, "She could be manipulative, and she knew how to use guilt to get what she wanted, unless we were smart enough to recognize when we were being guilt-tripped." Mona was "definitely feisty, but in a good way," added Troister, who'd come to know and love Mona after marrying her niece Debbie Baltman, daughter of Mona's sister, Barbara." "It was," he believed, "a character trait that led to her accomplishments."

Another nephew, Harold, son of Mona's brother Sydney, delighted in sharing a January 27 birthday with Mona. He saw his fellow-Aquarian aunt as possessing "traits shared by all Winberg women – very stubborn, very independent, very determined. They had a fiery independence and a fiery will in an era when this was almost frowned upon."

Michael Winberg, the nephew who'd suggested the name *Contact* for her cerebral palsy newsletter, became close to Mona "as a relative and as a friend" because of extensive time spent together. During the twenty years Mona and her mother lived together on Gilgorm Avenue in Toronto's Eglinton-Bathurst neighbourhood, Michael was often at the house and observed that she was "as independent as possible and never a burden to anyone." She would mix him a glass of Tang orange drink when he visited, and when he drove away, Mona and her mother would both come out to wave good-bye. He'd look back and, waving to the two women standing together, observe that his diminutive Aunt Mona was at least taller than her mother.

Because her beloved brother Wolfe and his wife, Norma, (Michael's parents) lived in the nearby Forest Hill neighbourhood, Mona and her mother joined them late Friday afternoon, making a family gathering of seven, with the four adults, the two Winberg boys, Michael and Martin, and daughter, Marla, until her death at age sixteen from leukemia on December 7, 1968. It was the next day, as described earlier, that Sarah Winberg died. Yet Mona kept coming, even after moving further away to live on her own in Willowdale, travelling the distance by bus. "Even if the conversation or the celebration of Passover sometimes bored her," recalled Michael, "Mona would still smile." She was simply content to be in a convivial family setting.

Mona and her great-nephew Seth, son of Harold and Barbara Winberg, were "obsessed" with the Star Trek series and its characters. Once, when Harold and his family lived in the Toronto vicinity, they went to a huge Star Trek convention, Mona getting herself photographed sitting in Captain Picard's chair, amidst cardboard characters in their space uniforms.

Mona's nieces and nephews, their spouses, and their children in turn, understood the importance of "Auntie Mona" in their families' lives and genuinely adopted her as their adored own. And they liked having fun; on Halloween, Michael Winberg's childhood rounds of trick-or-treating always included a scary call at the Gilgorm Avenue house.

Michael had become so close to Mona that, as she told me, "He knows what I need before I do." Because he in fact no longer thought of her as disabled, Michael had not even thought to mention his aunt's condition before bringing his fiancée, Allyne, for an introductory visit.

"I was surprised at our first meeting," recalled Allyne. "I discovered a wonderful and warm woman who was extremely intelligent and creative, ready to talk about anything. She was interested in me because she cared deeply about Michael as she cared about all her family."

Allyne was impressed, as well, by how Mona "kept up with the times, first using a huge IBM clunker of an electric typewriter to bang out letters, then using computers, and then becoming hopeful when voice recognition equipment first appeared, at least until she found it could not handle her pattern and pace of speech." Allyne was struck by how Mona "went out of her way to thank people, could find the silver lining in any cloud, and was always complimentary." At the same time, she was just as impressed that her candid aunt by marriage "thought for herself and did not pull punches, but would say it like it is."

When Mona began writing her weekly newspaper column, Michael and others in the Winberg family saw a new side of her emerge. "She now had a real job. It was a full-time job for her, interviewing people and transcribing the results, because of the time and effort it took to write a new column each week."

Her family discussed the issues Mona wrote about during the *Toronto Sun* years. She was interested in others' opinions or thoughts, in order to help form her own or to acid-test her take on things. Brother Wolfe was agitated by the hypocrisy of how the benefits system hurt the very disabled people it was supposed to help. Nephew Harold had soulful conversations with her about Tracy Latimer's murder. Nephew Michael's wife, Allyne, discussed the difficulties of school integration for pupils with disabilities.

"She was passionate about the Latimer case," said Harold. "Once Mona made up her mind, it was fixed. Her views were not superficial. They were very genuine. And they were supportive of what she believed to be good and true for people with disabilities."

Allyne especially enjoyed talking with Mona about subjects that came up in her more personal columns, "perhaps because I was learning more about my family connection, but also because they had for me, as no doubt they did for many others among Mona's large *Sunday Sun* readership, such strong human interest."

The family connection was directly reinforced over the years when the whole Winberg tribe got together. They did so whenever logistics or pretexts, like the January 2007 joint birthday celebration for Mona and Harold, permitted. Sid Troister, often a spokesperson for the family, rose to deliver an impromptu speech: "Of course, we are celebrating Mona's birthday – and Harold's. But the event does much more than that. It has brought together the Winberg family, Mona and Norma of course, but as well, the children and grandchildren of Wolfie, Barbara, and Syd – all connected in large measure because of the continuing love and affection all of us, the children, the children by marriage, and the grandchildren, have for Mona."

Several of Mona's "favourite things" fitted well with family parties. She relished Chinese food, loved ice cream, and had a sweet tooth, especially enjoying a large amount of "sinful" chocolate on her birthday cake. She enjoyed, it was reported, "a good gossipy story."

Mona "was always interested in learning things, such as the connections between astronomy and astrology, and had a strong interest in people," said Allyne, "forever asking questions. She was curious, but humble, and had a sense of humour."

Her nephew Harold Winberg noted, after the death of Mona's two brothers and sister, which left her the last one standing of her generation, how she became "the family matriarch around whom we all rallied."

Harold and Mona were close and over the years he recognized her dominant qualities. "Mona would fight, get into scraps, and it never mattered who it was or the person's size or prestige." Their phone calls would last an hour between Toronto and Richmond, B.C., "back when they cost $1 a minute." So the advent of emails opened up an entirely new dimension for constant and cheaper contact. "With the Internet it is easy to pump out a message, except that in Aunt Mona's case I knew how long it took her, and the toll it claimed on her physically over time."

Whenever Harold went into her small apartment and saw walls displaying the Terry Fox Award, the King Clancy Award, the Order of Canada, and other honours, he had been "humbled by what she was able to accomplish in her life." As for those qualities of independence and stubbornness, he saw how the two fused into a single characteristic. He correctly foresaw that she would never leave her apartment, where she had perfected as much as anyone could the art of independent living. "It represents what her life is all about," he said years before she died. "To leave her apartment for a nursing home would be waving the white flag, surrendering to her disabilities."

Mona herself often repeated, "My biggest blessing is the love and support of a very caring family. They have given me freedom and independence. Yet, when I need them, they are always there for me."

The magical balance that independent living required had been achieved. For even within her deeply beloved and all-important family, Mona maintained her independence from them and was never pandered to by them. She had her own life to live and lived it.

— 21 —
Conscience of the board

Because Mona's interest in the world was that of a participant observer, being a board member offered a perfect channel to translate her observations into actions. It was a channel she fully utilized.

She engaged board work avidly because the meetings had agendas she could prepare for in advance, they ran on pre-set schedules enabling her to plan her time and transportation, and the boards drew together other like-minded individuals who invariably became respectful of her and usually became friends with her as well. Board work gave Mona responsibilities whose execution in running community organizations left her with a sense of accomplishment. Mona felt needed.

The first of many boards on which Mona served was that of Bellwoods Park House in Toronto. This was not only an initiation for Mona, who joined this board in 1954 at age 22, but for the board itself, since it was in charge of the pioneering venture of operating Canada's first residence for disabled adults. A decade later she was also elected second vice-president of the Adult Cerebral Palsy Institute of Metropolitan Toronto, the operating body of Bellwoods Park House. Additionally, Mona chaired Bellwoods New Directions Committee, whose members sparked with ideas and innovations about how to define and establish new priorities for Bellwoods and its residents.

In 1976, as noted previously, Mona left the Bellwoods board after more than two decades of service, when joining the board of directors of Participation House in Markham, becoming, as well, chair of its committee that decided who should be admitted to the facility. These positions she held until 1982.

During the 1970s she was also serving on boards and holding offices in the Ontario and Canadian cerebral palsy organizations, among others.

In 1982, ready for a new board to challenge, Mona was elected a trustee of the Victorian Order of Nurses, Toronto Branch. She had become devoted to the VON for the quality of care its nurses provided to shut-ins and disabled people in their homes. Mona remained active on this board for the next three years, and served on the VON board's Quality Management Committee.

Her work on these boards was intrinsically important for the results achieved with each organization, but Mona's experiences also provided great training for bigger things to come.

By the early 1990s, Anne Golden, who chaired the United Way of Greater Toronto, had resolved to diversify her organization's board. She wanted it more proactive in the community and, certainly, to include a person with disabilities in its makeup because many of the organizations supported by the United Way served the needs of citizens with disabilities. It seemed almost inevitable that Mona would be elected to the United Way's board of trustees, as indeed she was in 1991.

Had the tipping point been reached where disability was now an advantage? This delicate question consists of one-part cynicism, one-part realism, and one-part illusion.

"The most difficult part of having cerebral palsy is being accepted by my peers," Mona reflected. "Among militants, I'm considered passive. They say I must feel like the token disabled person on all the boards I'm on. My answer is that I've got so many disabilities, I wouldn't know what one I was the token of."

Never was Mona Winberg a "token" disabled person on any of the boards to which she was elected. On April 24, 1994, after three years on the United Way board and as many as forty years' service on other boards, she wrote that one of her "favourite things" was serving on boards that welcomed her questions "about how they provide services," boards "willing to be challenged on any preconceived ideas about disabled people."

She dug in and told it like it was, which was the only way Mona, daughter of Sarah, knew how to be. The fact that she actually knew what she was talking about, when she stuck to her agenda on behalf of people with disabilities, made her an authoritative player. The fact that many people without disabilities would have low expectations of her provided an advantage, as did their unspoken, almost morbid fascination with her.

If anyone thought Mona would be a token appointee for disabled people, such an erroneous assessment could not have lasted long. From the day she joined the United Way board in 1991 until the day she left it in 1997, Mona made a real impact, becoming a stellar if unconventional member of the working board and even a "poster girl" for the United Way's annual fund-raising appeal.

"Mona did not let a thing go by," recalled Anne Golden. "She was not unchallenging as a participant. She spoke at every meeting. With forty people on the board, and her halting speech, which was not easy to listen to, there was a real clash. The room was filled with high-powered people, CEOs of banks and the like, who wanted speakers to get directly to the bottom line. But Mona caused everything, and everyone, to slow down."

In all Mona's years on the board, "She never asked a frivolous question. She always had a point and got to it. Mona Winberg was very, very smart." She did not mind being solitary in her courage to advance views and hold her own. "Some decisions were unanimous, but for one vote."

As board members came to recognize her qualities, however, and accept that she was introducing a new perspective of accountability into their deliberations, they settled into a different pace, at least when an issue that had been raised by Mona was in play. "Everyone had great affection for her," smiled Golden in remembering. Other board members during Mona's tenure with whom she worked especially well, because of their interests and backgrounds, included Ruth Grant, a past chair of United Way and a leader in children's health through Care Canada and The Hospital for Sick Children; Donna Dasko, the Environics opinion pollster attuned to how Canadians were thinking; Ross DeGeer, a shining part of Ontario's Big Blue Machine who became Ontario's agent general to the United Kingdom; Hon. David Crombie, the popular Toronto mayor who became a federal cabinet minister and chair of the Terry Fox Hall of Fame; and George Fierheller, a past chair of the United Way.

All members developed respect for Mona, and it wasn't just because of her particular approach to agenda items for which she always prepared herself thoroughly. Those who once grumbled about getting up at 6:00 a.m. for a 7:30 board meeting now learned that Mona had to rise at 3:00 a.m. to begin the lengthy process of getting ready, then standing by for her Wheel-Trans ride that might materialize anytime between 5:00 and 7:00 o'clock. Sometimes, if her ride only came near the end of that range, Mona was lucky to get from North York all the way downtown to the meetings at 26 Wellington Street East on time. Sometimes she was even lucky to get there at all. One morning during a period when, as she laconically noted later, the quality of Wheel-Trans service had "slipped," she was literally dropped onto the ground.

In a setting such as these United Way board meetings, an individual from the disabled community intent on not being a mere token might have been tempted to "showboat." Not Mona. "She had a common sense approach," explained Golden, "that came through in her respectful but pointed questions." Looking back, the former chair observed how Mona's lens for viewing any issue before the board "consistently had three aspects: the diversity side, the allocations side, and the needs side."

"The first huge impression we all had of Mona was one of enormous empathy for the sheer amount of effort that went into each physical gesture, act, every single word," added Golden. "I never heard a single expression of self-pity. Mona was very confident. She took no guff. She took the issues of the day, such as the murder of Tracy Latimer, very seriously."

Mona attended every meeting, "did her homework" before the board meetings, and was attentive throughout their two and a-half hour duration. As well, she served on the Leading Women Advisory Council of United Way, and attended all its meetings.

The 1988 United Way Campaign in Toronto raised $39 million, the largest amount in its 30-year history, and more than a 10 percent increase over the prior year's haul, outdoing every major city in North America. At the United Way's annual achievement dinner in the Sheraton Centre that November, Mona received a standing ovation for her role in the campaign's film and advertisements. She jokingly told a cheering audience, reported Anne Dawson in the *Toronto Sun*, that United Way had put her in a real dilemma. "Whenever I go out, if a man I don't know smiles at me, I don't know if he has recognized me from the video or whether he has got something else on his mind."

Because Mona appeared so unlikely a candidate for a naughty scenario, and because most people excluded contemplation of sexual expression involving individuals with disabilities, she had, once again, tricked expectations and brought the house down with laughter.

Mona's six years on the board of trustees generated "tremendous respect" on her part for the organization. She had "never encountered a more dedicated group than those who make up the United Way." There was something else. Mona's work with United Way also gave her "an opportunity to write columns about disabled people in Toronto I might not otherwise have been exposed to."

If there was a theme to Mona's role with the United Way, said Golden, it was that she served as "the conscience of the board, and she knew that that's what she was."

— 22 —

All in the family circle

On the bright morning of June 8, 2005, Mona headed expectantly to Brampton's new Grenville and William Davis Court House. Her niece Deena Baltman was about to be sworn in as a judge of Ontario's Superior Court and she was cheerfully determined to witness the event.

2005, June: Mona's delight in seeing her niece Deena Baltman sworn in as a judge of Ontario's Superior Court was matched by the joy Deena felt at her aunt's presence for the ceremony.

The prospective judge had let everyone know in advance her aunt had special needs. The administrators of justice were quietly pleased to learn this, because their new facilities had been constructed to accommodate people with disabilities, including space for wheelchairs at the front of the courtroom.

"I don't want to sit up front, but at the back," protested Mona on arrival. "If I'm at the front it will be a distraction and this is *your* day. I just want to witness it."

Shy Mona could not escape at least some attention, however, once Ontario's newest judge began speaking about "my indomitable Aunt Mona," celebrating her as "a renowned champion of persons with physical disabilities, an accomplished journalist, and a recipient of numerous honours including being inducted into the Terry Fox Hall of Fame and the Order of Canada. She has successfully taken to task numerous politicians, bureaucrats, and public figures." It was on that basis, Madame Justice Baltman reassured her amused courtroom audience, "If I make a mess of things in my new job, I will be hearing about it from Aunt Mona long before the Court of Appeal gets a chance to straighten things out."

Reflecting upon that humorous truism several years later, Deena added, "That's just another way of saying that, when it came to matters of social justice, I feared her wrath more than any other authority."

On the frequent occasions when the two got together in private, Mona cherished Deena's company. No intimate topic was off limits. Because of Deena's particularly liberal outlook on life, Mona felt comfortable speaking openly with her about personal matters, including sex and the challenges people with disabilities encounter in the tortuous realm of romance and making love.

Close familial connections that gave Mona such joy were inevitably the source of deep sadness, too. She was devastated by the deaths of her two brothers, her sister, her niece Marla, her mother, her niece Debbie. Mona, a sensitive person in a closely-knit family, grieved their deaths. Beyond this lurked an unspoken fear that, with each death, another peg essential to holding her "independent living" support system together and keeping her out of an institution, had disappeared.

Mona not only outlived her three siblings, perhaps to be expected because she was the youngest, but she outlasted them in years of life as well, sailing on to just days short of her seventy-seventh birthday whereas they had died at younger ages, two in their fifties and one aged seventy-one.

Throughout their lives, Mona's ten-years-older brother Wolfe had been a companionable presence exerting a cheerful influence on her life. When Mona first landed her "Disabled Today" column with the *Sun*, she couldn't wait to tell him. Wolfe and his understanding wife, Norma, had always given her "a love with no strings attached." They helped boost Mona's self-confidence because they believed in her and, above all, in her "freedom to live my life in my own way."

When Wolfe Winberg died in July 1994, Mona's friends rallied in support as she, bereft and distraught, made a Herculean effort to write her next column by deadline. At the same time, affection and support flowed from her newspaper family, headed by managing editor Michael Burke-Gaffney and *Sunday Sun* secretary Pauline Mason. The column was about her brother, "the finest person I knew." Wolfe, she said, was "an excellent judge of character" who "could spot a phoney five miles away." She'd always looked up to him. She'd revelled in his dry sense of humour that never deserted him, even in final years of declining health. Wolfe had "all the qualities I most respect in a person: honesty, fairness, and conscientiousness. He was truly a man of integrity, one of the very few individuals I've ever associated with that word."

Wolfe and his wife, Norma, "were true pioneers," added Mona, "because, even today, disabled people are not given the opportunities I had. Without their love, encouragement, and constructive criticism, I would not be the person I am now."

Her gratitude for that external support – from her mother, her brother Wolfe, and all the other family members – was a force which Mona channelled back into her own life by resolving *to live as independently as possible*. "To do anything less would be a complete betrayal of all the love and faith my family has always had in me."

The circle was complete.

23

Wanting what we don't have

Mona was a petite woman with short, wavy, light brown hair. She'd always wanted long hair, she told Ryerson journalism student Kathleen Morland, "but mine's too thick and curly." After a pause, Mona added, "but we always want what we don't have."

What Mona did not have was a very cooperative body. As years passed, her head would tilt more and more, and her body became increasingly misshapen.

When asked about how she dealt with her disabilities, Mona would sometimes ask the inquisitive person to pick up a pen and write their name, but without using their thumb. After a shared laugh at the failed attempt, she would then ask, "It's not easy, is it? That's one of my problems. I can't use my thumb. Imagine if you had to do up buttons like that."

When Mona reached her early forties, she began finding it harder to make out what others were saying. Dangerously, she could no longer hear sounds around her very well. Mona was becoming deaf. Always the pioneer who liked to take advantage of the latest thing in assistive devices, she struggled with the streamlined newest models of tiny hearing aids, until in frustration she had to abandon their promise of something "discreet and elegant." Her hands simply could not cope with the small batteries and the tiny hearing aids. She got, instead, a primitive-looking model, a large unit whose voice receptor hung around her neck against her chest, with wires leading to amplifiers in her ears. Unlike the model that went directly into her ear, this hearing aid was rechargeable. Yet the large, easy-to-wear device was also industrial grade. Mona had style. So she created different patterned fabric covers for the oversized instrument that would match her outfits. "When you live alone and you've got to be independent," said matter-of-fact Mona, "you have to make sacrifices."

Some years later, Mona added another device to her independent living repertoire. Subscribing to the Lifeline Personal Response Service at $35 a month, she got a "help" button that she wore around her neck like a pendant, hanging beside her big hearing aid. When she pushed the button it activated an automatic, two-way voice communicator installed in her apartment.

The "Lifeline" was specifically designed for individuals having limitations in hearing, seeing, dexterity, or mobility. A distress signal picked up in Lifeline's response centre enabled the operator to identify Mona's location in the city and talk with her through the speakerphone, even if she were lying on the bathroom floor.

Depending on the situation, a neighbour might be contacted or 911 called, but most "alerts" were not emergencies like falls or fires but the "social calls" encouraged by Lifeline to ensure subscribers were fine. About eighty percent of all Lifeline call-ins were in this "chat" category, which was how the service monitored the well-being of its subscribers. If Mona did not make the twice-daily call, a response centre operator would call her to check up. Sometimes there'd be a recorded message to welcome Mona home when she returned from an outing. The bottom line was independence.

Lifeline enabled Mona, who used a wheelchair and was prone to falling, to live more confidently on her own. She never felt isolated, even when sleeping, because Lifeline heightened her sense of security. Understandably, Mona also promoted this remote contact equipment in "Disabled Today." Lifeline was yet another component in her growing campaign for independent living – the model she was providing for others, even as she continually worked to upgrade its operation.

Although she wore that large hearing aid and filled her apartment with many other assistive devices, not all of Mona's steps to overcome her disabilities involved mechanical or electronic appliances. She also programmed herself, including learning to read lips. "It gave her extra clues," explained Michael Winberg. "She was always trying her best to overcome her hearing difficulty and understand what people were saying to her."

Mona had weak tear ducts, which meant a problem seeing through watery eyes, not to mention tears running down her cheeks giving the impression she might be overwhelmed by sadness or joy when in fact she was neither. She would get eye drops administered, and lie down until the problem cleared.

Mona's speech caused people to avoid her or limit contact. She had experienced this phenomenon even with specialist doctors. Though one might expect members of the medical community at least to have sympathetic understanding of the situation, several times when Mona visited these doctors' offices, "they couldn't wait to get me out of there. They get so uncomfortable. Cerebral palsy, especially my kind, is not socially acceptable because it affects my speech, the first thing anybody notices."

But for those patient enough to listen, Mona's struggling voice seemed, in a quiet way, sweetly, gently intimate. It had its own rhythms. Her slowed-down and strung-out pattern of speaking resulted in emphasis on certain words in a sentence that one might not usually stress, but they coincided with the end of a segment she could complete. The unexpected pitch and emphasis gave an overall effect of poetic musicality.

She often asked those to whom she was speaking if they were having trouble understanding her, offering to repeat missed words. She explained, slowly, that disabled people "are happy to repeat ten times if necessary, until we're understood. What's frustrating is someone nodding and pretending to understand out of embarrassment. You end up no further ahead."

"You're going to laugh," she said, beginning to chuckle herself, "but sometimes when I play a tape back, I can't understand myself what I'm saying."

Mona did not like it when people finished her sentences for her. Does anyone? How does one person know what another is going to say next, unless they've lived together for years? Mona lived alone. No doubt those who jump in to complete someone else's slowly emerging sentence think they're helping, making it easier. Often what others supposed Mona was going to say next was not, however, what she had in mind, which then required slow and deliberate backtracking. Even when the proffered conclusion to her sentence did resemble what she'd herself expected to say, such acts of impatient intervention diminished her dignity.

Whether this urge to do the talking for someone with a speech impediment may be close to a conditioned response in today's hurry-up society of high-speed communications, or is a means of staying in control of a social moment, or both, it also denotes the intervener's sense of superiority, perhaps subconsciously, to the person of hesitant speaking ability.

Only when Mona was with close family members or particular friends, she sometimes might not mind one of them finishing her sentences, "because sometimes I do get really tired and it's okay. But mostly I don't like anyone to do it."

As for her face, no one had a sweeter smile. Yet I never saw her smile in meek compliance, as vulnerable or dependent individuals often do, if something important was not right or something serious was being treated as a laughing matter. The clear force of Mona Winberg's mind always trumped sentimental folly.

24

The writer who couldn't write

Mona's younger years, filled with dreams of being a writer, awakened into an adult life filled with the work of writing. She was lucky, as all aspiring writers are, to make the transition from dream to reality. However, as fortune's necessary forerunner, Mona first had one significant hurdle to clear. She could not physically write.

Mona's challenge was not as extreme as that of French writer Jean-Dominique Bauby, whose letter-by-letter formation of every word, in the aftermath of loosing all bodily functions, required someone else pointing to each letter of the alphabet in turn, until he slightly winked his left eyelash, the only movement of which he remained capable, to signal that, yes, "h" or "w" was the next letter he was after.

Yet on the other hand, writing was certainly not as easy for Mona as for many whose fingers fly furiously across light-touch keyboards to pile up words of little interest and less importance. Unable to hold a pen or a pencil, the only way Mona could write anything was by painstaking single-digit pecking at the letters on a keyboard. From high school days, a writing machine – first the adapted manual typewriter, then her IBM electric typewriter, then the adapted computer keyboard – became Mona's passport to the world of written communication.

By the late 1980s Mona got a computer. This meant, once she learned how to use it, that changes and corrections to her writing could be made more readily. Still, it was by no means an easy process.

Mona would sit at her keyboard, utterly focused on her piece of writing. First she looked up at the screen, even though her head was at such an angle the text must have appeared more upside down than right-side up. In the days of hot-metal linotype, typesetters and printers could read text that appeared upside down and backward (the reverse image one sees holding a newspaper in front of a mirror) about as fast as they could read words the way they appear on this page, and perhaps over the years, in something akin to that cognitive adaptation, Mona had acclimatized herself to reading at an atrocious angle. Or, if not like a printer with his type, then perhaps like an aviator seeing the horizon in a steep turn yet staying in control of her airplane. However she managed, Mona was definitely not looking at her computer screen in any way that resembled normal.

After studying the screen, she moved her arm until her index finger hovered above a key, into position from where it could drop down through an opening in the hard clear plastic template over the keyboard. The template's individual holes gave access to each letter or number, while simultaneously shielding the entire keyboard so that a slip of Mona's hand would not create alphabet soup on the screen.

Then she paused after the letter was typed. Then she looked up again to study the screen and ensure the right key had been hit. Then she repeated the determined manoeuvre, again holding a finger over a single hole above the keyboard for the next letter of the word she was typing. Then came a strike on that key. Then followed another verification gaze up at the screen. In the course of several minutes, Mona had added the word "to" and with persistent effort and much more time, her carefully pecked letters formed the words "the need."

At that keyboard, using the adapted equipment of our age, year after year, writing column after column for the *Sunday Sun* about people with disabilities, one letter at a time, she turned out more than 600 instalments of "Disabled Today." One of her short columns of 340 words took 1,740 individual typed letters to complete. One of 500 words, some 2,450 characters. Even with computer advances that helped, Mona had to work on her column full time. Whatever new software appeared, she had only a single finger to work it – for each of those 1,470,000 letters over her dozen years as a columnist.

Just as when she spoke, invariably getting to the point with directness, so in her writing Mona made every word count. If words are hard to come by, their preciousness requires they be spent with precision.

"Mine was a weekly column," she quipped, "because it took a week to write."

That included time spent on interviews. As noted earlier, Mona conducted most interviews for "Disabled Today" by telephone with a tape recorder attached. Recording what people said entailed the usual problem of lining up the person, preparing her questions, getting consent to the interview being recorded, then hitting the right

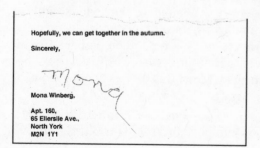

Hopefully, we can get together in the autumn.

Sincerely,

Mona Winberg,

Apt. 160,
65 Ellersile Ave.,
North York
M2N 1Y1

Mona left a legacy of writing, and yet she could never write by pencil or pen. With limited control over her hands, and no use of her thumbs, the best handwriting she could manage was to sign a typed letter. This one from 2001 shows Mona's signature.

buttons and pushing them hard enough to start rolling the tape, then getting the questions out as fast and clearly as she could speak, while straining to hear well enough what was being said in response. In the place of quick exchanges or rapid pursuit of a point, these interviews were protracted, deliberate, and unique.

The interview done, Mona proceeded to transcribe it, sitting for hours and listening through earphones to the recording over and over again. Being unable to write by hand, she had not even been able to jot down, like most journalists, abbreviated notes of what the other person was saying during the course of the interview that might now trigger memory of the statement or indicate when in the interview something she was after had been stated. Steadily, she transformed the recorded words she heard into text, typing one word at a time, letter by letter, for hours.

"I have to rely a lot on mechanics, because I don't have good use of my hands. How do you like that? A writer who can't write!"

– 25 –

Keen about Jill

Mona's life evolved through interaction with friends she made over the years, such as companions Jill Keenleyside and Barbara Hickey.

In January 1986 Mona met Keenleyside for the first time upon arrival at CBC's Studio 7 in Toronto to be a guest on a cerebral palsy benefit telethon, although they had spoken quite a bit by telephone leading up to the broadcast.

Running CBC public relations for the telethon, Jill had been immersed in the cerebral palsy subject for a couple of months by this point. Back in November the 29-year-old publicist had first been informed that "Weekend with the Stars" would be broadcast on CBLT-TV over a mid-January weekend. "Just another TV show to promote," thought Jill as her mind tripped through the routine: "Get people to watch. Promise them performers and touching images. Make the public aware. Get the job done and move on to the next assignment."

Somebody at CBC said, "You should talk to Mona Winberg, because she's a writer with the cerebral palsy organization. You could phone and talk to her."

Learning that Mona would not only be an information source for her, but also a guest on the show, Jill, the ardent young career woman, researched her background. She became mesmerized as she read about a woman with cerebral palsy "who was damned if that was going to stop her: she lived on her own; she was editor of the OFCP's newspaper *Partici-Paper*; she was on the board of at least five organizations for the disabled. Mona with a disability was working harder than any two people without one."

Realizing she potentially had a great story with which to promote the telethon, the publicist telephoned Mona, nervous about making the call because she couldn't see her. "I kept saying things over, babbling nervously, and it became embarrassing for me, afraid I wouldn't be able to understand her. And for about ten seconds, my mind really blocked what she was saying, probably out of fear. I think that happens to people, just because we think we do not understand what is being said.

"Then her warmth came through and I started to relax and to realize the problem was with me. Mona was charming and I had no problem understanding what she was saying at all, if I listened patiently and calmly. It was Mona Winberg herself who actually broke through my normal ways."

It was not just Mona, but others Jill contacted as well, who began to open a new vista for her. She spoke with Harry Miller, by this time Mona's successor as president of OFCP, whose affirmative action program included retrofitting work spaces to make them accessible, a step in the larger project of making job opportunities available to the disabled, with a focus for employers to hire on the basis of ability, not disability. She talked with Ann Snyder, whose Ottawa store, Handi-House, offered disabled customers a range of products that included wheelchairs, prostheses, special adaptive clothing, a collapsible bath seat for travelling, and a one-handed can opener. She contacted two thoughtful and enterprising London nurses who designed and made stylish clothing suitable for people with disabilities. She was touched by how Wayne Pronger and Tom Kelly, two men who would be guests on the telethon, partnered so that Tom sang the songs Wayne wrote, lending Wayne his voice because, with Wayne's cerebral palsy, his fine lyrics became a jumble of distorted words whenever he talked or sang. What she saw was, for Jill, a revelation.

Keenleyside had only been assigned "to do normal publicity for a typical show" to be broadcast from Toronto, but having spoken with Mona and learned about the accomplishments and needs of others like her, she now found herself emotionally involved in the story. "It started to really mean something to me."

She had encountered more than one disabled person while preparing to publicize the telethon, "but it was really Mona Winberg who inspired me because of her attitude about life. She impressed me so much. All of us have our own issues and complaints and wake up every day with something we're dealing with, but what I learned talking by phone with Mona, who had so much more to contend with, was not just a 'positive attitude' but a strong philosophy for living."

Thus, despite Jill's initial trepidation about dealing with a victim of cerebral palsy, by the time of the telethon she had undergone a complete reversal of feelings, a 180-degree turn triggered by her contact with Mona. "She was such an amazing human being. I was just enthralled by her attitude. I *wanted* to be her friend."

Getting on with her job, the CBC publicist pitched the *Toronto Star's* Family Section editor to run advance coverage of the broadcast. "Would you consider doing a story on the cerebral palsy telethon?" asked Keenleyside, adding how in preparing for the program she had changed her own attitudes toward the disabled, describing the impact Mona had had on her.

"Would you consider writing it yourself?" quizzed the harried editor, short on time and staff, but long a believer in opportunity. The *Star* ended up running Jill Keenleyside's by-lined confessional under the heading "Disabled taught me a lesson" in its January 15, 1982 edition, on the eve of the telethon, as a Family Section front page feature.

Jill admitted to *Star* readers her embarrassment at encountering so many remarkable people who cared and did things she had known nothing about. "I discovered in preparing for the telethon that the real disability didn't just afflict people with cerebral palsy. It afflicted me. The slogan 'The greatest handicap of the disabled is your attitude' applied as much to me as to the bully who taunts a child in a wheelchair.

"I was never mean or cruel. I didn't turn away in disgust from handicapped people. What I did was worse. I felt sorry for them. If I met a disabled person I was so nice, regardless of whether I liked him. If I wasn't feeling pity, I was feeling awkward. And showed it. If he had a speech problem, I raised my voice and slowed my words, assuming he couldn't also hear. Or worse, that he wasn't very bright. Or both.

"Most of the time I didn't give the disabled a second thought. I never considered discrimination, or lack of job opportunities. I never imagined sitting in a wheelchair at the bottom of a flight of stairs. I watched the telethons, yet didn't know one set of initials – CP, MS, or all the rest – from another. The performers drew me. In my own little world, the disabled didn't play a part. So what did I care?"

"Where had I been?" she puzzled in print. "I was coming across people, attitudes, and ways of life I didn't realize existed." Stating that Terry Fox "affected us as much as any Canadian ever has," she added, "What I didn't know is there are thousands of Terrys out there. He knew it. And he tried to tell us." What had started out as "just a job" to touch the conscience of the public was finished. "I didn't know it would work so well," Jill ended. "On me."

Thereafter Mona and Jill got together every few months, Mona at first travelling to the Keenleyside house in Toronto's west end. One special day Jill and husband Denis adopted children. Mona, who always wanted to go for rides, was able to find an excuse to come along. "They were very young and hadn't really met anybody disabled before and were perhaps a little taken aback at first but within seconds that changed," recalled Jill. "It was very moving for us to see, because kids are so honest and react completely with emotion. What if they had been frightened by her because she looked different from what they were used to? But Mona was Mona and put them at ease, completely winning them over with that huge smile of hers."

When together, Jill would sometimes notice how something was bothering Mona a lot, but when asked she didn't want to talk about it. "Then I realized it was one of those typical dumb little things we all complain about and thought, 'This is not fair!' She has all this other major stuff to deal with, and she still deals with the itty-bitty, stupid stuff we all complain about every day, too. But Mona has the greatest attitude of almost anybody I've ever met." There are people for whom the cup is half-full, others for whom it is half-empty. Jill thought of herself as a cup half-full, definitely a positive, person. "But a friend of mine who had multiple sclerosis, and Mona who had cerebral palsy, both lived life with the attitude 'My cup is overflowing.' I don't think Mona resented anything. Her attitude was that she'd been given a gift and was going to experience life and live it to the fullest."

Someone like Mona brought out the best or the worst in people, Keenleyside observed. She watched so many people who would be formally polite in social settings completely envelope Mona when they greeted her. "They just loved her, you could see instantly. They were so glad to see her again, and completely comfortable with her." She compared it to how people's normal polite reserve evaporates when a tragedy happens, or the electric power's gone off, or there's a major crisis, and suddenly they connect as humans. "That's what it was like with Mona. With her disabilities she would break through the veneer of social reserve and bring out what was really inside people." Yet these good moments were also offset by the reality that at other times, in other places, "her disability brought out the ugliness of people who didn't understand, were afraid, and reacted cruelly towards her."

If Mona was giving a lot to her friend Jill, it was a two-way street. "If it hadn't been for Jill's constant prodding, I would never have had the audacity to write to the Toronto newspapers and suggest they begin a column for and about disabled people, or to mention that I would be interested in writing it. I am convinced that without Jill's encouragement, the column and everything that resulted from it would never have happened. We all need someone in our lives who can make us aspire by directing our vision to the stars. For me, Jill was that 'someone'."

Even after Mona became fully occupied writing "Disabled Today," she still continued to see her friend Jill whenever possible. Mona would go to the Keenleyside home for dinner in the mid-1990s, or Jill would go to her place, since that was often easier for Mona.

Spaghetti kids: Mona visited the home of friend Jill Keenleyside, whom she'd met in 1982 through a CBC cerebral palsy telethon, during the 1980s and into the mid-1990s. Mona enjoyed dinner and happy times with the Keenleysides' son, Damion.

They would sometimes go to a restaurant, because Mona liked the social aspect of being out, but only if the eatery wasn't very full. Busy restaurants were difficult for conversation because Mona's hearing aid didn't filter out background noise, especially the clattering dishes. Every once in a while there'd be a sudden, sharp noise. Her whole body would jump. "That happened a lot," recalled Jill. "It was hard for her. She couldn't help it. This reaction was completely involuntary, a shock to her system."

Such outings stopped because of Mona's increasing problem with balance. The angle of her head contributed to her starting to fall over when she went out. It made walking difficult, and especially caused her to be nervous about winter ice.

"Mona had enormous dignity, enormous," said Jill. "She just wanted to be able to eat for herself, to do as much for herself as she could. She wouldn't bemoan when somebody had to help her. We spent so much time eating together I saw that she was very conscious of her dignity at the table. Table manners were very important to her, also eating, and the way she dressed. Even the little fabric purse-like holder for her hearing equipment would match whatever she was wearing. Appearance was important to Mona."

After Jill moved to Ottawa, Mona sent her feel-good emails, "the friendship ones and the sunny-day ones, to brighten my morning." That was Mona's attitude. Despite her own many difficulties, she was able to lift the spirits of others, including people who were fully able-bodied.

− 26 −
Bonding with Barb

Mona first met Barbara Hickey, executive assistant to United Way president Anne Golden, in the course of her work as a board trustee. The two began with the most practical of matters, such as coordinating Wheel-Trans rides for United Way meetings, but soon this connection blossomed into a strong and lasting friendship.

"There was a picture of Mona Winberg in the boardroom," recalled Barbara, "which was an odd photo that seemed to emphasize the brace around her neck. That was not the person I saw, not the bright, fun, crazy, healthy person I knew Mona to be."

Barbara noticed little details. She saw (as apparently every woman did) how the fabric pouch Mona wore around her neck to hold her hearing aid always matched her clothes. She observed how, with the Lifeline monitoring system which required Mona to check in twice every day, "the girls who answered the calls vied with one another to take her call – 'Hi, Mona, what's doing today? Who's visiting?'"

In 1995 Mona and Barbara decided to visit the Metropolitan Toronto Zoo, long an aspiration of both women. Barbara had not realized, however, just how far east in the city the zoo was located and arrived late, panicked by the thought of poor Mona, on her own and helpless. When she spotted her friend, Barbara witnessed how Mona's "independent living" translated into arriving at the zoo on time, chatting with strangers, calmly understanding about a delayed rendezvous, and just being happy finally to see the zoo, even though the lions were asleep in the summer heat.

There were times Barbara went to Mona's place, witnessing her at the computer "firing off emails" and, with her help, sending letters to board members or others whom Mona believed needed to see her latest column because of the issue it raised that was relevant to their life or public responsibility. For visits like these, Mona had a gin-and-tonic ready to melt Barbara's self-described "reticent nature," and not reluctantly joined her guest to sip one herself.

Mostly, the two went out to events with Barbara a very willing escort. They liked seeing movies, their game being to go to a theatre where admission was a bargain price. One outing to Silver City cinema challenged them, however, because a thunderstorm had knocked out Yonge Street's traffic lights and cars were flying by in the heavy rain, sending a misty spray everywhere. The duo stood at the curb waiting urgently to cross Yonge and get to the theatre before the early matinee half-price admission ended. Finally, with Mona's daring, they risked their lives and crossed through all the traffic, staying alive, saving some money, and enjoying a British comedy.

From sleeping lions to roaring traffic, their outings seemed always to include something memorable. In the case of the Terry Fox luncheon in 1995, it was an injured arm. Barbara escorted Mona to the luncheon award ceremonies, where they chatted with Terry Fox's mother, Betty, his brother Fred Fox, champion skater Kurt Browning, Wayne Gretsky's dad, Walter, and the Hall of Fame board members.

When the ceremonies began, Barbara took special care to prevent Mona from falling because, as both women understood since each suffered from osteoporosis, her bones were brittle. "It was a nightmare," recalled Hickey, who had been shepherding Mona up to the stage. "A big guy from the *Sun* enthusiastically embraced Mona and she lost her balance and fell."

Stoic Mona, "not uttering a single complaint," was gratefully inducted into the Terry Fox Hall of Fame, delivered her brief remarks, then with Barbara went by taxi to the North York Hospital for her fractured arm to be treated, finally returning home happy, a cast on one arm and her trophy clutched in the other.

During Mona's years on the United Way board, she and Barbara talked "shop" a great deal, addressing both issues and people. When leaving the board, Mona feared that without things to talk about, her friend would drift away, underestimating just how much people loved being in her company. As the years passed, the two continued to have much to discuss and share.

"Mona had a good sense of how to deal with problems," Barbara recalled, thinking about United Way issues but also matters in her own life. "It was tragic for Mona when her brother Wolfe died, and when that happened, for the first time, I felt I was actually able to be there for *her*."

– 27 –

Practically anything and everything

Independent living never meant flying solo. VON nurses, Meals-on-Wheels providers, Wheel-Trans drivers, Winberg family members, *Toronto Sun* and United Way friends were supplemented as the years advanced by such further services as the Senior Care program and the women who monitored Mona daily through the Lifeline Personal Response system.

Most directly, however, independent living became supported by paid visiting helpers who accompanied Mona through the chores on her journey of self-reliance.

Always on the vanguard in such matters, in 1989 Mona became one of the participants in a pilot project for the Ontario government's Direct Funding or Self-Managed Attendant Care program. Under this scheme, money went from the Ministry of Health and Long-Term Care to the Centre for Independent Living. It, as program administrator in the Toronto region, in turn distributed these funds to disabled citizens. They, in turn, used the money to hire help.

It was quite a distribution chain for the money, but it worked, with appropriate accountability, to link the user and the provider of the service directly. This self-managed attendant care program empowered individuals with disabilities and fostered independent living. The amount each qualifying person got was based on his or her needs, according to an individual evaluation. Because of her severe disabilities, Mona received the maximum hours allowed for attendants' services.

Whomever Mona hired as her own caregivers, after holding interviews with applicants, would come to her apartment for a set number of hours each day. There was a preset schedule, with one caregiver coming in the morning, another for the afternoon and evening. They were paid at a wage rate set by the ministry. Laura Lorenz, between working shifts for the Toronto Police, was Mona's bookkeeper for the program, keeping track of the hours attendants worked and the money paid them.

Mona liked to engage attendants around 50 years old, "because women of that age are mature and know about household tasks, especially if they had children."

They helped Mona take a bath and dress, shopped for groceries and other items, did general housecleaning, wrote out notes and letters she dictated, helped her get to bed, and did "practically anything and everything, as long as it was not too strenuous." A good attendant kept her eyes open for ways to be helpful. If she saw that Mona was not eating enough, she would fix her a snack. One caregiver, after coming for four years, had become extremely adept at anticipating Mona's needs.

She did not feel that having help undermined her independent living. "Disabled militants refuse help if they can do something themselves, but I accept it."

"It was not all bright and rosy. When you work so closely and the work is personal, you become at least attuned to their moods, too. They're not always cheerful and don't always feel like talking. I had caregivers, too, who stole money and other things from me. I'm a bit of a fool. It took me a while to catch on," Mona ruminated. "Some caregivers," she added, "have given me a little bit of lip and abuse, too." Then Mona's irrepressible upbeat attitude about living rounded out her explanation, "But heck, it's part of life."

During a power blackout in 2003, Mona was without electricity for more than a day, leaving her vulnerable since many of the operations at her apartment were electricity driven. Fortunately, her two caregivers made it through, and they improvised in the darkness.

In November 2003, Ontario's debt-saddled government capped the number of hours available to a person needing attendant care. The government also announced that no new applicants would be accepted into the program beyond those then enrolled, which in Toronto numbered 668 people. Mona grew more careful about the things she asked her attendant to do. She worried, too, that as people in the program got older and needed more help they'd be stymied, and that younger disabled people wanting to live independently would be excluded from this worthwhile program.

"I live in constant fear regarding my future needs, and the very real possibility that I may not be able to continue to live in the community," she emailed me in September 2005. "My anxiety is heightened by the deplorable fact that the groups which are working with and for disabled people are uninterested and uncaring regarding many of the challenges confronting their older and most vulnerable members."

Sue Skinner, Mona's afternoon and early evening caregiver at the time of my various visits to Mona's apartment, said that working with Mona "reinforced her conviction that disabled people and seniors are happiest and able to make more of a contribution to life when in their own homes rather than institutionalized." Sue accompanied Mona to many public events, such as the December 2003 Citizenship Court ceremony where Mona addressed new Canadians, and she helped Mona find and photocopy materials for this book, in which she shared Mona's interest. In February 2006, Sue suffered a brain aneurysm and was unable to work for Mona thereafter.

Digna Hernandez, Mona's morning caregiver in her final years, was adamant about nursing homes and that Mona "had no place in them."

Dorothy Daniel, her physiotherapist, was a key person in Mona's support team, working with her (or as Mona quipped, "enduring me!") from 1978 until the summer of 2006. Dorothy was convinced, based on her experience and what she'd witnessed, that "physiotherapy helps disabled adults maintain their physical abilities and thus their independence." In February 2006, she was also convinced of something else: she "read me the Riot Act regarding all the typing I have been doing. It is hard on my muscles, especially my arm," said Mona.

Exercising her body and not straining it unduly in harmful ways were essential for Mona's continued wellbeing. Through July of 2006 I worked with her to find affordable replacement physiotherapist services. Getting physiotherapy was key to slowing her physical degeneration. By this stage it had become best to reach Mona by email because her use of the telephone had become quite problematic.

In addition to her visiting attendants, Mona's independent living continued to be supported by the assistive devices and amazing configurations of equipment in her apartment. She constantly upgraded the equipment around her in a sustained effort to remain independent. In April 2005 she emailed, "Just to inform you that I'm receiving a new computer today. For the first time in my computer-using life, it will not be an Apple. Please do not be alarmed, therefore, if you do not hear from me for a couple of weeks. When it comes to computers, I'm a slow learner!" A number of days later, a further email: "It's a good thing I have a head of heavy hair – because I've been tearing it out working on this new computer! Sue is helping me and we're both becoming a little exasperated! But we shall overcome."

Mona loved Star Trek and perhaps part of her connection with the television series was how her apartment resembled the high-tech command centre of a spaceship. She, of course, was its captain.

"Let's face it," Mona said, "nobody wants to go into a nursing home or other institution."

She never did. In her years of independent living, Mona would reside for 39 years on her own, thanks to her resolute determination and the individuals and services helping her maintain self-sufficiency.

Even when Mona had such difficulties with caregivers and other support staff in the last half year of her life and institutionalization loomed, Barbara Ostroff came to the rescue. From Circle of Care, a not-for-profit provider of in-home health and support services, Ostroff was instrumental in revamping Mona's whole network, complete with Mona's move into a two-bedroom unit in the same building so a live-in caregiver could manage her increased needs. Barbara worked closely with Mona's nephews and nieces to put together the new support system and Mona remained free from a dreaded institution.

Paying tribute to solitary courage

Mona Winberg's frail and misshapen form defied, for many, any suggestion that she was a leader, but there is no question that this pioneering woman created a path for others to follow.

Her special pull as a leader involved feelings she kindled in those who knew her, met her, or even just read her columns – a rare mixture of inspiration, respect, intelligence, humour, and fearless advancement of new thinking, rounded out with fear of her disapproval and topped off with a melt-your-heart smile.

Increasingly, Mona's leadership became publicly recognized. She began to receive awards and distinctions for her tireless efforts to improve the lives of people with disabilities and to upgrade government services intended for their benefit.

In 1984 these tributes began with an award from the Canadian Cerebral Palsy Association, followed four years later with 1988's splendid trio: the King Clancy Award, the Canadian Rehabilitation Council for the Disabled Award, and the Ontario Government's Office for Disabled Persons "Community Action Award."

The King Clancy Award, a prestigious honour created by the Canadian Foundation of Physically Disabled Persons and presented by the Toronto Don Valley Rotary Club, recognizes outstanding contributions for work in the community. Winning it was, Mona told reporter Enzo Di Matteo of the *North York Mirror* in May that year, "exciting, nerve-wracking, and memorable. I had to make my acceptance speech in less than one minute, and you wouldn't exactly call me speedy in anything I do," she joked.

Even if she did speak haltingly, Mona always considered her voice as being for a cause larger than her own. Thus, while the King Clancy Award for the writer of "Disabled Today" was an important personal achievement, she saw its greater significance. "The biggest focus right now is bringing to the attention of people the abilities of the disabled," she said in her brief remarks. "That is what the column is all about."

At that February 1988 gala award presentation for the King Clancy Award, Mona met another of Canada's trailblazers against discrimination, Hon. Lincoln Alexander, lieutenant governor of Ontario, for the first time. After that, they met more times and corresponded.

Lincoln Alexander, air force pilot in war and lawyer in peacetime, whose own solitary courage led him to break down many barriers while upholding and inspiring others, came to early national prominence as the first black citizen elected to Canada's parliament. When appointed to cabinet, he set a further benchmark as the first black minister of the crown in our country. He continued achieving additional breakthroughs against racism and discrimination over the decades, in the legal profession and policing, rounding out further leadership roles as Ontario's lieutenant governor and University of Guelph's chancellor. Sometimes he saw Mona at an event and would have his driver stop the car, get out, and come straight over to her. This was not done for a photo opportunity. Lincoln Alexander was just genuinely glad to see her. He would write, in his Foreword to this book, that Mona was "a woman who made a difference," that she was "a stream of inspiration."

On November 18, 1988, Mona was one of a dozen Ontarians to receive the Community Action Award from the provincial government. Remo Mancini, Minister Responsible for Disabled Persons, referred to the determination and resourcefulness of these "exemplary citizens," noting in Mona's case how "she has increased public awareness and understanding of disability issues through her column 'Disabled Today' in Toronto's *Sunday Sun.*"

In May 1989, Mona won the Ontario Association for Community Living's media award for her "Disabled Today" column. Harry Zwerver, the Association's executive director, said "Mona's experience

with her own handicap gives her writing an incredible sensitivity and awareness. She is extremely thorough and can take complicated issues and turn them into a very readable story." Mona, presented with this media award plaque in the Jupiter Room at the Regal Constellation Hotel, bore it proudly home to be mounted on the wall of her small apartment.

Several years passed. Mona continued to plug away. Then in 1995 came a major acknowledgement that the world was a better place because of her efforts, when she was inducted into the Terry Fox Hall of Fame. The Hall of Fame

2003: Hon. Lincoln Alexander greets Mona Winberg at a public event.

had opened the year before, in February 1994, with Vim Kochhar its founding chair, to honour individuals who have worked for Canada's citizens with physical disabilities.

1988: Mona was front and centre to receive a Community Action Award for her "Disabled Today" column in Toronto's *Sunday Sun* from Ontario's Office for Disabled Persons. Applauding at left is Mona's Willowdale MPP, Gino Matrundola, while applauding at right is Hon. Remo Mancini, Ontario's Minister Responsible for Disabled Persons. Between, l-r: Mona's brother Wolfe Winberg; Janet Burke-Gaffney, wife of Mona's editor at the *Sun*; Mona's sister-in-law Norma Winberg; Mona's niece Debbie Troister; and Michael Burke-Gaffney, editor of the *Sunday Sun* who hired Mona to write a weekly column about disability issues.

When being inducted, Mona was described as "a dynamo, in print and in person" and "a source of inspiration and a tireless fighter for the disabled." Her disabilities "have never stood in the way of her ability to communicate. Wherever Mona goes, her warmth and sense of humour, her conscientiousness, and her determination have won her the respect and love of many friends and admirers."

Two years later, Mona was back in the awards news for being designated the 1997 Gardiner "Citizen of the Year." June Callwood, a journalist and ardent advocate for social justice whom Mona considered "a warm and gracious lady," was present when Mona received this award.

"Mona, you have a great sense of humour," smiled June.

"I have found it useful to break down barriers."

Shortly before she died, June Callwood wrote to describe Mona as "a woman of dignity and compassion" and saying "this fine book is all about finding a path that has heart in it."

All the while, her column "Disabled Today" continued to attract recognition from committees of judges deciding upon newspaper and journalism awards, such as the Special Media Award she won in 2000.

All these honours were glowingly touted by the *Toronto Sun*, and the newspaper's stories were just as proudly clipped by Mona's helpers and pasted into her growing number of scrapbooks. As a news organization, the *Sun*, keen to feature her journalism awards, also fully understood the strong human interest aspect of this story-within-a-story. Those running the paper ensured that the *Sun*'s many photographs over these years, even if showing she was disabled, never failed to get that great Mona smile on her face.

Also in 2000, her status as a VIP nudged higher when Mona joined the ranks of notables listed in the *Canadian Who's Who*. Mona Winberg was really becoming a Somebody.

1995, September: Mona Winberg is inducted into the Terry Fox Hall of Fame. She slowly speaks words of acceptance, while chair of the organization Hon. David Crombie holds the microphone for her. At centre is founding chair Vim Kochhar, and at left, Ontario's Lieutenant-Governor Hon. Hal Jackman.

The following year she reached the pinnacle of public recognition. The February 14, 2001 announcement from Rideau Hall that Mona Fleur Winberg of Toronto would be admitted to the Order of Canada was a real valentine for Mona. "I can't quite believe it. I'm having trouble believing it," the *Toronto Sun*'s Kevin Masterman quoted "a jubilant Winberg" as saying in the next day's paper.

Taking stock of this highest recognition that can be bestowed upon a Canadian, Mona credited the "Disabled Today" column as being her greatest accomplishment. "It gave disabled people a voice they never had before. I always remembered I was speaking for those who couldn't."

In Ottawa for the ceremony, an excited Mona met up with people like Bob Rae, whom she'd interviewed when he was premier, reconnected with friends like June Callwood, and met for the first time people like Dalton Camp, among others being installed that day. After the formal part of the Rideau Hall ceremonies ended, Governor General Adrienne Clarkson came over to Mona, bent down, and gave her a kiss.

"Mona went to another stage in her career in 2001 at Ottawa, with the Order of Canada recognition, her participation in a press conference, and in her columns after that," observed Burke-Gaffney, looking back. Her editor at the *Sun*, whose interest in disability issues and media connections found him consulting with the Canadian Association for Community Living at this time, was certainly close enough to the action to know.

2001: Mona Winberg received Canada's highest civil honour when Governor General Adrienne Clarkson conducted her investiture into the Order of Canada at Rideau Hall ceremonies in Ottawa. Also inducted were Mona's friend June Callwood, left, and former Ontario premier Bob Rae, below.

The press conference featured two new members of the Order of Canada. "With Dalton Camp and Mona, we had a press conference in which these notable Canadians spoke about disability issues," recalled Burke-Gaffney. "Though it was not well attended by the media, it was one of the last public things Dalton Camp did, speaking personally in public about his brother who was institutionalized in New Brunswick. Mona spoke and was very impressive."

"That was the first press conference I addressed," said Mona of the event. "All the rest I'd attended before had been as a journalist." Focusing on the Latimer case, then a national sensation and in large part the rationale for the press conference, Mona stated, "Tracy Latimer's father assumed she wanted to die. We don't really know that, but we do know she had no choice in the matter." She added, "The unfortunate thing is that some people still equate what he did with euthanasia."

Attending ceremonial events and being publicly honoured for the contributions she made in speaking up for people with disabilities did not mean Mona would, or even could, stop taking the positions that had brought her to public attention in the first place.

All these award ceremonies were public presentations, but after they ended the gratitude they had directed toward Mona remained with her. She reflected at times like these on the determination and love of her mother, Sarah. She thought about how much she owed to individuals like Mike Burke-Gaffney. In her apartment, the growing number of plaques and award certificates crowding her walls competed for space with existing photographs of her beloved family members, pushing the next generation of Winbergs onto the window sills.

Recognitions continued. Mona was recipient of the Queen's Golden Jubilee medal in 2002. She was designated a Paul Harris Fellow of Rotary International in 2003.

Yet she did not care to be singled out as an over-achiever or someone who had overcome tremendous trials, just because she happened to have a job and cerebral palsy. "Many people are inclined to think of disabled people as either extra wonderful or extra nobody. The truth is we are just like everybody else in strengths and weaknesses."

29

Over and over again

Not just as an award recipient but in other ways as well, Mona Winberg was increasingly being recognized as a leader and spokesperson for the wider community. Even if these events were ceremonial in nature, such as a citizenship court ceremony, that did not prevent Mona, always the advocate, from using the occasion to advance the cause.

December 3 is the Day of Disabled Persons, and on this day in 2003 a special Citizenship Court session was convened in Toronto for new Canadians to officially receive their citizenship certificates. Mona was the co-presiding official with Judge Agnes Ugolini Potts, as well as being a featured speaker. Mona welcomed 83 new Canadians from 33 countries.

"You likely have hopes and aspirations about what your new life will bring and I know you are determined to reach most of your goals," began the slow-speaking Canadian in addressing her new fellow citizens. Given the diversity of mother tongues present, another challenge in spoken communication faced Mona, but she pressed on with her clear message.

"However, you must also be prepared for difficulties and disappointments. Unfortunately, there are some narrow-minded persons who may find fault with you because you are not a native-born Canadian.

"This is very similar to the way that some disabled people are treated as second-class citizens," continued Mona in her soft, intermittent voice. "The more conspicuous the disability, the more that one has to prove that one is equal . . . over and over again."

Respecting the impediment that required her to say the most in the fewest possible words, Mona concluded her address by simply appealing for leadership and courage:

"We are breaking down the barriers of fear and ignorance to make a better future for all disabled people – just as you must walk firmly and steadily in your chosen path so that you can make it easier for all those who follow in your footsteps."

The following day I visited Mona and she was ecstatic describing the events of the day before. Accompanied by helper Sue Skinner, they'd been driven to the ceremony by Wheel-Trans. Mona felt thrilled by the impressive presence of Royal Canadian Mounted Police constable Howard Adams in full-dress red serge tunic. She was happy to be with her friend Vim Kochhar who, as another leader for people with disabilities and an earlier immigrant to Canada himself, also spoke. She enjoyed seeing the different expressions on the faces of people becoming citizens of Canada.

But she also reflected, in the day's aftermath, more sombrely on the moods and actions of those present. Some of the new Canadians had ignored her, she told me, others raced right past. When I expressed disappointment about this, Mona countered with uncommon understanding, "You have to remember, some come from countries where disabled people are not seen in public."

The ceremony had concluded on a high note, in any event. Mona had been given a standing ovation upon completing her speech, then presented by citizenship court judge Ugolini Potts with a patriotic clock inscribed with Citizenship and Immigration Canada's motto: "Canada, We All Belong!"

2005, December 3, International Day of Disabled Persons: Mona Winberg, a featured speaker at a Toronto citizenship court, greeted new Canadian citizens from 33 different countries. Behind her: helper Sue Skinner, RCMP constable Howard Adams, Vim Kochhar, and citizenship judge Agnes Ugolini Potts. Man at left not identified.

30

Eclipse of the sun

Mona cited the eight-year maximum time in office for presidents of the United States when explaining why she thought it important not to overstay one's usefulness in any particular role. If the need for renewal and vigour applied to that important office, it must surely apply to all lesser positions people occupied, too. Yet moving from theory to practicality, how long should she remain a newspaper columnist? Already she was well past the eight-year mark.

Four or five factors conspired to keep her at the *Sun*. One was her unswerving determination to speak out on issues facing disabled Canadians. Another was the knowledge that, in the realm of disability issues, hers was pretty much the only established media voice keeping interest up and pressure on. A third was that all her life she'd wanted to be a writer, a line of work with no mandatory retirement age so long as the juices kept flowing. As well, the succession of awards and the public recognition Mona received for "Disabled Today" gave her entrees, additional forums, and speaking opportunities to advance the cause of independent living and to promote measures enhancing the dignity and security of citizens with mental and physical disabilities. Finally, what else would she do? The status she had from the column, and the direct outlet it provided for her agenda, could not be achieved in any other way, so far as she could see. And, hadn't she gone on record a number of times saying, "I'll keep on going as long as I can and as long as I am needed?"

It seemed that "as long as I can" would be the determining factor.

New Century: At the start of the twenty-first century, Mona connected with a large world from her "command central" apartment and its communications systems and assistive devices. Here is where she wrote "Disabled Today" for more than a dozen years in Toronto's *Sunday Sun* -- and emailed her friends, surfed the Internet, and spoke with family, friends, and colleagues by adapted telephone.

Working on "Disabled Today" for days on end, suspended awkwardly over her keyboard like a human praying mantis, had exacted an ever-greater toll on Mona's health. Her spine curved. Her body increasingly twisted in shape. She became badly bent over. This changing shape in turn meant her balance was thrown off when she tried to walk, while her head, despite mechanical supports, tilted further. Though Mona Winberg still had plenty to say, and despite the fact her voice needed to be heard and heeded more urgently than ever, there was a limit, even for her.

The irony was that even as advances in technology helped her do interviews more efficiently and speeded things up with her computer, these gains were offset as her deteriorating body, made worse by all the time she sat contorted at her keyboard, slowed her down in equal measure. This regime meant Mona never had a respite, and seldom got a holiday. It still took a full week to write a 400-word column.

A dozen years of this was all she could take.

"The long hours I spend at the computer," she told her *Sun* readers when saying "Goodbye, folks" in her sign-off column of August 29, 1999, "have resulted in much physical pain and bodily wear and tear," a remarkably candid note from a woman who never complained.

"I also do not know how much longer I will be able to enjoy the privilege of living on my own," she confided to her public, again revealing a true state of despair for one whose life's purpose had revolved around independent living. "I want to spend the remaining time free from the responsibilities of weekly deadlines."

Her *Sun* newspaper family, and her weekly readers, truly missed Mona Winberg. Many letters-to-the-editor poured in with tributes. Michael Burke-Gaffney said, "The experience with Mona was the highlight of my career in journalism. I encouraged her to be an advocate, a fighter, and stayed in the background." Years after Mona retired, no longer making her memorable weekly appearances at the newspaper's offices, hard-bitten reporters still asked after her with affection and interest: "Where's Mona? Does anybody know what she's up to?"

After her retirement, Mona intermittently was up to contributing articles to the *Sun*. The most extensive was on a topic especially urgent to her: an analysis of the murder of Tracy Latimer, who like Mona had to contend with the effects of cerebral palsy, the several trials of her father Robert Latimer, and the swirl of public sentiment about it all. During income tax season, Mona put together a column of tax tips for people with disabilities. She contributed book reviews. In one case an editor at the *Sun* asked her to do a review and gave her a 48-hour deadline. The problem, apart from reading the book first, was that it required 49 hours of typing by Mona.

After she surrendered her column, opportunities for Mona to hold up the flag for people with disabilities became increasingly rare, and therefore all the more important. Her final "Disabled Today" may have appeared in print, but her mind did not stop working nor her concerns diminish. Her voice had been made quiescent by force of circumstances, not because she had run out of things to write or because she felt the battles had all been won. It was just the opposite. Her frustration mounted the more that silence filled the space she had once occupied, and she despaired that others were not coming forward to be heard.

"Where are the voices of people who should be protesting?" she demanded when I visited her in mid-February 2004, the day an auditor general's report disclosed millions of wasted dollars that could have gone, she said, to social and health programs. "I feel guilty I'm not still writing my columns. But I'm not the only one who knows. Where are their voices?"

The *Toronto Sun* did not replace Mona Winberg with another columnist to carry on the disabilities beat, even though if a sports, gardening, or cooking columnist left the scene, the subject would not be abandoned but a new writer hired.

"We could likely never find another person like Mona," said Burke-Gaffney, which left one wondering whether this observation should be categorized as tribute or excuse. "It was a dozen years of advocacy we won't likely see ever again, given the change in contents and style, ownership, and financing of the media," he added, again a doubled message that could be either tribute or lament, but was probably both.

To the extent this was true of Canada's news media in general, it paralleled a similar change in parliament where focused interest in issues affecting Canadians with disabilities also declined. This parliamentary shift was noted by William Young, parliamentary researcher with the Committee on the Status of Disabled Persons at the height of its activity in the 1980s, and today Parliamentary Librarian with a unique overview of Parliament's shrivelling disabilities agenda.

The demise of Mona Winberg's fabled "Disabled Today" column marked, as it turned out, the end of an era. It was not a setting sun from which Mona, ever the realist, could take any solace or satisfaction, despite all she had done. "It is the future that fills me with despair now," Mona wrote me five years later, in mid-November 2004. "Like the rest of the population, disabled people are living longer. On top of their original disabilities, the infirmities of old age are now added.

Worse, this is occurring in an environment of severe government cutbacks to social services. Most appalling, however, is the fact that most groups that work with disabled people are indifferent to the needs of their most vulnerable people."

Mona noted that when she'd started "Disabled Today" in late 1986, "there were not the appalling cutbacks in services to disabled people that exist today. What makes me really apprehensive about the future is that many of the voices that should be protesting these injustices are silent."

– 31 –

Mona on her good days

Although her close friend Jill Keenleyside spoke of Mona's "cup runneth over" attitude to life, Mona herself appreciated her limits. She always stressed that people with disabilities, like others, have strengths and weaknesses.

During the winter of 1993 she'd read *Days of Grace,* the autobiography of tennis great Arthur Ashe, who had contracted AIDS through a tainted blood transfusion. When asked by people if he wondered why this misfortune had befallen him, Ashe replied that no, he did not, because then he would have had to ponder why all the good things happened to him in his life as well. Mona acknowledged that she could not match his "noble spirit."

"Mona," effused Jill, "was one of the angels living on earth." I'd once said something like that to Mona myself. She smiled, then answered, "Don't forget, you only see me on my good days!"

Sometimes Mona awoke in the morning upset after a bad dream. Raquel San Jose, her caregiver from the Philippines, would talk with her about it. Mona shared a great deal with Raquel in easy-flowing conversation, the way people find it easy to be utterly open with a complete stranger or someone whose background is far removed from that of immediate family or close friends. Sometimes Mona looked back at her life and became cast down or upset. Raquel would urge her to look forward, working her back into a better frame of mind.

Other times, Mona's retrospectives produced a more balanced assessment. "I can look back through my columns and see what I did with my life," she told me. "I consider that my greatest achievement is that I was, and still am, a very fussy writer. I think, without that column, I would have gone through life wondering if I had lived up to my potential."

Those columns, extensively sampled in Part II, provide benchmarks not only for her life, but also for Canadian society. They reveal a woman of solitary courage, of intelligence and humour, and of unrelenting advocacy. They document the quest for a better deal for Canadians with mental and physical disabilities, and the many triumphs over them. They are an enduring legacy from a woman whose fate in 1932, but for a mother's love that defied a doctor's best advice, would have been life in an institution instead of being a force in the world.

People who encountered Mona Winberg remained deeply touched by her character and courage, or her clearly held views, or her smile, or her perky humour. Very few ever forgot her.

– 32 –
Slipping away

One week before her seventy-seventh birthday, Mona Winberg's family and friends, some sixty in number, gathered on a cold and overcast winter's day in the Benjamin Funeral Chapel at the northern edge of Toronto for final tributes to her life. Mona's remains lay in a plain wooden casket, its simplicity and quality honouring the woman inside. After two weeks in hospital, Mona had died from pneumonia on January 19, 2009. The service proceeded in the time-cast traditions of the Jewish faith.

When Cantor Marshall Loomer called for "messages from the heart," Mona's nephew Sidney Troister came forward to speak on behalf of the family about her life, public contributions, relationships with others, and "accomplishments which are almost legend." He finished by recalling Mona's witty trademark opening for many of her public speeches – "If any of you were expecting a Sunshine Girl,

I am sorry if I am a disappointment." – in order to offer his heartfelt rejoinder: "She was *never* a disappointment."

Mona's niece Deena Baltman then proceded to the front, gained her composure, and recited the Mary Elizabeth Fry poem, "Do Not Stand at My Grave and Weep." On this day Deena would also describe a gold locket she'd been given by Mona, who'd been presented with it years earlier by her mother. Engraved on the locket were Mona's birth date and the quotation "But Oh, The Thorns We Stand Upon." Within, facing one another, were two black-and-white pictures, one of Mona, the other of Sarah. Because her mother had very little money for jewellery, this had been a very deliberate endowment. "Whatever thorns she stood upon," reflected Deena, "Mona nonetheless seemed invincible."

I looked around at others present: the colleagues, close friends, and cherished family of Mona Fleur Winberg. Everyone seemed calmly united in a spirit of solemn reflection . . . His Honour Lieutenant Governor David Onley . . . Hon. David Crombie . . . Michael Burke-Gaffney of the *Toronto Sun* . . . Mona's relatives whom I'd come to know and those from British Columbia whose faces I could finally match to names and voices known before only by telephone . . . writers like Irene Borins Ash who had a chapter on Mona in her 2003 book *Treasured Legacies: Older & Still Great,* and Carolyn Blackman who would write an extended obituary of Mona's life for *Canadian Jewish News.*

When Mona's mother defied Dr. Aaron Brown's advice in 1932, it had been an act of courage as well as instinctive maternal love. In that era, what a doctor said usually had the force of scripture. The power of medical personnel, the structures within which they operated, and the escapist use of institutions and asylums, all constituted a solidly entrenched order. It was especially astounding for a female to challenge that established order and the value system that went with it in a society where women had been acclimatized to a secondary status and generally evinced deferential attitudes. The fourth life that Sarah Winberg had given birth to, and then saved, and then attentively nurtured over the years into another human being as resilient and courageous as herself, had now ended.

At the Bathurst Lawn Memorial Park cemetery, beneath a late morning monochrome grey sky, our procession made its way to the newly dug grave awaiting Mona's simple casket. The pallbearers, her six strong nephews, had no difficulty with the coffin's weight. Mona was a slip of a thing. Their feet crunched on the packed snow over a path ploughed between the close rows of grey granite and black marble tombstones.

A cluster of dark coats and heavy boots took shape around the open grave, against the white snow background, beside the frozen pile of upturned brindle-brown earth. Graveyard workers, in honey-brown work coats that almost matched the raw earth in colour, moved silently through their routines. The four men steadily lowered the casket on supporting ropes, two on each side. When it settled below, two on one side pulled up deliberately to quietly remove the lengths of rope, then all four stood back.

The melodic voice of Cantor Marshall Loomer, unhesitatingly advancing the brief interment ceremony into its next phase, carried across the cemetery's snow-filled expanse, dissipating somewhere over the serried rows of grave markers where others had arrived before Mona. Members of the Winberg family stepped forward, a few at a time, taking turns to shovel some earth down into the grave, symbolically beginning the covering of Mona's coffin.

The frozen lumps were hard to break free. Several fell from the end of shovels with a loud bang on the wooden box below. Not a summer funeral with soft earth to sprinkle easily, but a hard-lumps exit, deep in the Canadian winter, the same frigid season in which Mona's frail, noble life had first begun.

PART II

Mona in Her Own Words

Introduction
A bumper harvest of newspaper columns

Every week for more than a dozen years, from November 2, 1986 to August 29, 1999, Mona was writing columns for Toronto's *Sunday Sun*. She produced some 273,650 words that appeared in print, each one laboriously typed, a very slow single letter at a time, but by the end of it all, she'd created more than 600 columns.

Only one in four of them appears in this next section of *Solitary Courage*. While 150 or so columns is just a fraction of what she wrote, it is still enough to provide a substantial and representative sampling of her work. These "Disabled Today" columns that are republished in this book appear with the kindly given consent and collaboration of the *Toronto Sun*, a newspaper courageous enough to hire Mona a quarter century ago and proud of her enduring messages today.

Some omitted columns involved subjects that Mona returned to frequently, important for a columnist over the spread of more than a decade as she tried to keep issues before her readers, but repetitious if combined in a single book. Others referred to places, individuals, and events that are now simply too dated or particular.

Some columns are included because they show how a principle took on meaning in a specific situation, even though they contain illustrative details or specific references that may be slightly dated now. In some cases that has been addressed by providing supplemental current information in a footnote, but all Mona's columns themselves remain as she wrote them.

Although her most recent columns are just a decade old, others stretch back to the 1980s. This entire body of work preserves an invaluable record of social history, political imperatives, and emerging issues for Canadian citizens affected by mental and physical disability at an important stage in our country's evolution. A particular value of such an historical record is how it helps us now see in sharper relief those recent times and the lessons emerging from their patterns.

The 156 columns which follow are arranged into 20 thematic chapters. They begin with large framework topics such as government, the cost of cutbacks, advocating for disabled persons, and adapting.

The next selection covers essential aspects of "independent living" such as education, educational integration, housing, accessibility, and assistive devices, but also transportation, work, sports, and recreation.

Following that come chapters confronting the dark side, such as the tragedy of Tracy Latimer's murder and the abuse and neglect of disabled people, and finally ending with brighter chapters about getting away, remarkable achievers, love, and friendship.

Altogether, they are the best of Mona Winberg, in her own words.

– 1 –

A Newspaper Columnist

When conveying her analysis of happenings in the public sphere, Mona's skill as a writer was on display each week as she mixed clear thinking with the emotions of human joy and disappointment, rounded out with insight or anecdote from her own experiences living with disability. Sometimes she even wrote about writing "Disabled Today" itself. These first two columns, bookending a decade of Mona's writing for the Sunday Sun, *help provide a framework for her hundreds of other weekly offerings on specific issues.*

A year of fighting injustice
October 30, 1988

This is the second anniversary of the column and, as becomes a custom, I will look back at some of this year's noteworthy events.

It has been the best of years and the worst of years. It has been difficult because I have had a great deal of pain in my neck due to arthritis and disc problems. Thus far, the only solution I have found is to wear a therapeutic collar. I am hoping that the medical profession will begin to take more interest in the problems faced by people with cerebral palsy as they age, similar to how they have been alerted to the challenges relating to post-polio syndrome.

One of the most notable events has recently occurred: people in institutions who have intellectual limitations or who are psychiatrically disabled were given the right to vote. This is a big step forward. The expectations of people can help them achieve their highest potential – and we can overcome the practical problems if we are willing to try.

The Thomson Social Assistance Review Committee gave its long awaited report. Despite its deficiencies, the report made some excellent recommendations. If provincial and federal governments implement them, it will help make life easier for disabled people— many of whom are living with incomes well below the poverty line. You can bet this column will keep reminding the government of its responsibility to follow through on this report, which took three years and $3 million to produce.

During the past year, I have had the opportunity to interview many interesting people—everyone from the inventor of a new wheelchair to a blind artist, in addition to politicians, musicians, doctors, and the drivers and staff of Wheel-Trans. These interviews have been conducted in such wildly dissimilar places as the Royal York Hotel, a gym, and on the beach in St. Petersburg, Florida.

It has been a special privilege to participate in the 1988 United Way campaign as a spokesperson for the United Way. This has introduced me to the many fine people involved in this organization, as well as others who contribute donations. People who have never met a handicapped person before are now being made familiar to a person with a disability. Since many problems are caused by fear and ignorance, I hope this exposure will result in better understanding and knowledge of the abilities of people with a disability.

My involvement with the United Way has also been the cause of many unusual experiences: Everything from giving speeches four times in one day – which was a little tiring even for someone who likes to talk – to almost falling off a truck, and being taken on an unforgettable tour of the beautiful greenhouses in the City of York.

As for the future, wherever there is an issue to fight, an injustice to expose, or human-interest story to tell, that's where this column will be.

Finally, my most sincere "thank you" to you, the readers. It is your interest that encourages me and your concerns that give me ideas for the column.

Celebrating ten years of writing "Disabled Today"
November 3, 1996

Today marks the 10th birthday of this column. I've been writing about the concerns of disabled people and their families for a decade. Hard to believe, isn't it?

My first column appeared the day Rick Hansen wheeled into Toronto following his triumphant Man in Motion tour. It's impossible not to be charmed by Hansen's handsome face and articulate speech. However, other people with disabilities who may not be as easy on the eyes—such as those with cerebral palsy or developmental handicaps—are still striving for inclusion.

Among my favourite columns were ones that dealt with Becky Till and Emily Eaton and the battles they each waged to get an integrated education.

Another memorable article concerned Tracy Latimer and her father, who killed her. The public, and particularly the media, condoned this tragic act and thereby unleashed the outrage of disabled people across Canada.

This column has seen three changes of government provincially in Ontario and two federally—and been impartial in its criticism of all of them. A common denominator of all governments today is the slashing of services that benefit their most vulnerable citizens. This will continue until we all rise up and shout: "Enough!"

Looking back over the years, I discover that my happiest memories are of the people I've been privileged to meet.

I will always be grateful to four fine gentlemen for their kindness, warmth and encouragement. Two are former lieutenant governors— Lincoln Alexander and the late John Aird. The other two are David Crombie, chairman of the Waterfront Regeneration Trust, and former Etobicoke–Lakeshore MP Patrick Boyer.

I am also thankful to Vim Kochhar and the Canadian Foundation for Physically Disabled Persons for giving me, in 1988, my first honour: the King Clancy Award.

I appreciate the affection and understanding of everyone at the *Sun*. A special thanks to our helpful *Sunday Sun* secretary, Pauline Mason, and associate managing editor, Mike Burke-Gaffney, who hired me. Mike looked beyond my disabilities and gave me a chance to show what I could do.

— 2 —

Educating the Public

A primary function at "Disabled Today" was public education, and in this Mona moved on two levels. One was to address specific issues relating to disability and provide readers with important information about them. The second, essential to true education, was the opening of peoples' thinking and perceptions about the nature of society and individuals with mental or physical disabilities. Mona knew only too well why it was essential to confront and change attitudes amongst the general population towards disability.

Shattering the age-old stereotype

January 4, 1987

A dictionary I have defines the word "myth" as "a fictitious, traditional story or legend."

Over the years, many myths have evolved about disabled people. One of the most ingrained is that they are all happier in each other's company. Nonsense! Disabled people are no different than any other group of people. A disability—even the same disability—does not ensure that the individuals having it will also share the same views, aspirations, and sensitivities. Does anyone expect engineers to always remain together? Or clerks? Or bus drivers?

Another myth places disabled people in either one of the two extremes: Happy, smiling Pollyanna types or sad dejected figures of tragedy. The truth is that disabled people—like other people—are sometimes happy and sometimes a little in between.

Depending upon circumstances and events, a morose disabled person will have times of gaiety and light-heartedness. Whereas the most "well-adjusted" individual can, occasionally, experience despairing thoughts like, "How am I going to manage the rest of my life?"

A myth that is being shot down with great frequency is that of the permanently unemployable disabled person. Futurists tell us that we are moving into a mechanized, computerized society where the thinking process, not physical ability, will be important. Thus, it is anticipated that more disabled people will find work that is both rewarding and productive.

On the other hand, it is erroneous to believe that disabled people who do not work have nothing better to do than watch television all day.

Patricia Walsh has no 9-to-5 job. Yet, she is one of the busiest persons I know. She is a book reviewer for *The Companion,* a monthly publication of the Franciscan Fathers. As well, she is active with several groups and committees that are enabling disabled people to live fuller, meaningful lives. All this, despite the fact that she is in a wheelchair, with hands and speech that do not always respond as she wishes.

"I want to make the best use of my time that I can," Walsh explains. "To me this means helping others."

When I looked up the word "myth" in another dictionary, it had this brief definition: "An imaginary person."

Up until recent years, few disabled people have been a part of the mainstream life. With increasing integration in all levels of society, the "imaginary people" are now being replaced by those we all know: Fellow students, co-workers and friends.

Mona also came up with some guidelines about how to treat people with disabilities.

The 12 Rules of Respect
November 4, 1990

If you've ever wondered what you can do to make life easier for a disabled person, here are 12 useful tips:

1. Don't get one disability confused with one another. For example, if you see someone in a wheelchair, don't talk loudly to him. That person has difficulty in walking, not hearing.

2. However, if you are speaking to someone who is hearing impaired, it is important that you face him, talk a little slower and not cover your mouth. Many hearing impaired people read lips.

3. Don't automatically assume it's a prank or a nuisance call when you answer the phone and hear someone talking in a different manner. The caller may have cerebral palsy or another disability that affects his speech. DON'T BE TOO TIMID TO ASK.

4. After you've tried and you still cannot grasp what somebody with a speech disability is saying, don't feel reluctant to ask him to repeat it.

5. If you are having a prolonged conversation with a wheelchair user, it is easier on him if you sit down so that he doesn't have to strain his neck by looking up continuously.

6. Make certain that the respective owners approve of where you are placing their wheelchair or crutches. Their mobility depends upon these devices, but they're not going to do them much good if they're beyond their reach.

7. If a parking lot is full, don't take the space reserved for disabled people even though you believe you'll only need it for a short time. A handicapped person could come along and not be able to get out of his car because you are illegally taking his place.

8. When you are talking with a disabled person and his able-bodied companion, direct your conversation equally to both. It is hurtful and humiliating to the handicapped individual when you ask questions of his companion about him and generally treat him as if he were invisible.

9. No matter how great a temptation it is, be careful about offering unsolicited advice. It is a maturing experience for handicapped people to be responsible for their own successes or failures... just like everyone else.

10. Please give a disabled person a fair chance when he applies for a job. He may make up in determination and resourcefulness what he lacks in dexterity and speed.

11. People need more in common than being disabled to be compatible. Consequently, you should not take it for granted that all handicapped persons prefer each other's company. RESPECT INDEPENDENCE.

12. Above all, don't feel rebuffed if your offer of assistance to a disabled person is refused. Some people feel that they must do things for themselves. However, it is essential that you are not discouraged from extending help to another handicapped individual who may really need it.

To give her readers a clearer appreciation of the situation with disabled persons, Mona occasionally used her column, as in this example from 1988, to present statistics that could speak with their own eloquence.

Latest stats disturb

July 31, 1988

Statistics can be confusing—even boring—but I have some today that you really must know about.

Statistical Profile of Disabled Persons in Ontario, a bilingual booklet just released by the Office for Disabled People in the province, identifies disabled adults aged 15 or over, and disabled children aged 14 and under, with both groups together representing 20 percent of the population—considerably more than has ever been estimated.

Disabled adults are older than non-disabled adults. Thirty-six percent of disabled people are age 65 and over whereas there are only

9 percent non-disabled people in this category. It is interesting to note that 79 percent of the 152,000 unmarried disabled Ontarians over age 64 are women.

It is evident that both government and organizations who work with disabled people must include, in their long range planning services, provisions for both a disabled and an aging population.

The disabling conditions most frequently identified were musculo-skeletal conditions, arthritis/rheumatism, heart and circulatory problems, and disorders of the nervous system and sense organs. In terms of specific individual conditions, the most common were hearing disorders (20 percent) and back problems (17 percent).

Among children, asthma (11 percent), learning disabilities (16 percent) and hearing disorders (11 percent) were the most frequently reported disabling conditions.

The most commonly mentioned disability was mobility, followed by limitations in agility, hearing, and sight. It is interesting to note that hearing problems are mentioned in all three of the above-mentioned categories.

Among disabled adults, 54 percent are mildly, 23 percent moderately, and 15 percent severely disabled.

On the subject of assistive devices, 38 percent of disabled people needed technical aids but did not have them because they were too costly.

The difference between having a technical aid and not having one can sometimes mean an independent life or one spent in an institution. The Liberal government must expand its Assistive Devices Program to include disabled adults of all ages so that no one in need of aid is deprived.

Government financial assistance for architectural or other modifications would, as well, help disabled people to remain in their own homes. The *Statistical Profile* shows a total of 159,000 disabled Ontarians lack special features in their homes, such as ramps and handrails, to help them move around. An additional 280,000 disabled people have problems using appliances and fixtures in their homes.

The survey showed that 48 percent of disabled adults are completely dependent on personal assistance for some activities.

It is regrettable that 39 percent of disabled adults have eight years or less of schooling, while the comparative figure for non-disabled adults is 16 percent. Many of today's jobs rely on mental, not physical, abilities.

Of 63,000 disabled students, 42,000 (70 percent) attend regular classes, 14,000 (23 percent) attend mixed classes, and 10,000 (17 percent) are in special schools or classes. There are still too many students in "special" settings.

At the time of the survey, 41 percent of mildly disabled people and 74 percent of severely disabled people were unemployed. In this latter group, almost 58 percent reported incomes of less than $10,000 in one year—a poverty level existence.

Finally, an estimated 44,000 disabled adults need special transit services.

Not only does this book give a picture of disabled Ontarians, but it also shows where the Liberal government must act to improve the quality of their lives.

In her efforts to improve awareness of disability issues among the general population, as well as to advance the lives of those with disabilities themselves, Mona advocated increased social integration of people with handicaps, and their heightened representation in the news media.

TV needs to bring handicapped into the picture

July 13, 1997

Television is in the Dark Ages as far as its attitude toward disabled people is concerned.

When was the last time you saw a person with an obvious disability in a regular TV series?

Like the old and realistic CBC *DeGrassi* school programs that had a student who was a wheelchair user. Or the excellent former ABC series *Life Goes On* and its engaging star, Chris Burke, who has Down syndrome and portrayed a character with the same disability.

Where the role calls for a character with a disability, it's not always necessary to cast a person with the same disability in the part. After all, not all disabled people can act, any more than all non-disabled people possess acting skills.

I vividly remember the truly magnificent performance non-disabled actor Daniel Day Lewis gave in the feature film *My Left Foot* as real-life author Christy Brown, who had cerebral palsy.

Shows like CBC's newsmagazine *Disability Network* do a good job, but have a specific audience in mind—disabled people themselves. However, I like a series where the disabled character is one of a variety of other characters, as they usually are in real life, who can be enjoyed by anyone in the viewing audience.

More than a year ago, the CBS soap *Guiding Light* introduced a new story line of a couple who have a baby with Down syndrome. This series can show the little girl at various stages of development and will educate its audience almost without them being aware of it.

I've been told that sponsors shy away from shows that have conspicuously handicapped characters. However, these same sponsors should realize we are consumers too.

When comedienne Ellen DeGeneres admitted she's gay on her ABC-TV series *Ellen*, the show's ratings skyrocketed and television congratulated itself for taking such a bold step. Perhaps if we disabled people came up with a program idea about our sexuality, this would make us more attractive to TV.

Television and its sponsors have a choice: they can contribute to our isolation, or help us as we strive for acceptance and inclusion.

While Mona took others to task for actions that negatively affected individuals with disablilities, she did not hesitate to turn her critical eye on programs designed to assist disabled persons, or on people with disabilities themselves when she felt their attitudes or actions hurt the cause.

Call for independence
August 6, 1995

"Many rehabilitation programs do not teach people with disabilities how to be independent in any real way. What they learn is how to be dependent on different systems."

Those are the words of Scott Seiler, who is both learning disabled and visually impaired.

"People with disabilities are taught to ask rehabilitation specialists for assistance but not taught how to help themselves. If disabled people become too self-reliant, we would not need these specialists who want to keep their jobs by keeping us dependent. In most cases, they are not even aware of doing this," he said.

Our entire society likes to look at disabled people as children and objects of pity. We are not considered full human beings and because of this, we learn to be dependent.

This can lead to over-reliance on other people to solve all our problems.

People with disabilities expect government and the law to remove barriers into the work force and the community. Instead of complaining to the people who have created the barriers, we believe that somebody else or one of the systems should intervene on our behalf.

If we do make a complaint to the Ontario Human Rights Commission, it could take years to overcome a barrier in only one place.

"We have laws and precedents around integration. The laws are beautiful pieces of legislation and court rulings to force integration as something that should be done. But in many instances, laws and precedents are 20 years ahead of actual practice.

"Integration is assimilation into the community, but this has not happened because we're trying to force assimilation through legislation.

"Though some people feel legislation is the key to opening doors, there is still a big discrepancy between what the law says and what is happening in reality," declares Seiler.

When disabled people are in a new social situation, many of them wait for other people to make the first overtures of friendliness. They don't feel any responsibility in encouraging this to happen.

We are teaching disabled people there will always be somebody else or a law there to help them out of any difficulties.

"People with disabilities should be taught to solve their own problems and to advocate for themselves by the acquisition of skills. This training has to start early in childhood and must be faithfully maintained by parents," says Seiler.

Handicapped by bad attitude
January 28, 1996

Some persons with disabilities have such unpleasant attitudes they make life difficult for other handicapped people.

Recently, I was in a Wheel-Trans taxi on a blustery and cold day. Another rider sat in the front seat with the driver.

We then picked up a woman who demanded to sit in the front seat. The driver patiently explained that the man sitting there already needed it and helped her into the back seat. All the way to her destination, she complained because she couldn't sit where she wanted.

If she had to climb up and down subway stairs or wait on windy, snowy corners for tardy buses, she might appreciate the comfortable and accessible service that Wheel-Trans provides.

There's also the danger that other disabled people may be classified, along with her, as selfish and self-centred.

A friend of mine was on the subway one day when she noticed a man with a white cane ahead of her. She walked over to him and asked if he would like help down the stairs.

He became angry, lifted his cane in a threatening manner and told her in no uncertain terms to mind her own business.

Said my friend: "It will make me reluctant to offer aid to another person with a disability."

People like this man seldom realize that their own rude reaction may deprive another disabled person of much needed assistance. Whether we like it or not, we who have a disability are more conspicuous. How we choose to behave can educate non-disabled people in a positive fashion or else reinforce every negative stereotype they have heard about us.

A while ago, I was waiting for a friend at a movie theatre that has two levels when I observed a woman with a brace on one leg slowly make her way up the stairs of the second level, accompanied by another woman. It was five minutes before the film on their level began.

Because of the slowness of their ascent, a crowd soon formed behind them. About 15 minutes later, they reached the top and the crowd was free to surge inside the theatre.

Why couldn't they have arrived at the theatre earlier so as not to delay anyone who wished to see the beginning of the movie? This would be similar to the way airlines pre-board persons requiring special assistance.

We disabled people possess rights, but so do other people.

A person who's a wheelchair user once said to me: "When we request our rights, we are assertive. However, when we forget that other people have rights too, we are aggressive."

Indifference is the greatest threat
March 31, 1996

Disabled people are in danger.

It's not government cutbacks so much that have placed us at risk—it is our own apathy and laziness. We don't seem to care that accessibility to decent, affordable accommodation, transportation, and assistive devices which enable us to become independent, contributing members of society is disappearing.

There have been no voices raised explaining how these services allow us to stay healthier, find jobs, and get off social assistance.

One of the latest assaults on our well-being is that homemakers can now often spend only one hour with each client. If an individual needs help with laundry, bathing, and meal preparation, the homemaker cannot possibly accomplish even one of these tasks satisfactorily. As one homemaker pointed out to me: "I will spend more time traveling to and from different homes than I actually do with my clients."

Relatives and friends are expected to take over homemaker duties. But what happens if these persons live out of town or are experiencing health problems of their own?

Their silence forces me to believe disabled people are indifferent to this gradual deterioration in our services that could eventually make it impossible for us to live in the community or ever get out of institutions.

So-called advocacy groups have also not protested what they must surely recognize as the whittling away of the gains it took disabled people and others years to achieve.

Perhaps these organizations believe their silence will save them from more government cuts. However, they will not be spared when government sees how spineless they are. Even worse, some of them are squabbling among themselves as old jealousies and rivalries come to the surface. They are not truly interested in disabled people—their sole concern is to maintain their own power and status.

Some of you may think that columns such as this one and other favourable coverage in the media are fighting your battles for you, and that all you have to do is sit back and reap the benefits. However, the media get involved in other issues and cannot give any one matter their sole, undivided attention.

We must wake up to the jeopardy we're in. We must enlist the assistance of non-disabled friends to spread our message by talking, demonstrating, and writing letters. Even government will be forced to give way to a strong, united, and effective force.

After all, the one thing they do care about is our votes.

As a social critic anxious to help improve the lives of people with disabilities, Mona resolutely pointed her readers to problems wherever and whenever she saw them. Yet she was just as quick to use the power of her columns to celebrate people and programs that advanced the cause.

The Secret of Shhh

May 2, 1993

Toronto's Young People's Theatre skilfully combines the drama of a believable story with fantasy and adventure in the new, one-hour play, *The Secret of Shhh*. It ushers in May, Hearing Awareness Month.

The tale concerns two children, Mimosa and James, both hearing impaired. While James' hearing aids make him a target for ridicule by school bullies, Mimosa's hearing problem has not yet been identified. She is regarded by everyone as stupid and inattentive.

The play was commissioned by YPT's artistic director, Maja Ardal.

"Through my friend Mimi Shulman, who is hard of hearing, I became aware of the great need for communication accessibility," Ardal told me. "Her hearing loss has been increasing over the years so I've been getting an education in the process about this supposedly invisible cause of so much distress.

"During her childhood, Mimi felt that everyone had a secret which they didn't want to tell her. This was before she knew she had a hearing loss," she said. Ardal then asked Marcy Rogers, another friend of Mimi's, to write a play based on Mimi's experiences. The character of Mimosa is patterned on Mimi.

This delightful play also features an eccentric street entertainer and her sidekick, a magical cat who can speak seven human languages, despite being hard of hearing. The pair whisk Mimosa and James off to the "Land of Your Biggest Fears" where the children learn that confronting their problems can make them disappear.

"An important point made in the play is that it is essential for people with hearing problems to see the faces of the persons they are communicating with so that they can speech-read. It's not a matter of shouting, but of speaking distinctly," Ardal stresses.

"I hope that this play gives children with hearing impairments a better feeling of self-esteem and that it provides other viewers with new knowledge and insight," she said.

Kids get lessons in living

June 10, 1990

The students in Grade 6 of Pleasant Elementary School in North York have learned something this past year not usually taught in schools: They now know that disabled people and seniors are just like everyone else and that they can be active and functioning members of the community.

It all began when Patti Durkee left Senior Care—an agency that provides Meals on Wheels, homemaking, and other services to seniors and disabled adults of all ages—to become a Grade 6 teacher at Pleasant.

"Since my students didn't know much about disabled people or seniors, and because some people also have an unfavourable impression of today's children, I felt both groups could benefit by learning more about each other," she said.

To help Durkee with her idea, Arnold Foss, Senior Care's co-ordinator of the intergenerational and volunteer visiting programs, set up a pen-pals program that has disabled people and seniors corresponding with the students in Durkee's class. As a client of Senior Care, I participated in this interesting project.

"Before the program began, I asked the students what it means to grow older," recalls Durkee. " I received answers like—being older means frail, it means being sick, it means you're going to die.

"We also discussed disabled people and we felt that part of the problem is that the students don't understand the causes of why someone may look or act differently and therefore, they end up not liking that individual."

The pen-pal project fits smoothly into a VIP—Values, Impressions and Peers—program that Durkee is teaching too. It deals with many moral issues, such as saying no to drugs.

"The children also learned about the importance of volunteering and how essential agencies like Senior Care are in helping disabled people and seniors to stay in their own homes and out of institutions," Foss notes.

The pen-pals finally met a couple weeks ago at an intergenerational tea at Pleasant school. There were lively and sometimes very intense conversations going on at each table, with the students obviously enjoying their roles as hosts and hostesses.

What I particularly observed is that the students felt quite comfortable with those of us who were visibly disabled.

"The students got to know the hearts and souls of the disabled people and seniors when they corresponded with them. Therefore when they did meet, the children saw only the person and not the disability," says Vivian Shapiro, principal of Pleasant.

"We can become a little closed world if we don't bring various people into our school. By having this contact, our students now realize that over the past disabled people and seniors are a part of the community in which we all live," she said.

— 3 —

Government

Because government funding and various public laws, rules, and programs impact so profoundly on the lives of people with disabilities, Mona frequently ended her week by turning into The Sunday Sun *a column about government and politicians. All levels of government, and all parties, came under Mona's exacting scrutiny. In the first columns below, the federal government and its policies are examined.*

Tories' policies disappointing

October 23, 1988

Two words came to my mind after assessing the way the Tory government in Ottawa has treated the concerns of disabled people the past four years: disappointing and ineffectual.

I say that despite the efforts of Tory MP Patrick Boyer and despite some progress, such as the fact that a disabled person and an attendant can now fly on Air Canada using one ticket.

David Baker, executive Director of Toronto's Advocacy Resource Centre for the Handicapped (ARCH), shares my disappointment.

In 1985 the Supreme Court of Canada ruled that the Canadian Human Rights Act contained no obligation to make reasonable accommodation for disabled people or others. The then minister of justice, John Crosbie, said that the government would take immediate steps to remedy the situation. It is now almost three years later, and still nothing has been done.

Reasonable accommodation means meeting the special needs of a disabled person up to the point where it would impose undue hardship on the employer, landlord, or service provider. It could involve ramping an entrance to a building, a telephone with an amplifier for a hearing impaired person, or a special training program so that a developmentally handicapped person can perform a job.

The government does not want to amend the *Canadian Human Rights Act*, not because of this issue, but because it doesn't want to deal with the issue of sexual orientation, says Baker. There have been several recommendations that the *Canadian Human Rights Act* include protection for gays and lesbians. If the government were to amend the act for "reasonable accommodation," it would be under pressure to include these changes on the issue of sexual orientation as well. It is not willing to do that. As a result, disabled people have been deprived protection under the Act.

The *Ontario Human Rights Act* and several other provincial acts include both reasonable accommodation and protection for gays and lesbians. Yet the federal government, which should be taking the lead in this matter, is burying its head in the sand and hoping the issue will go away.

They will have done very much the same in the income security area for disabled people, observes Harry Beatty, ARCH lawyer.

In January 1987, the federal government increased its Canada Pension Plan (CPP) disability payments. However, if recipients also received social assistance under the Canada Assistance Plan (CAP), Canada Pension payments had to come off dollar-for-dollar because of some CAP restrictions. In some provinces, CPP disability payments went down. This shows how the different programs do not work together.

CAP also limits liquid assets for a single disabled person to $3,000. This has been unchanged since 1980. The earning exemption has not been increased, either, since 1982. This means a single disabled person who receives the top GAINS-D allowance of $693 per month can only earn a monthly $125 and keep 50 percent of the next $100 of their earnings.

These asinine rules serve as a disincentive to anyone wanting to get off social assistance and enter the job market. There are also extra expenses for special aids a disabled person may require to perform a job.

What is needed is a federal government that will work with the provinces and disability groups to make the CPP and CAP plans compatible and raise the ceiling on liquid assets and earnings to a more realistic level. This will result in more handicapped people experiencing the fulfillment and self-esteem that only comes with satisfying work and adequate wages.

Grits don't merit our votes

June 1, 1997

The Liberals do not deserve to be re-elected tomorrow.

They have a dismal record with regard to disabled people.

By dismantling the Canada Assistance Plan (CAP), under which many programs for people with disabilities were funded co-operatively with the provinces, they disgracefully abdicated their responsibilities to handicapped persons.

CAP was replaced with the Canada Health and Social Transfer, which not only gives progressively less money to the provinces each year but also makes no provision for disabled people. As a result, the provinces are not compelled to do anything for us.

In a last-minute attempt to get our votes, the Liberals recently announced various measures that would benefit those disabled people who have significant incomes and therefore pay income tax. However, since most disabled people are unemployed and live below the poverty line, these concessions are useless to the vast majority of us.

By abandoning its leadership role in the provision of services and assistance to disabled people, the Liberals have made us one of the prime targets of the cost-cutting measures of the provinces.

Our concerns have also been ignored by the other federal political parties, mainly because most of our so-called advocacy groups have been silent. They are afraid of losing their government funding. What they should ask themselves is: Are they more interested in perpetuating their own existence than in speaking up for the people they are allegedly serving?

The groups composed of my fellow disabled are just as ineffectual. By narrowly focusing on their own interests, they cannot see that governments throughout Canada are bent on turning the clock backward. They want to save money and have concluded that cutting programs that help disabled people and other vulnerable groups is the easiest way for them to do this because we don't have a strong, united voice.

Ontario is a particularly complacent, do-nothing province. Governments are making services so difficult to come by that soon many of us will be forced into institutions.

The New Brunswick and Quebec governments have already started along this path and Ontario is following with its "levels of support" plan.

However, no matter how powerful they are, governments eventually have to call an election. We can show our dissatisfaction with the Liberals by returning fewer of their number to power. If we continue to do nothing, we will deserve whatever we get.

Changes are few
June 14, 1992

The Canadian Association for Community Living (CACL) is more concerned with the issues that the new federal disability bill does not address than the changes it does make.

"It doesn't go far enough," states Diane Richler, CACL executive vice-president, of the omnibus bill now before the House of Commons.

The first legislation to deal exclusively with disabled Canadians, the bill is the result of a legislative review by the Canadian Disability Rights Council and its subsequent recommendations.

"We have been very anxious to see changes made in the Immigration Act but nothing is mentioned in the omnibus bill about them," Richler said.

"There's currently a provision that excludes people from immigrating to Canada if they are likely to place undue hardship upon health and social services. That's being interpreted to mean anyone with a disability.

"This suggests that people with a disability are a drain on society and, if we had our druthers, they would not be part of our community. It also implies that the Canadian government views people with a disability as a burden rather than as contributing members of society," she said.

Some amendments are going to be made to the medical criteria of the *Immigration Act* but, at time of writing, it's not known what they will be.

Changes to the *Elections Act* are another major concern to CACL.

"One of the changes would allow electors who are unable to read or who are blind, visually impaired, or so physically disabled they are unable to vote in the manner described in the Act, to request the assistance of the deputy returning officer. But this does not include people who have an intellectual disability," says Richler.

Other, more positive, changes to the *Elections Act* include mobile polling stations for people living in institutions. Also, candidates with disabilities who are running for public office will not have to include disability-related expenses within their election spending limit.

As well, the Criminal Code is being amended so that disabled people can give testimony from behind a screen or outside the courtroom if seeing the accused would prevent the complainant from freely testifying.

"The Secretary of State and Minister Responsible for the Status of Disabled Persons, Robert de Cotret, is aware that some improvements can be made to the bill," says Nancy Lawand, executive director of the Status of Disabled Persons Secretariat.

He is also willing to look at a proposal by CACL to seek an order-in-council regarding disability issues so that any future legislation is sensitive to disabled people.

Feds must show will to act

November 24, 1996

One of the key recommendations in the report of the National Task Force on Disability Issues is that the federal government continue to play a leadership role in matters relating to disabled people.

"It also states that discussions with the provinces are necessary around co-ordination to ensure there is a consistent approach and policy regarding disability across Canada," says Melodie Zarzeczny, acting executive vice-president of the Canadian Association for Community Living (CACL). He is acting in this role because the federal government has seconded Diane Richler, the CACL's executive vice-president, for a few months, to give policy advice and work on new initiatives for Human Resources Development.

There are significant disability-related costs, such as attendant care and transportation, that can act as disincentives to employment. In addition, people may also lose government benefits when they take even low-paying jobs. This prompts them to say, "I can't afford to work!"

Zarzeczny observes: "People in the workforce have so much personal satisfaction—from the pride and dignity of having a job to the economic and social benefits. What is critical around labour market integration is that we ensure people with disabilities have access to training opportunities and insurance-sponsored programs that lead to employment."

She adds, "This is particularly important for people with intellectual disabilities who have had no former attachment to the labour market. The current programs are targeted at putting people back to work who have been in the workforce previously."

Many disabled people are sceptical of the value of this task force. They say government already knows what needs to be done from previous task forces.

They also feel it may be a ploy to get our vote for a coming election. Zarzeczny, however, stresses: "We must continue to push our agenda forward. Now is the right time to do it because our programs are being reformulated. We must make certain we're there delivering our message. At the present time, there's a window of opportunity to make some change."

She says, "Disabled people are citizens of Canada first. It's up to this government to guarantee they receive the same rights under our Canadian Charter of Rights and Freedoms as the rest of the population."

This report is entitled *The Will To Act*. The federal government has all the information it will ever require.

Now, it must prove it has the will to act.

Given the primary role provinces play in health care, education, transportation, housing, and social services, policies of provincial governments across Canada were also frequently addressed by Mona in "Disabled Today."

Now act on equity, Mr. Rae

January 27, 1991

"We must remember that for people who are disabled, there's always been a recession. Therefore we can't use that excuse to not move ahead." This was Premier Bob Rae's response to a question I asked him about whether now, in the middle of a recession, was an appropriate time for the NDP government to bring forward its employment equity legislation.

"First of all, we appoint an employment equity commissioner. That person, together with a group that he or she pulls together, shall be responsible for consulting widely with the business community and other people about the type of legislation we are about to introduce.

"We're obviously going to look at other laws—for example, the American Congress' legislation that deals specifically with disabled people," explained Bob Rae.

I asked whether quotas will be included in the legislation. "It is not a question of quotas. It's a question, first of all, of rights, then it's a question of access, learning, and training," Rae replied.

"We're looking at getting employers and employees together and setting targets, goals and objectives. This will necessarily include the assurance that the workplace reflects the types of people in the general population. We're talking about reducing the unemployment levels among disabled people dramatically during the nineties," he says.

As it is now, if disabled people want to supplement the social assistance they receive by finding a job, the government punishes them by allowing them to earn only very small amounts.

Is the NDP planning any changes to this program it cost-shares with the feds?

"The federal government has severely limited its spending under the Canada Assistance Plan, so I'm not sure we can use the excuse anymore that we have to wait for them to make changes," Rae said.

"People who are disabled should have an assurance of the level of income that is adequate to them. At the same time, I don't want policies in place that are going to continue to penalize and discriminate against people who are able to find employment."

He told me that one of the most important things he's learned is that disability can happen to anyone—regardless of income and background.

"This was really brought home to me when my younger brother who, in addition to having cancer, was struck by a syndrome that causes temporary paralysis," he stated.

"Here was somebody who, until he was 31, never thought that he would be disabled. Yet he was in a wheelchair for the last year of his life. Any one of us can become physically or mentally impaired. Therefore, when we talk about programs we want to bring into place, we should bear in mind any one of us could benefit from them. We share the human condition, so we should all try to improve it," Rae said.

His many years in opposition have given Rae a good understanding of the needs of disabled people. However, just how much he and his NDP will do about them, remains to be seen.

Fighting New Brunswick's care classification system
May 11, 1997

The province of New Brunswick is depriving disabled people of hard-won rights and forcing them into institutions.

"Government has adopted a medical model that judges people according to the level of care they require. As a result, they are being placed in nursing homes," says Julie Stone. An educator, Stone is president of the Canadian Association for Community Living (CACL) and lives in New Brunswick.

"People with an intellectual disability are not ill," she says. "They may need different levels of care, depending upon individual circumstances."

Both the New Brunswick Association for Community Living and CACL are fighting the New Brunswick government on this matter. A challenge under the Charter of Rights and Freedoms has been launched, on the grounds that taking away a person's right to choose where they live is against the Charter. But this will take time to resolve.

"It all began when an assessment was made of everyone who uses New Brunswick government services," Stone explains. "Everybody who was given the numbers 3 and 4—persons needing round-the-clock care—would only be served in a nursing home.

"If the community in which they lived did not have a nursing home or if there were no empty beds, people would be moved away from their community to where nursing home beds were available," she explains.

In New Brunswick, the ministries of Health and Community Services are combined, and the minister is a medical doctor.

The majority Liberal government of Premier Frank McKenna was getting so much heat about this matter that it stated anyone living in their own home now would be allowed to continue to do so. But disabled people who are newly requesting services as of April 1 must go into nursing homes if they are in categories 3 and 4.

"New Brunswick's classification and categorization system is also taking place in Quebec," Stone says.

"B.C. has a new welfare act that separates disabled people and gives them their own funding. However, CACL is anxious about it," Stone says. "We are concerned that government may eventually decide they are spending too much money on these people and it would be cheaper to place them in an institution."

It has been proven many times that disabled people who are warehoused in institutions are at risk of physical and emotional abuse. Be aware that the New Brunswick system is heading for Ontario, where a "levels of support" program is already in the works here.

The dignity of the individual is an important underlying theme for people with disabilities, and dignity is closely connected to privacy. Despite the relentless erosion of the residual island of personal privacy in our age, Mona was consistently clear about the need to challenge any removal of individual privacy by government.

Down with this data project
June 8, 1997

In a flagrant invasion of privacy, Ontario's Ministry of Community and Social Services (MCSS) is requesting personal information about disabled people in a questionnaire being sent to agencies.

This levels-of-support project, as it's known, involves a computerized data base where MCSS will establish a list of disabled people who receive services, such as those provided in group homes and supported by independent living programs.

"The data is focused on negative characteristics like bowel and bladder functions," says Stan Woronko, co-chairman of the Family Alliance Ontario. "Non-disabled people would not tolerate having their personal medical files accessible to bureaucrats. This is targeted at people with disabilities and is totally unacceptable," he says.

Obviously, the aim is to find a way to provide services at their lowest possible cost. The ministry wants to fund only the most basic, custodial care. By categorizing people into the level of support they require, MCSS will be able to allot a certain number of dollars of support to them. The need for personal development, opportunities, and a satisfactory quality of life are not being taken into account.

MCSS is asking the staff of agencies that provide services to fill out the questionnaires. However, disabled people themselves have been disgracefully ignored and have not been asked for their consent.

The Family Alliance is instructing disabled people and their families to call their agencies and forbid the release of this information.

"MCSS claims this is just research into finding out how much things cost," says Woronko. "But we neither believe nor trust them. We think it's an indicator of tragic consequences ahead," he adds. "It's a measure of this government to spend as little money as possible on people with disabilities," he says.

Ultimately, this will affect every disabled person in Ontario who relies on some type of MCSS-funded service.

"Government will provide only the most minimal support, oriented to a person's physical needs around eating, drinking, dressing, undressing and toileting," Woronko says.

They are not treating disabled people as human beings who want jobs, independence, and the chance to make a contribution to their community.

"A project that regards people as biomedical statistics is completely contradictory to MCSS stating they are in favour of individualized planning and funding and looking at what each person needs," Woronko says.

"We must fight this to the very end—we cannot allow it to go through."

Fear of fingerprint plan

May 19, 1996

On June 19, Metro Toronto councillors will vote on whether Metro's welfare recipients—8,000 to 10,000 of whom are disabled—will be fingerprinted. After fingerprinting, each welfare recipient would be issued a debit card to be used in all financial transactions. This is being publicized as an anti-fraud measure by Metro.

The proposal is raising fears about the invasion of privacy and about the potential harm such a move could do to former psychiatric patients.

"No more than 3 percent of welfare fraud can be proven," says Scott Seiler, co-ordinator of the Income Maintenance Group. "I have very grave concerns about the privacy of a person who is fingerprinted. If government privatizes the delivery of welfare, people's information would not be subject to the municipal or provincial Freedom of Information and Privacy Acts. Information could be sold, without any consequences," he warns.

He also says that the financial institutions which will be involved (some of them American) can make a profit through service charges and by being rewarded by the government when they identify fraud. "What business is this of the banks?" he asks. "Are they becoming the police in Canada?"

Fingerprinting will very much frighten psychiatric survivors because they will be suspicious of how the fingerprints are to be used. In other cities like San Francisco, these individuals refused to even try to get welfare. They usually ended up on the streets. The lifespan of anyone on Metro streets is three to five years.

"Psychiatric survivors compose 24 percent of the disabled people on social assistance. Fingerprinting will result in a mass exodus by these people from the system. This will unfortunately be perceived by the public as justification for the government claiming that these people never needed help in the first place," Seiler says.

By selecting some of the weakest groups in its population to be fingerprinted, Metro will be treating vulnerable and disadvantaged people as if they were criminals.

"This is precisely what happened in Nazi Germany before the Holocaust. Jewish people, gypsies, persons with disabilities, and homosexuals were given a number, label and fingerprinted," he says.

Anyone who is opposed to fingerprinting should make their views known to their Metro Toronto councillor.

Sometimes Mona also found things to celebrate about government and politics. The election of Gary Malkowski, the first deaf MPP in Ontario's Legislature, was one.

Sign of times for the deaf
September 16, 1990

"It's a great victory, not only for the deaf community but for disabled people all over the world."

Those were the words of a jubilant Gary Malkowski when he became the first deaf person, who uses sign language, ever to be elected to political office in North America. He took the Metro riding of York East, a Liberal stronghold for many years that fell to the NDP in the recent provincial election.

"Communication accessibility will be one of my top priorities," Malkowski told me. By this, he means the use of sign language interpreters, computers, signalling devices, and closed captioning TV to ensure that he can fully participate in the political process.

He will also continue to press for the acceptance of American Sign Language as a language of instruction option in deaf education. Deaf students, he says, are looking forward to this change.

He feels that one of his greatest challenges lies in obtaining sign language interpreters because their shortage has now reached a national crisis.

"My being a deaf MPP will bring into sharp focus the twin difficulties of getting language interpreters and the lack of sign language training programs at a university level," he predicts.

However, he won't be an MPP who is only interested in the concerns of deaf people. "In our riding, the big issue will be tenants' rights," Malkowski says. "We have a record high number of senior citizens and, therefore, the huge increases in rent are a real problem. I'm also interested in ways to improve the environment."

Malkowski paid tribute to Richard Johnston, former NDP Scarborough West MPP for 11 years, for his interest and support of disabled people.

"I also want to thank the Bell Relay Service which, I believe, was a key factor in my election, because it allows deaf people to function in a hearing environment," he said. (I interviewed Malkowski on the phone with the assistance of a Bell Relay operator).

He has worked for several years as a vocational rehabilitation counsellor at the Canadian Hearing Society.

"Deafness is a disability that people have never really looked at," says Denis Morrice, executive director of the Canadian Hearing Society. "With Gary as an MPP, this will make it much more visible. The public will be very impressed with him and his knowledge of the issues and, as a result, this will open more doors to other disabled people.

"In the deaf education review that was conducted in Ontario, Gary stressed that deaf people should be having a say in matters that affect them," noted Morrice. "Therefore, he will certainly be pushing for government legislation and policies that will give more control to disabled people in concerns that influence their lives."

Malkowski's election shows parents of handicapped children that assessments are not always correct. He was labelled a slow learner and had to attend special classes for 10 years. It also proves to us, his fellow disabled, that our handicaps set no limitation to the contribution we truly wish to make to life.

The new NDP government should consider naming Malkowski as the minister for disabled persons.*

---

* In fact Gary Malkowski was not named to the cabinet of Premier Bob Rae during his five-year tenure in office, but he was appointed parliamentary assistant to several different ministers before his political career ended when most NDP members were defeated in the ensuing general election. Further details of Malkowski's life in politics are found in chapter 10 of Part III.

The cost of cutbacks

Government cutbacks to social services are a constant cause of concern for those in need, particularly citizens with disabilities. Mona devoted many columns to such cutbacks and their wide-ranging effects on the disabled, seeking both to make her readers aware of these issues and trying to rally public opposition to spending cuts.

Cutback threats still loom
January 19, 1992

The words were reassuring—but I still feel uneasy.

After reading media reports warning of Metro Toronto funding cutbacks in such essential programs as assistive devices, homemaking, and nursing, I spoke to Ray Lazanik, Metro's general manager of social services.

"None of the assistive devices or health-related programs have been cut. They will be considered in the total review of the budget in April but, at the moment, there's very little likelihood they will be cut. Metro council is very cognizant of the importance of these programs," he told me.

"I also think homemaking and nursing services will be low on the hit list. But I don't know that—nobody does yet," he admitted.

People with disabilities have always made easy targets for governments when they are in a cost-cutting mood. The federal government's decision to limit the increase of its transfer payments to Ontario, British Columbia, and Alberta is a good example. Many programs that benefit disabled people are cost-shared between federal and provincial governments and are included in the transfer payments.

"Money spent on homemaking, nursing, or Meals on Wheels services for disabled people and seniors are not frivolous expenditures," says Michael Scheinert, executive director of Senior Care, one of the largest multi-service agencies in Ontario. "If government, at a provincial or municipal level, wants to cut services across the board, the hardship will be felt most keenly by those persons already facing physical or health difficulties," predicts Scheinert.

Senior Care provides home support programs like Meals on Wheels, homemaking, housekeeping, and relief for caregivers of pensioners with such illnesses as Alzheimer's disease. This organization came into existence in 1974 and now serves 3,000 Metro seniors and disabled people in a year.

"It would be devastating to cut back on these programs—not only for the individuals who receive them but to their families as well. Many families depend on the type of care that we provide to help their relatives maintain their independence and remain out of institutions," Scheinert said.

Members of some families may be getting older and experiencing health problems of their own. Or they may have full-time employment. Either way, they are unable to take on the care of a disabled person or senior as well.

"It seems highly likely that government is going to continue to cut back on the number of institutional beds. They also want patients discharged from hospitals earlier. But you cannot just place people in the community and not offer them care. You must make certain that there are programs and services available that can maintain people at home in reasonable comfort and dignity," said Scheinert.

To reduce community services at a time when we have an increasingly aging population makes no sense at all.

"There is no doubt that the demographics indicate that a significant area of service development will be for the aging population. It would be a big mistake if these services were to suffer the scalpel," Scheinert observes.

I know from first-hand experience as a person with cerebral palsy how necessary these programs are. I receive Meals on Wheels and homemaking services from Senior Care and a nurse from the Victorian Order of Nurses. It is these programs that have enabled me to function in the community.

"It's been very difficult to bring the services up to a decent level of support. To cut back on them now would be a sad and serious error and undo the progress we've made over the past few years," says Scheinert.

Feeling of betrayal
November 29, 1992

Shock and betrayal. That is what the Ontario Association for Community Living (OACL) is feeling over reports that a devastating $1 billion will be cut from the budget of the Ministry of Community and Social Services over the next three years.

One year ago at a NDP government consultation, OACL asked to be told if there was a problem with finances so that they could decide where to make cuts, streamline activities, and take responsibility for conducting business differently. Instead, OACL was informed only after the ministry cut $5 million to sheltered workshops.

"They totally, completely, absolutely ignored every word we said," says OACL executive director, Barbara Thornber.

Also hard hit were programs that assist and support developmentally handicapped people to live in the community after their years of being shut away in nursing homes and institutions.

"OACL accepts the need to economize, but feels that not enough is being done to curb unnecessary waste. For example, more than $228 million is being spent annually to keep 3,020 people in institutions. That works out to $75,530 per person.

"Since 1987, community resources have grown considerably, often with insufficient funding allocations. Institutions, on the other hand, have seen a 24 percent decrease in the number of people they house. Yet, their staff has only decreased by 7 percent," Thornber says. Institutional staff earn 30 percent more than people doing comparable work in the community, though both are funded by government.

She fears the cutbacks to sheltered workshops will lead to increased segregation of people because workshops will not be able to continue with the reforms they had planned.

The minister of community and social services, Marion Boyd, told me that the sheltered workshop program was reduced by $3 million, while $2 million has been redirected to supported employment.

"We have been consulting regularly with OACL and our other stakeholders on the entire range of issues regarding developmentally handicapped people," she said.

As for the exorbitant amount of money being spent on institutional care, Boyd said efforts were being made to divert some of it to the community.

During their vigorous "Yes" constitution referendum campaign, the NDP and the feds spent millions of dollars without even a murmur about fiscal restraint. If it's something that it wants to do, government finds the money.

Anger over cutbacks

November 28, 1993

Outrage and anger have greeted the recent Ontario Ministry of Health cutbacks to the availability of artificial limbs and various supplementary aids funded under the Assistive Devices Program (ADP).

Among other changes, the minimum replacement period for artificial limbs has been doubled from two to four years for those 19 years of age and older. Also, the ADP will no longer fund such interface products as stump socks, prosthetic underhose, and knee guards.

It is obvious that this adversely affects those on limited incomes, while wealthy people will be able to afford the products they want.

"They are trying to reduce expenses in the wrong way," points out Edwin Greenfield, assistive devices administrator for the Ontario March of Dimes (OMOD).

"The ADP funds 75 percent of the cost of the assistive device and the individual is responsible for the other 25 percent. In some cases, people don't need this subsidy. However, whether somebody is earning $50,000 per year or merely surviving on a disability allowance, the funding remains the same. If they want to trim expenses, the funding should be determined by the individual's income," he said.

I wondered if this would be regarded as an invasion of privacy.

"It may be," he replied, "but it's also tax dollars we're talking about and that's a public affair. People who ask for funding should not have anything to hide. Financial need is one of our eligibility criteria."

The OMOD helps fund the 25 percent that is owed by individuals to the ADP, using dollars from the United Way, service clubs, and other donations they receive.

Under the ADP, a person is allowed one new wheelchair every five years, but wheelchairs don't always last that long. If an individual needs a wheelchair before the five years are up, he or she turns to OMOD or another agency for financial help. However, because donor dollars are down, Greenfield predicts the time is coming when people will be turned away if they need wheelchairs.

"All government programs must be reduced by 4 percent," says Layne Verbeek, a spokesman for the health ministry. "The only way to do that in the ADP is to make criteria tighter, which means not giving new equipment every three to five years automatically, but only when it's necessary, and to pay the maximum on the best available price. We don't plan on making this program geared to income because we already have co-payments in the ADP."

If the NDP had the guts to protect those who sincerely need subsidies and to prevent others from abusing the system, this would ensure assistance to those who require it the most.

We're paying the price
October 16, 1994

Once again, it is disabled people and seniors who are being forced to pay the price of a deteriorating health care system.

Medical Data Sciences (MDS) recently announced a charge of $15 for each home visit for the collection of laboratory specimens. This is not covered under OHIP. By charging for this service, MDS joined most other lab companies in Metro Toronto.

"We've had a 17 percent reduction to our fees and a further 7 percent reduction is going to occur over the next two years," explains Wilma Jacobs, MDS' director of corporate communications.

MDS and other laboratories are paid for the laboratory tests they perform based on a fee schedule set by the Ontario Ministry of Health. However, some disabled, elderly or ill persons cannot get to the specimen collection centres. For example, some people must have a blood sample taken in the early morning before eating or drinking. They may find it difficult to go out under these conditions, even with the help of Wheel-Trans.

It's hassles like these that force vulnerable people into institutions.

Government money doesn't cover the extra costs and time involved in sending a technician to a home or the expense of maintaining a car.

"No patient will be refused because of an inability to pay—that is in our policy," says Jacobs.

"For some people, this charge may qualify as a tax deductible medical expense. There's a lower fee for people who are 65 or older. It all depends on the patient's personal circumstances and we're going to be very sensitive to this," she says.

Persons who are on the Ontario Ministry of Health Home Care Program do not have to pay this fee. The health ministry suggests patients ask their doctors to do business with labs that don't charge. However, there are only about two in Metro Toronto in this category.

"The Ministry of Health is aware of the problem and plans to begin discussions very soon with the Ontario Association of Medical Laboratories. It is hoped that a solution to the problem will be arrived at quickly," says Barbara Selkirk, the health ministry's spokesperson.

This problem would never have arisen if the Ontario NDP government were as committed as they claim to be to maintaining disabled people and seniors in their own homes as long as possible.

Home Care has been cut
November 27, 1994

Ontario Health Minister Ruth Grier recently took me to task for stating that homemaker services are being reduced.

She wrote: "... the NDP government is committed to spending $133.5 million to expand integrated homemaker programs to all parts of the province. The programs served 29,000 people during 1993-4, of whom 6,700 were served by 18 new sites."

However, we're talking about two different issues.

Grier is correct in her assertion that the homemaker program now serves more clients. But I am also right when I say that, here in Metro Toronto, the number of hours homemakers spend with their clients has been decreased.

"Many years ago, a person received four hours of help on a given day. Then, it was reduced to three hours. Now, most people get only two hours a week of help," explains Jerry Berman, Director of Home Services for Senior Care, an agency serving both elderly and disabled people.

Two hours may be enough for those clients living in bachelor apartments if they only need help with light housekeeping and laundry. But the homemaker cannot possibly do everything for people who require aid with bathing, shopping, laundry, and housekeeping.

"This places a great deal of pressure on the homemaker to work as fast as she can. She has no time to talk and it may mean that the clients cannot have everything done that they wanted," Berman points out.

Since some disabled people and seniors live alone and see no one but their homemaker, this can make their existence a very difficult, lonely one.

"I wish to emphasize I am not blaming the agencies that purchase homemaking services like the Home Care Program and Metro

Community Services. Their budgets have become very tight and they simply don't have enough money to help everyone the way they used to.

"Instead of placing people on waiting lists, they are spreading out what they have more thinly," Berman said.

I receive Meals on Wheels and homemaking services from Senior Care. Every cent spent on these vital services pays a rich dividend: it prevents disabled people and seniors from having to enter costly institutions.

Unkindest cut of all

March 12, 1995

"Devastated," is the word Diane Richler uses to describe her reaction to the funding cuts in the recent federal budget.

She's the executive vice-president of the Canadian Association for Community Living.

"There will be a reduction in the amount of money the federal government will make available to the provinces for social services. That payment will no longer be made on the basis of cost-sharing in the actual services the provinces provide," Richler said.

"Instead, the lump sum transfer payment will include money for health, post-secondary education, and social services. People with a disability are going to lose out to the much stronger power bases of the medical establishment and universities," she warns.

However, one potentially positive implication is that the provinces will now know how much money they have available with no federal constraints on how they use it. An excuse the provincial governments used for being unable to change from institutional services to more flexible, community-based ones for intellectually disabled people was that the federal requirement under cost-sharing programs tied their hands.

"The federal government has maintained an ill-defined mechanism called the Human Resources Investment Fund, where all their existing programs' dollars in social services and employment are to be amalgamated. Some of the possibilities for the use of this fund include continued demonstration projects, research, and support to the voluntary sector," she notes.

"What we've lost in this budget is the amount of money going into the system and the fact that there are no longer any dollars protected for social services. This is the most critical issue.

"There will be very little going into this area because the provinces will be subjected to so many other pressures. In social services, people with a disability will be absolutely at the end of the line," she said.

The federal government is also planning to amalgamate the transfer payments that were available under the Canada Assistance Plan (CAP), Established Programs Financing, and other health payments into one Canada Social Transfer. The last year CAP will be in existence is 1995-1996.

"Most of us knew there were many problems in the current system. Now, we have been given a blank slate and the challenge will be what we're able to create on it.

"It will be a year before these changes take effect. More than ever, all of us in the community have to consider what we want the new system to be like and make certain our voices are heard," she stresses.*

Get ready for cuts in services

March 26, 1995

Cuts to Ontario social programs that benefit disabled people are coming because the recent federal budget reduced transfer payments to the provinces.

That's the prediction of Andria Spindel, executive director of the Ontario March of Dimes.

"We won't have national programs with common principles and minimum requirements any longer. There will be no minimum, acceptable threshold for which people receive service," Spindel warns.

"With programs that are provincially designed and driven and away from any federal involvement, one province may offer services that can't be obtained in another one," she observes.

Under the Canada Assistance Plan, there was at least a definition of the social problems that required attention. Without national leadership, each province will be able to do what it wishes.

"It's a wonderful theory in this country that people should define what they need at their local level. However, if you have a physical

---

* A brief synopsis of the changes that followed restructuring federal transfers to provinces and territories in 1995 appears in Part III. For fiscal year 2010-2011, transfers from Ottawa to the provincial and territorial governments were increased under Prime Minister Harper's Government by $2.4 billion, bringing total federal support to $54.4 billion a year, the highest level ever.

impairment, you need to be able to cross the street no matter where that street is," she points out.

Ontario will soon have an election that may result in a change of government. "The question I would ask any candidate right now is what will you cut when you have a $2 billion debt?

"People should articulate what cherished values they wish to preserve to all political parties in Ontario. To pour money into everything will not necessarily improve the situation. We need to decide which are the most important services that we want funded," Spindel said.

She's critical of what she terms the "infrastructure legislation" of the Ontario NDP government. It adversely affects the workplace by making the lives of employers complex and difficult and is very expensive for government to administer.

"We're not putting money into services anymore—we're pouring it into infrastructure. It's not even infrastructure that will last, like building a highway. We're building an attitude and it's costing a great deal of money because along the way it's alienating people," she says.

She feels disabled people should organize a caucus to present their views in a meaningful way both to the government and members of the opposition.

It is only by acting in a prompt and united manner that we can try to prevent further erosion of services essential to our well-being.

Redefining disability will hurt pocketbook
October 29, 1995

The Ontario Ministry of Community and Social Services (MCSS) is in the process of redefining disability.

Fears are it's going to be a very strict medical definition that removes the social and economic factors which affect a person's ability to work.

"This will eliminate people who have, for example, psychiatric disabilities where heavy abuse is a contributing factor. Abuse is not a medical condition but a societal one," explains Scott Seiler, co-ordinator of the Income Maintenance Group.

Another issue concerns people who have a facial deformity or epilepsy. Is the condition itself why they are unable to work or is it the attitude of other people? It is people like these who may not be allowed to remain on the Family Benefits Allowance (FBA).

"The Ontario government is beginning the process of cutting the number of people with disabilities on FBA by changing the definition of disability," charges Seiler. "You can reduce the number of people with disabilities on FBA by forcing them on to the General Welfare Allowance (GWA). The government changes the definition and suddenly, these people are not disabled under the law."

A person on FBA in the Metro area receives $930 per month. On GWA, an individual gets a considerably lower monthly $510.

"People who have mild, moderate or invisible disabilities will be thrown off FBA onto GWA and because they are not classified as disabled, also ineligible for such programs as assistive devices and vocational rehabilitation services," warns Seiler.

There are around 170,000 people in Ontario on FBA. A large number have psychiatric problems and some may not even be able to participate in workfare.

The Common Sense Revolution of the Ontario Harris Government favours removing disabled people and seniors from welfare and placing them in a new category. It could result in a small percentage of severely disabled people being in this group.

MCSS communications assistant Catherine Melville says: "We are looking at clarifying the definition of disability so we are protecting the system for the truly disabled." She adds: "The government remains committed to moving seniors and disabled people off the welfare system. We are considering setting up an income supplement program that's better designed to suit their needs."

MCSS recently sent out new rules stating that unemployability would no longer make a person eligible to receive FBA. Though it later said this statement was an error, some of us believe it was a trial balloon.

The painful cuts of 1995

December 31, 1995

If I had to sum up 1995 in one word, it would be "cuts."

Last fall, hundreds of disabled people and their friends protested the cuts to Wheel-Trans contracted taxi service by marching on Queen's Park.

The Toronto Transit Commission (TTC) decision to cut the taxis left more than 13,000 ambulatory riders uncertain of rides to work, school, and other vital destinations. At that time, the TTC blamed reduced funding from the Ontario Progressive Conservative government for the cuts. However, as *The Sun* later discovered, the TTC did have enough money to increase the salaries of some of its staff. The TTC is as adept as government at finding money for projects it wants to fund.

The Employment Equity and Advocacy Commission legislation of the old NDP government was scrapped by the Conservatives. Though the legislation was flawed, it also had several helpful features that now will be lost to us.

Some disabled people and seniors were adversely affected when the Conservatives reduced the General Welfare rates by 21.6 percent. I have often wondered why governments—both federal and provincial—have a law that doesn't allow a disabled person receiving Family Benefits to earn more than $160 per month. This ridiculous ruling penalizes those handicapped people who wish to help themselves.

A couple of new words were added to our vocabulary in 1995: "Tuna Dave." This was, of course, a reference to Minister of Community and Social Services, Dave Tsubouchi and his tuna fish diet recommended to single people on welfare.

The diet, though practical, does not consider two facts: disabled people and seniors cannot always walk or get rides to stores with bargain prices; and, some disabled people, like those who have cerebral palsy, burn up a great deal of energy and therefore require extra nourishment.

On a national level, Robert Latimer was unsuccessful in his bid to get a lighter sentence from the Saskatchewan Court of Appeal for the murder of his disabled daughter, Tracy. Many people regarded hers as a life not worth living, but none of us has the right to make that decision for anybody else. To approve of her death diminishes the lives and contributions of all disabled people.

My closing words are for Premier Mike Harris: cuts are only popular with the people not suffering from them. If they continue relentlessly and irresponsibly, they will hurt everyone. Premier Ralph Klein in Alberta was wise enough to back down from further cuts to health care. I hope you have his political smarts.

May we all experience good health and good fortune in 1996.

Vulnerable pay the price for promised income tax cuts

February 2, 1997

"The downloading of funding for long-term care is a potential time bomb," warns Anne Golden, president of the United Way of Greater Toronto.

"People are living longer and with hospital cutbacks, growing demand, and reduced services, these costs are going to increase," she predicts. "We have an escalating concern about how Metro Toronto will cope and what the impact will be on our most vulnerable people," she says.

Recently, the Ontario Tory government announced it would assume the funding responsibilities of education. In return for this, it has slapped municipalities with a host of new financial obligations.

For example, municipalities which paid nothing toward long-term care will now be expected to fund it 50 percent. In homes for special care, serving mainly psychiatric survivors, the change is even more dramatic: municipalities will have to fund them 100 percent, compared to a financial commitment of zero before.

Municipalities are also responsible for 50 percent of the cost of General Welfare, compared to 20 percent previously. With Family Benefits, they will assume 50 percent of the cost; before, they paid nothing.

Toronto's United Way believes these changes hold the following implications for Metro:

- Increasing demand will drive up the cost of providing services;
- Municipal property tax rates will rapidly increase or services will deteriorate.

To get a provincial perspective on this financial restructuring, I next spoke to Scott Seiler, co-ordinator of the Income Maintenance Group. His concern is that because both levels of government are funding General Welfare and Family Benefits evenly, they will want to move people off the more generous Family Benefits to the considerably more parsimonious General Welfare.

"Services for people with disabilities that municipalities help fund are going to be in great jeopardy, especially in the poorer regions of the province, because those municipalities do not have a property tax base big enough to pay for them," he says.

"This is a way for the provincial government to save all kinds of money and place the cost and responsibility of the cuts on another government. It's what the feds did to the provincial governments," Seiler observes, referring to finance minister Paul Martin's landmark 1995 budget.

The Ontario government is funding its promised income tax cuts by abdicating its responsibilities to the province's most vulnerable citizens: disabled people and seniors.

– 5 –

Advocating for the disabled

Although publicizing and advancing action on disability issues, whether by campaigning for the rights of people with disabilities, fundraising for organizations, or advocating for a disabled individual who requires assistance, is a worthy cause, such activities can generate a great deal of debate. Stakeholders often hold conflicting opinions about the best course of action for achieving optimal results. Seeking to provide a compass through this minefield, Mona covered all these activities, and the debates surrounding them.

Stick with the Man in Motion

January 11, 1987

Please don't jump off the Rick Hansen bandwagon. Courageous Hansen is no stranger to adversity, but he had to take some especially hard knocks from critics last week on the CBC program *The Fifth Estate*.

The television program was an incisive look at Hansen's Man in Motion tour to raise money for spinal cord research, rehabilitation, and wheelchair sports. While not detracting from Hansen's personal charisma, sincere motivation, or remarkable achievements, the show revealed some real concerns about this type of funding.

In several hard-hitting interviews with disabled people, as well as Health and Welfare Minister Jake Epp and others, program host Eric Malling questioned the donation of thousands of dollars to Hansen while cutbacks to other research projects were the order of the day.

Peter Kavanaugh, a freelance journalist in Sydney, N.S., was born with a hip defect, then got polio, and now has arthritis. He watched

Hansen roll through town and wrote an article called "Stunts detract from the real issues." Kavanaugh predicted that the next time an organization wants to raise money, it will have to figure out some sort of stunt to get it. The public may become hardened—therefore, the stunts will have to become more extravagant and spectacular.

Allan Arlett, president of the Canadian Centre for Philanthropy, agreed. "We can't have these quick flashes of money," Arlett said. "We need a steady flow of funds into medical research, not Band-Aid solutions that are out there to grab the media interest."

Everyone interviewed expressed personal admiration for what Hansen was accomplishing and a great liking for the man himself.

Hansen and George Cohon of McDonald's, one of Hansen's original and biggest sponsors, were also interviewed. Their dedicated commitment and belief in what they are doing are unmistakable.

Norman Kunc, a well-known lecturer and author who has cerebral palsy, had a provocative query: "What happens if, say, people with cerebral palsy want to do their fundraising and they're not as glamorous as Rick Hansen? Does that mean the public gives more money to Rick Hansen than they give to cerebral palsy? Then the whole medical research is turned into a beauty contest."

I asked Eric Malling about his own reaction to this form of fundraising. "I seriously question a society that allows its members to suffer the pain and physical strain that Hansen is undergoing for the purpose of raising money," Malling replied.

The concerns voiced on this program were all valid but they may have overshadowed the most important fact of all—that Rick Hansen has inestimably increased public awareness and knowledge of disabled people. This can only be beneficial to all of us in the future.

Many thanks, Rick

May 24, 1987

This is a public "thank you!" to Rick Hansen. He has made it acceptable to have a disability.

This is the most important and far-reaching result of his fabulous Man in Motion world tour. Certainly, he has raised a great deal of money. He has also shown remarkable courage, stamina, and determination—which would be noteworthy even in an able-bodied athlete.

However, he has done more to increase knowledge and understanding about people with disabilities than any agency,

organization or the government. We have our own homegrown hero—
one who uses a wheelchair, too. He did not have to go elsewhere to
prove his worth before returning to Canada. In fact until recently he
has been largely ignored by the U.S media.

While the public in Canada has taken Hansen to its collective heart,
it is interesting to me that the disabled population is divided on the
real worth of his accomplishment. I discussed Hansen recently with
Joe Knapper, a computer programmer with Environment Canada. He
is a wheelchair user as a result of spinal injuries a few years ago.

"I am a great admirer of Hansen and what he has achieved," said
Knapper. "However, one fact should be remembered—Hansen was
an athlete long before he became disabled.

"Therefore his endeavour and its successful outcome came more
naturally to him than it would to someone without his background.
I am concerned that other disabled people may experience a lack of
self-esteem because they are unable to do what he has accomplished."

Hansen has several other assets: an intelligent, diplomatic way
of speaking, and a handsome, downright charming face. Not all
disabled people are as easy on the eyes, however, or as appealing
to the other senses. Some of us have to work—with great effort and
concentration—merely to obtain a small measure of integration in the
community.

Hansen's real achievement lies not in the many countries that he
has wheeled across and not even in the millions of dollars he has
raised. His real gift to both disabled and able-bodied people is that he
has brought the two together by showing them how they each share
abilities and limitations.

Most of us can never aspire to Hansen's fame and success. But
we can all take pride in his accomplishment—not only because it
is a magnificent feat for a disabled person but because it would be
a glorious achievement for anyone. Thus he has shown the utter
uselessness of judging a person only by his outward appearance.

A couple of weeks ago, I was waiting in a line-up in the Willowdale
Post Office when I accidentally dropped an envelope.

"Isn't Rick Hansen wonderful?" the woman behind me beamed as
she went down to pick up the envelope and then place it in my hand.

This remark showed not only a relaxed recognition of disability
but also a comfortable ease in mentioning it.

Therefore, I say it again: "Thank you, Rick!"

Group plots the future

October 6, 1991

It's always exciting to tell you about the beginning of a new and innovative project.

The Future Advocates Association was born last May at a conference of young adults with Down syndrome held in conjunction with the national parents' group convention of the Canadian Down Syndrome Society.

"A variety of programs are available to children with Down syndrome but, at the age of 21, special education ends and then what? We are faced with a critical situation in the lives of not only disabled persons but in their families as well," says Dr. Mary Waksman-Cooper. She's a psychologist who's on the foundation advisory board of the national Down syndrome parents' group, and is director of The Canadian Centre for Cognitive Education in Toronto.

"I spoke to some key people in the organization and suggested it was time to do something for the adults. When we work with children, we sometimes forget that they grow up," said Waksman-Cooper.

TV actor David MacFarlane, who has Down syndrome, helped organize the Future Advocates Association and is now assisting Waksman-Cooper start up a Metro Toronto chapter of the FAA.

It is both interesting and significant that the young adults did not wish to have the words Down syndrome in the name of their new national group.

"We did not want to stress the disability because we do have some abilities. Our wish is for other people to do things with us instead of for us. We are human beings and want to be treated like everyone else," MacFarlane told me.

Why is the word "future" used in their name?

"It's a reminder that we need programs and services now and in the future," he explained.

One of the most moving roles of MacFarlane's acting career came when he had a guest role on ABC's hit television show *Life Goes On* last season. This series has an American actor with Down syndrome, Chris Burke, as one of its stars.

"New statistics suggest that, because of medical improvements, the lifespan of people with Down syndrome is now over 60 years of age. It's worth investing in the future because there is a future," points out Waksman-Cooper.

She provides group therapy in Ottawa for adults with Down syndrome.

"It's a sad story, but very few of my psychologist colleagues can relate adequately to people with Down syndrome because of their communication disabilities. Even worse, they have some preconceived ideas about their abilities. We now know that there are people with Down syndrome who have IQs of close to 100. So, when we talk about Down syndrome, we don't mean low-functioning individuals. We are referring to a range of IQs from 55 to 100 and more," she said.

The FAA has members from all over Canada and is for people who are age 22 and over.

The best of luck to the FAA!

While publicizing and promoting organizations that advocated for disabled people, Mona had to walk a tightrope. Sometimes such groups encountered problems themselves and criticism was required, not simply for balance and fairness, but rather because it was necessary, as seen in this 1995 case, to be clear-minded about changes that could help such organizations proceed more successfully in the future.

Shove comes to push

February 12, 1995

It's that old double standard again.

Amid charges and counter charges, PUSH Ontario (Persons United for Self-Help), has gone bankrupt. About $1 million, mostly obtained from the provincial government, has gone missing.

PUSH's board of directors was composed entirely of disabled people. This makes it very vulnerable to criticism. People with disabilities must constantly prove themselves. If they fail, they are judged more harshly than non-disabled people.

Having said all this, I also feel that PUSH Ontario must accept a fair share of the blame for its own difficulties.

"PUSH didn't have the leadership or the training it needed. Nobody knew what they were doing," says disability rights activist Beryl Potter, who was active in PUSH's early years.

"People should become board members or obtain jobs because they're qualified, not because they are disabled. "You cannot place an inexperienced person in a position of responsibility for $1 million. What made it worse was that they were not accountable to government.

"When the Liberals formed the government in Ontario, they funded the Ontario Action Awareness Group and I had to account for every cent I spent. They gave me a yearly $250,000 and I submitted financial statements every six weeks," she said.

It's an honour to be a board member but like everything else, there are responsibilities attached. An unfortunate aftermath of PUSH's collapse is it may cause other disability organizations to have their own credibility questioned.

The lost $1 million could have benefited so many other groups. If it had been injected into the Special Services at Home program, it would have enabled more parents to cope with their special needs children in the loving environment of their homes. It could also have been used to expand community services to increase the number of disabled adults who live on their own or make it possible for them to leave costly institutions.

PUSH's downfall is a misfortune. But the unwise manner in which government spends our money is a tragedy.

In the 1990s, Ontario's NDP government introduced an Advocacy Act designed to help those with disabilities fight for their rights themselves. Although the Act's new model of advocacy was initially seen as a positive step, the statute nevertheless became the target of criticism from those who felt it failed to adequately protect people in need. Next the government's choice of commissioners to administer the Act was widely criticized. Then objections arose over how the commission sought to expand its role by taking over the advocacy functions of other entities. Because of the centrality of this novel Ontario advocacy regime for the status of disabled persons, Mona returned to its role over several years, as seen in these next four columns.

Advocating advocacy

March 15, 1992

Ontario's proposed new Advocacy Act has the potential to help vulnerable adults resist abuse—as long as several safeguards are in place.

"It creates a structure to provide non-legal advocacy services to people with a broad variety of disability labels. The design ensures that advocates are independent of service providing agencies or government ministries," explains David Giuffrida, acting provincial coordinator of the Psychiatric Patient Advocate Office. He's also a member of the Ontario Advocacy Coalition, which represents 30 self-help or advocacy organizations for disabled people.

The Ontario Advocacy Commission, whose majority of members will be disabled themselves, is to have responsibility for the advocacy system. The commission's purposes include contributing to the empowerment of vulnerable persons, and promoting respect for their rights, freedoms, autonomy, and dignity.

"The type of powers advocates should have and, to a large extent, are given under the Advocacy Act are access rights—a right to have access to the client and to documents relevant to the client's care. However, if a client asks an advocate to leave, the advocate must leave," says Giuffrida.

The coalition is concerned because the act excludes anyone under the age of 16 from advocacy services. Children, particularly those in care facilities, can benefit from advocacy, as can those receiving mental health treatment in the psychiatric wards of general hospitals.

"The cornerstone of the commission will be client-instructed advocacy. Some of the most vulnerable people, however, will be those who are unable to express any wish. The Advocacy Act should make better provision for clients in need who cannot instruct advocates," says Giuffrida.

Advocates are not guardians or substitute decision-makers. Even with non-instructed advocacy, the role of the advocate is to explore options and possibly make authorities aware of abuse and neglect. It's not to impose their view on a client.

The Advocacy Act is part of wider companion legislation that includes the Substitute Decisions and Consent to Treatment acts.

A big concern with advocacy is how to prevent advocates from assuming too much control, especially in non-instructed advocacy.

"This is a very difficult issue that we're trying to grapple with right now," admits Elaine Ziemba, Ontario's minister of citizenship with responsibility for disability and seniors issues. "All of our experts are coming in to talk to me about how we can include this in the Act in a way that protects vulnerable persons and yet gives them the advocacy they need," she said.

The Advocacy Act is expected to be proclaimed into law by year's end.

Advocacy arrives
November 1, 1992

When it is made into law shortly by the NDP government, Ontario will be the first jurisdiction anywhere to have an Advocacy Act that helps safeguard the rights of vulnerable people.

Orville Endicott, the legal counsel of the Canadian Association for Community Living, explains why he is optimistic about the act and the commission that will guide it: "The majority of members of the advocacy commission will be people with disabilities or seniors. To be appointed to the commission, one will have to be nominated by groups in the community representing people with disabilities, senior citizens, or patients' rights.

"To my knowledge, this is the first time that a commission has come into being under statute in which nobody will be appointed because they have gained the favour of the government of the day. Instead, they will be nominated by the very community that the legislation is designed to serve. The Advocacy Act admits that the people who know the best advocacy are persons who have the need for advocacy."

The legislation empowers individuals by giving them an advocate who can help them articulate concerns about their own life, communicate their wishes, and assist them to become self-advocates. By creating the advocacy commission, it also empowers groups.

To avoid conflict of interest, only agencies that provide no other services to vulnerable people can become involved in advocacy. Both paid and volunteer advocates are necessary to provide advocacy to everyone in Ontario who needs it.

"It's going to be a monumental undertaking to advocate for the many different types of disabled people," predicts Scott Seiler, co-chairman of the Ontario Advocacy Coalition.

The advocacy commission will also perform systemic advocacy— address problems that face more than one individual because they are issues inherent in a system itself.

"Legislation with respect to people who have disabilities has always been based on paternalistic philosophies. The Advocacy Act turns it the other way around. It says that these people can tell us what they want, instead of us telling them what they need," says Endicott.

I hope that the people who are appointed to the commission and advocates themselves will have two special qualities—empathy, so that they understand what needs to be done, and foresight, so that they train vulnerable people, whenever possible, to be their own advocates.

They're appalled
September 18, 1994

Many disabled people and their groups are appalled by the recently announced eight appointees to the Ontario Advocacy Commission.

There is no one with a developmental disability on the new commission.

Under the Advocacy Act, which will come into effect in 1995, the commission will be responsible for a province-wide network of advocates to help vulnerable adults, such as disabled people and seniors, make choices and exercise their rights.

The chairman of the commission is David Reville, who had a one and a-half year bout with mental illness in the 1960s. He has been a special adviser to Premier Bob Rae since 1990.

"Reville's is being seen as a patronage appointment among people with disabilities," notes Scott Seiler, who is himself disabled and has acted both as a voluntary and paid advocate.

Dissatisfaction with the commission is so widespread that in a joint statement to the media, eight groups—including People First of Ontario and the Ontario Coalition of Senior Citizens' Organizations—denounced the process to choose the commission.

None of the commission appointees is well known in the general disability community. A new underground newsletter, *The Probe And Nail*, calls them the "no-name commission." This is particularly appalling when highly regarded people like disability rights activist Beryl Potter and University of Toronto professor Ernie Lightman, author of an excellent report on unregulated residential accommodation, were not selected commission appointees.

Both the Advocacy Act and the commission come under the jurisdiction of Citizenship Minister Elaine Ziemba. She explained: "The nine-member Appointments Advisory Committee (AAC) was elected by advocates and peer groups across Ontario. It's a Schedule 1 agency—it operates at arm's length from government," Ziemba said.

After a lengthy process of interviews by the AAC, Ziemba chose the chairman and eight appointees from the names recommended by them.

There are still four persons to be appointed to the commission by Ziemba and Premier Bob Rae. It is hoped that at least one of them will be a person with an intellectual disability.

Allegations have been made regarding the AAC's fairness and the suitability of some of the appointees. The Advocacy Commission will have to prove itself, not only in the work it does but also to the vulnerable people it is serving.

Big Brother foils us again

November 13, 1994

With a complete disregard for the wishes of the people involved, the new and controversial Ontario Advocacy Commission will be taking over the Psychiatric Patient Advocate Office (PPAO).

"The government's plan is to make all paid advocates come under the commission," commission chairman David Reville told me.

"We will want to make sure that the folks in provincial psychiatric hospitals receive at least as good services as what they're now getting and, ideally, better," he added.

However, David Giuffrida, the acting director of the PPAO, expresses these concerns: "The PPAO is a mature program—we've been operating for 11 years and have an international reputation," he explains. "On the other hand, the commission is a very new organization that, hopefully, holds much promise. But it has not yet demonstrated how well it will function. It's unseemly for them to cannibalize an existing advocacy program for parts before they establish their own track record," he said.

The advocacy legislation is limited to people 16 years of age and up. But the PPAO program has a broader mandate—it serves adolescent wards in two hospitals.

In one incident, an advocate was alerted that an 11-year-old boy had been placed in the same ward as an adult sex offender. Because the advocate acted speedily, the situation was quickly rectified.

The PPAO is a quasi-independent program of the Ministry of Health, which pays the salaries of their advocates.

"The Advocacy Act restricts non-instructive advocacy to vulnerable persons who are incapable of instructing an advocate, if there is risk of serious harm to the health or safety to those persons. We're not limited by this. We can complain on behalf of a person who's tied in a geri-chair* all day, or about someone in urine-soaked clothes," says Giuffrida.

"No one ever contemplated that the advocacy commission would have a monopoly on advocacy.

"I am also concerned about a commission whose selection and composition have engendered the scepticism in the disability rights community this one has," he said.

The Ontario NDP has betrayed the trust of disabled people and seniors by the arrogant manner in which it has handled the commission.**

Hopefully, it will make us stronger to fight our own battles instead of relying on the uncaring government.

– 6 –

Adapting

The quest by people with disabilities to live independent lives, whether requiring a great deal of assistance or just a little, was something Mona celebrated in numerous columns. In the following selections she chronicles the lives of individuals who adapted to overcome their disabilities.

Taking control is important
June 28, 1987

Independent living is having control of your life—"It is NOT measured by the number of physical tasks you can perform without assistance."

That is what Dr. Irving Zola told me when I interviewed him at the recent Ontario Federation of the Cerebral Palsied staff conference, where he was the keynote speaker.

---

* Geriatric wheelchair.

** The Advocacy Act of Ontario, under which this Advocacy Commission had been created, was repealed in March 1996 by the Progressive Conservative Government of Premier Harris which replaced the New Democratic Party Government of Premier Rae.

Zola is a professor of sociology at the Brandeis University in Waltham, Mass., and a prolific writer of articles relating to his profession, including both fictional and non-fictional works about disability. He was one of the early proponents of the independent living movement in the United States.

"I have to admit that—in anything I do—I try to reach an audience that would not normally be interested in the issues that I consider important," he said.

"That is why I started writing short stories—it is a way of getting people to deal with disability who would not ordinarily pick up a book exclusively on this subject."

Zola is himself disabled as result of polio in 1950 when he was 16 and then an automobile accident in 1954. He now wears leg braces and walks with two canes.

After his accident, he spent almost a year in a body cast. At that time he was in junior year at Harvard. Not able to attend classes, his friends made carbon copies of their notes—this was in the days before tape recorders were allowed in classrooms. Zola's brother would pick up all the notes and bring them to him. Other family members would help with typing, and in other ways.

"This is where I first learned the importance of networking," Zola said.

He stresses the importance of risk-taking, saying it has taken too little a formal role in the lives of disabled people.

"Throughout history people with disabilities have been perceived as being vulnerable and in need of protection. Efforts have been made to try and shelter them from physical as well as psychological concerns. This is unreal—the nature of living involves both kinds of risks."

Zola feels that the pure civil rights approach to advocacy is not going to be effective much longer. "Many of the things that we, as people with disabilities, will win in the future will be done by making other people aware that it is in their best interests too," he said.

"For example, many difficulties that disabled people face are also experienced by people who are aging. People with disabilities are living longer. With more older people surviving longer, it is clear to me that the number of people with explicit disabilities is going to increase significantly."

Zola's latest endeavour is of great interest to those of us who are mystery fiction fans. After wondering how the general public develops the stereotypes of different groups and why they endure, he realized that mystery fiction is one of the most popular and longest lasting genres there is. Its characters are frequently getting beaten up, shot at, and losing limbs. Therefore, his recent writing concerns itself with a study in how disability is depicted in mystery fiction.

I found two of Zola's observations particularly pertinent. I agree that it is essential that disabled people have the freedom to take risks. I also feel that the more that disabled adults realize they are a group which is inevitably aging, the more able they will be to deal effectively with future challenges this process inexorably brings.

A hard lesson to learn

June 12, 1988

"Having my leg broken was the best experience that could have ever happened to me." Why would Patrick Boyer, MP for Etobicoke-Lakeshore, make a seemingly wild statement like this?

Boyer is chairman of the parliamentary committee on the status of disabled persons. The accident he was referring to happened almost a year ago when he was horseback riding and another rider's horse kicked him in the leg. His subsequent slow progress from wheelchair to crutches and canes gave him a personal exposure to disability that enabled him to directly experience what handicapped people must contend with every day.

"To get to a hotel convention hall in my wheelchair, I soon discovered that it was necessary to go down a freight elevator, then by the furnace room and through the garbage chute area, on through the kitchen, then up another freight elevator to finally arrive at the conference room," he says.

"I experienced how people with disabilities who want to get from point A to point B often have to go through the entire alphabet in making their journey."

This is not an uncommon scenario. Many disabled people are confronted by these and other complicating factors that frequently challenge their ingenuity and determination. Some of the people Boyer encountered were sympathetic and caring; others were made uncomfortable by his disability and did not know how to cope so they placed their eyes firmly on the horizon as though he was not there.

"When I went to a conference in Quebec City, I found that the taxis at the airport are small ones. We waited a long, long time before finally getting a larger car to accommodate me and my wheelchair.

"Everything one does takes more time when one is disabled—even making a cup of coffee or shaving oneself takes longer," Boyer said.

He feels strongly that disabled people themselves have to be involved in all aspects of planning new architecture and in anything else that affects their daily activities.

What are the three most important facts learned from this experience?

"FRUSTRATION—I learned what frustration is all about when you want to do something very badly and it takes so-o-o-o long and consumes so much energy.

"DEPENDENCE—You really do depend on other people.

"RESOURCEFULNESS—You have to be inventive in overcoming difficulties. Sometimes you have to improvise on the spot.

"Then I realized that the first letter of each of these words spelled FDR. Franklin Delano Roosevelt was a president of the United States who got to that high office despite the fact he had polio and could not walk."

Boyer's bout with disability was only for a limited time, while some of us have to live with it everyday of our lives. What is essential is that we must all work determinedly towards the goals of better access, attitudes, and communication for improved conditions that will ultimately benefit everyone.

Beyond the white cane

February 6, 1994

To mark the start of White Cane Week, I have a story of the human will triumphing over fear and adversity.

Randy Firth was 20 when he lost his sight in a car accident 14 years ago. Initially, many anxieties beset him.

"I was afraid about what the rest of my life would be like and wondered how people would react to me as a blind person. I didn't know if I could work again or have a few dollars in my pocket. Would women refuse to go out with me because I'm blind?" he said.

He then began to learn Braille and how to get around using a white cane.

"Without a doubt, the white cane travel was the most terrifying experience I've ever had. I felt like a fool with a white cane. I thought it drew attention to me—like a white flag I was waving, asking the world to look at me because I'm blind," he said.

So frightened was he of travelling with a white cane that he refused to take lessons any more from his instructor. He wanted a guide dog. However, a person must be a good cane traveller to be able to give the dog understandable commands. For example, a blind person has to listen to the direction the traffic is flowing in to be able to tell the dog when it's safe to cross the road.

"Fortunately, I met a friend at a CNIB (Canadian National Institute for the Blind) support group. Both of us entered a residential program offering a very intense learning experience. It was very advantageous for me. I had the support of my friend and wasn't practising white cane travel in my own neighbourhood, where my neighbours could see me bumbling around," he said.

After mastering cane travel, he got his first guide dog. He then took the social service worker program at Centennial College. Now, he's the manager of the CNIB Etobicoke office and was married last summer.

If you want to assist a blind person, ask him or her if they require aid and, if so, how they like to be helped, Firth advises. "When people ask me if I want assistance, I try not to react harshly. Perhaps I don't need help, but maybe the next blind person they encounter will."

If I get a seat on the TTC, I can tuck my guide dog between my knees out of the way of being stepped on," he added. He stresses that guide dogs are working dogs and should not be petted or in any way distracted, no matter how friendly they are.

Firth's closing words could apply to any disability: "I'm the same person I was before I lost my sight. People should look beyond the white cane."

Accomplished artist draws on courage
September 6, 1998

This is a story of talent, courage, and motivation.

At the age of 36, Montreal resident Nechama Werner was struck by a massive stroke that left her in a wheelchair with a paralyzed left arm and only partial use of her right hand. Yet today she is an accomplished artist who has had one a one-woman exhibit and two group shows.

Her second one-woman and first Toronto show will take place next week and is being sponsored by Early Canadian Furniture and the Canadian Foundation for Physically Disabled Persons.

The Toronto show has been arranged by North York art dealer and consultant Miriam Berke, who told me: "When I first saw her work, I was very impressed by its integrity—it displays more than a mere talent. She works hard and is extremely positive and committed. She doesn't take shortcuts and her good works do not look unfinished. This is a big accomplishment.

"She also sticks to her convictions and obviously has had to push for what she believes in," Berke said.

Werner works in acrylic on canvas, usually with a palette knife. It's a struggle but she manoeuvres and manages with incredible perseverance to produce her popular paintings.

Berke continues: "Everyone has different limitations—limitations that are exclusive to them. Nechama is working to the maximum with her limitations. She might be a representational, realistic artist if she didn't have physical problems—but that is irrelevant.

"She gets around her limitations by doing semi-abstracts. Her landscapes are clearly landscapes. You know they're either a seascape or landscape, you can even make out some fine detail. They are semi-realistic and semi-abstract.

"I've known Nechama for a long time and she is an intelligent, bright, and optimistic person who derives tremendous joy from her family and her work.

"I see a huge evolution in her work, which is what you look for in an artist. A good artist is someone who grows. Neither she nor her work are static," Berke said.

In her column on Ronald Satok, Mona celebrated someone who not only demonstrated remarkable success in overcoming his own disabilities, but also deep commitment to helping others with disabilities lead richer, more expressive lives.

Blind artist teaches others to paint

August 7, 1988

Ten years ago Ronald Satok seemed headed for international success as an artist. Then misfortune struck. Satok, at the age of 46, lost his sight due to glaucoma.

"I felt that the loss of my eyes was the loss of my being," he recalls. "There was no point in living."

Slowly, however, Satok began to realize that there were all kinds of problems other people had to cope with, such as a sickness and terminal illness.

"I learned a very important lesson," he says. "All of us are given a brain, spirit, and body to work with. I realized that I had been given a great deal. So, I said to myself, why don't you take what you know and teach it to people who have special needs and stop feeling sorry for yourself? That helped me a great deal."

Satok, who refers to his blindness as an "inconvenience," opened the Satok School of the Arts in 1981.

"As an able bodied person, I was arrogant," he says. "I was so intent on making it in the art world that I didn't have time to think of children and adults who had inconveniences. When I became one of them, I realized that there is a segment of the population that needs special people to teach them. And, who better than a person who is himself inconvenienced?"

Satok's brother, Mel, was a key player among the people who came to his support when he went blind. One of the first organizations to help the school was Shoppers Drug Mart. Satok went to Shoppers' president Murray Koffler and his wife told them: "If you help me to help myself, I promise you that I will dedicate my life to helping others."

In addition to art, the school teaches dancing, movements, mime, and acting. Watching Satok teach art is like seeing colour come to life. His fluid body depicts each colour with graceful, sweeping movements—evidence of both his natural talent as a dancer and his study of mime.

He paints from memory. Friends have told him that his memory is better than their eyesight.

Satok has been married and divorced twice. He has a grown son and daughter from his first marriage. Satok is the executive director of the art school and his son Michael Satok-Wolman (a combination of his father and stepfather's surnames), is both director of the school and the associate of public art.

Just over a year ago, the school designed a 20-foot-long mural called *Jeremiah-As-Go-Between* for Toronto's Jewish Community Centre and presented a play with the same title.

"Of the actors appearing in the play, half were disabled," Satok told me. "One had Down syndrome, one was a wheelchair user, one was emotionally disturbed, and the rest had other disabilities.

The school's most recent mural was dedicated last month in the Joey and Toby Tanenbaum Opera Centre on Toronto's Front Street. The mural took one year to complete and was made of Venetian and Byzantine glass. It is called *Force of Destiny* and was donated by Anne Tanenbaum in memory of her husband, Max.

Disabled students from the Metro Separate School Board (MSSB) and clients of the Donwood Institute worked on the mosaic, fitting together its close to 700,000 individual pieces. The MSSB special education division and the Donwood Institute for alcohol and drug rehabilitation are two of the Satok school's most faithful participants.

Satok says that many people suffer from the "genius" syndrome. They will not do anything in advance unless they are going to be good at it. This often applies to people with special needs.

"Don't worry about being good at it. Just do it for the sheer enjoyment of learning," he tells these people. "It's like expressing yourself in a different tongue."

Satok's sense of smell, touch and taste have all sharpened since he lost his sight. However, he does not have an uncomplicated life without sight. "Getting lost is a real fear with me," he admits. "I got lost when I went to dog school in New Jersey with Paisley my guide dog. I got lost in the basement when there was no one in the building. At that time, I didn't have the knowledge of how to direct Paisley. The thing I didn't realize is that a blind person has to know everything. You not only have to know the shape of this room, but you have to know the next room as well."

Satok feels that disabled people need powerful leaders to weld them together and shame the government about its spending priorities, arguing that money being spent on the defence should be spent helping disabled people get on their feet.

Satok has not allowed his blindness to either embitter him or slow him down. Instead, he has gone on to help other disabled people gain confidence and skills that they were never aware of possessing.

Despite some help from the government and other groups, funding remains a concern for the non-profit Satok School of the Arts.*

This 1997 column Mona wrote on Hugh Wilson and the Shopping Channel shows how small but focused measures by determined individuals, and a willingness to make adaptations, can have large consequences.

---

* Underfunding, and dependence on the individual founder, continued to be a concern for the Satok School of the Arts. This subject is revisited in Part III, chapter 11, where similar problems confronting other such initiatives to benefit people with disabilities are compared with publicly-funded and publicly-run programs.

Real life comes to TV

September 14, 1997

The Shopping Channel recently became the first channel of its type to show a model with a disability.

The channel's head of production, Hugh Wilson, was contacted about seven months ago by Sue Charness Talent, an agency that represents people who are disabled.

"She struck a nerve with me," Wilson recalls. "In our business, we're so busy making money that we forget to look around and think about who else we can help," he says.

Wilson's mother was disabled and he became used to wheelchairs at an early age.

"Sue sent me several pictures. I liked one in particular of a model in a wheelchair whose name is Spirit Synott. Sue sent her to meet me. But it was difficult to sell this idea to everyone," he admits.

People were nervous and scared because it was different. They were thinking: What if it doesn't work? What if somebody sees the wheelchair and goes "Yuk!"

He told them the wheelchair was part of her life and that she's as pretty as any other model and her modeling skills were just as competent as any of their other models.

"I sold my idea—eventually, everyone bought into it and the whole thing came together in the course of about three weeks," he says.

It is fortunate that the Shopping Channel is located in an accessible building on Highway 10 in Mississauga.

"I was at a meeting one day and explained to management why we had to give her a little bit of help because we wanted her to be a jewellery model," Wilson continues. But her hands showed some wear from using a manual wheelchair. All she needed was a manicure and to make sure that whenever she used her wheelchair, she wore gloves.

"I call it levelling the playing field," Wilson says. "We should give disabled people a break and teach them how to accomplish what we do," he says. "You have to look beyond the fact that it might cost you a couple of extra dollars for the moment. It'll pay you back.

"You cannot give a job to a person with a disability merely because of kindness and goodness—it has to make everyone money," Wilson says.

"This is more practical to the business world. A large percentage of our viewing audience is challenged. Both they and our non-disabled viewers regard this as realistic television," he adds.

If small adaptations in a business can improve the opportunities of those with disabilities, other simple adaptations, such as those Mona profiled in these columns on specialized clothing, can remarkably improve the lives of people with disabilities.

Firm takes the stress out of how to dress

April 29, 1990

You know the old saying, "Clothes make the person." Paula Smith and Angela Platt strongly believe in the dignity of disabled people and the clothes they design and sell reflect this attitude.

Smith and Platt were in training together as nurses and have known each other for 30 years. Their interest in clothes for people with special needs first began when they saw how difficult it was to dress their patients in nursing homes and hospitals because these individuals often had limited use of their limbs.

In 1987 they formed the Mississauga-based A.P.S.—Adaptive Preferred Styles. "We didn't go to the bank and borrow a great deal of money because we both wanted to sleep well at night," Smith laughed.

Instead, they each invested a small amount of money of their own in A.P.S. and money from sales was promptly put back into the business.

"Our customers consist of two types of people: caregivers and disabled people themselves," explains Platt.

"We have dresses and blouses that either open down the front or the back, wrap around skirts, and easy opening nightgowns and slips. A unisex track suit with side-opening pants makes for easier dressing. We also have men's shirts and pants. Wherever there's an opening, we sew the buttons on top of the garment and Velcro underneath. It's street-ready and looks no different from other people's clothes."

Though they would very much like to get into children's clothes eventually, they now possess neither the time nor the resources. They also are not able to take orders of specially designed clothes for one person because of the great expense involved.

"The manufacturing of our clothes is very difficult," Platt says. "We aren't large enough to go to a huge manufacturer, and yet we're beyond the scale of a person who makes one or two garments at home."

A.P.S. sales are all mail order. Platt and Smith have done their homework and say that their prices compare favourably with the prices of ordinary clothes.

"We want disabled people to feel proud of the way they look and feel good about getting dressed in the morning," says Smith. "This enhances the feeling of dignity that is so essential to one's self-esteem."

Wrapping up for winter
January 7, 1996

One of the reasons I dislike winter so intensely is because of all the extra clothes one must put on before going out-of-doors.

Therefore, it's a pleasure to bring you news that may make this process easier.

Patricia (Patty) Gillard of Brampton makes capes for disabled people. Here's how she became involved in this work.

"I have always liked capes and usually have one in my wardrobe," Gillard says. "My daughter and daughter-in-law both work in classrooms of disabled children and they told me how difficult it was to get the children into their coats. It took so much time—time that could have been better used doing something with the children."

She's been making capes for about two months and has sold four to disabled children. They are popular because they are so easy to put on.

"The capes are wind-proof and water-resistant. I always describe them as warm, washable, and wonderful! They are also versatile— you can wear one if you want to get dressed up, or with a pair of jeans," she points out.

They actually consist of two capes, one for inner and one for outer wear. Both capes can be worn together in the winter. The outer cape, which is water-resistant, can be worn by itself in the spring and the inner cape may be worn alone on a cool day in the fall.

"They come in colors of purple for the outer cape and light mauve for the inner cape, purple and dark purple, pewter and black, a rose outer cape and an ivory inner cape, or a rose outer cape and a burgundy inner cape. I can get other colours but it would take a little longer," she says.

For men, she would make them in such masculine colours as black, navy or brown. They come in small, medium, and large sizes for children. The same range of sizes is available for women and men, but the length varies according to the height of the woman or man. All the capes have hoods and sleeves.

Gillard usually has zippers in the capes but this could be changed to Velcro to suit the convenience of the customer. She can also make a matching, three-cornered scarf so that if a child drools, it can be washed more frequently than the cape.

"Everyone's needs are different—I am willing to adapt to whatever each person wants," she says.

− 7 −

Education

Education, and particularly the failure of the educational system to meet the needs of students with disabilities, was a major topic Mona repeatedly addressed in "Disabled Today."

Education report assailed

February 28, 1988

A report criticizing Ontario's secondary school system has itself come under fire from groups concerned with disabled people.

"Some people with disabilities are not even included in the report," says David Hasbury, associate consultant with the Centre for Integrated Education in Toronto's Frontier College.

The George Radwanski Report said that the current emphasis on *process*—learning at an individual pace—rather than *outcome*—specific knowledge and skills—is leaving students unprepared for an increasingly knowledge-intensive job market.

"People have to find their own individual pace for learning," says Hasbury. "To place them in situations that would lead to failure is not going to do anything for their schooling. What we must do is recognize what skills they already have and what skills they need to accomplish things like living in the community, getting a job, or going on to further education. If we focus only on the content we think they need to survive in society, we're going to miss the boat. The content will vary according to the individual.

"We're looking at what society needs of an individual when he or she leaves school, but instead we should be looking at what the individual needs to participate in society."

There are three streams or levels in the secondary school system: advanced level, which offers opportunities to go on to college and university; general level, which prepares students for community colleges and the workforce, and basic level, which concentrates on abilities to find jobs.

"When we think of mainstream education, we think of academic skills. We have trouble in thinking that people with disabilities can gain skills in these areas. We don't believe in their capacity to learn. They are not a part of our understanding as to what education is all about."

Radwanski also recommends that students in every grade be required to reach a certain level in all subjects. If everyone has to be the same, persons with disabling conditions are not going to be treated as valuably, says Roz Vincent, president of the Down Syndrome Association of Metropolitan Toronto. She was concerned that the report paid so little attention to disabled students—almost as if they are "invisible."

"As a parent of both a typical child and one with an intellectual disability, I feel that all children should be allowed to learn at their own individual style. We're all different—we think differently and we process information differently.

"Obviously, the author of this report is trying to put us all on an assembly line and make us all like robots. Individual differences should be valued, not scorned."

It is essential that we keep on reminding educators of the existence of students with disabilities who may not fit conveniently into preconceived slots. Otherwise, these students and their needs will continue to be totally forgotten.

Keith Whittaker, acting director of special education and provincial schools branch of the Ontario Ministry of Education, says that government will study the recommendations and then decide, if they are implemented, whether they will be in the best interests of the exceptional students.

In the meantime, according to Whittaker, the Ontario government will be interested in seeing the various comments from the parents' association.

Hearing-impaired demand change

November 5, 1989

Deaf people in Ontario are angry. They're sick and tired of waiting for the Ministry of Education to approve the use of American Sign Language (ASL) as an alternative language of instruction.

"Signed English, which is taught in schools now, is based on sound and makes it easier for hearing people to communicate with us," explains Gary Malkowski, Ontario Association of Deaf education task force committee chairperson.

· "ASL is a beautiful language which is based on facial expressions and hand movements. It can also express different inflections."

Malkowski also points out that there are definitely more deaf teachers needed to provide deaf children with positive role models.

Another problem is that deaf children are not prepared for higher education and consequently do not receive the opportunity to enter the professional working world, because of things wrong with the education system.

"Hearing children are exposed to the environment of sound daily and can master their English skills before they arrive in school. Deaf children are not exposed to sign language and they arrive in school with little or no English skills, excepting deaf children of deaf parents who have ASL abilities," he said. "ASL should be taught to deaf children in school so that they can develop a language base and then they can learn English as a second language."

However, Paul Barty, superintendent of the Ernest C. Drury School for the Deaf in Milton, said his school feels Signed English is an effective tool to improve English language communication. Many parents are comfortable using it to communicate with their deaf children, he says.

The Ministry of Education is conducting a review of the deaf educational system in Ontario, including looking into whether ASL should be offered.

"Depending on what the review says, I would be more than willing to investigate whether the use of ASL as one of the languages of instruction would be helpful to our overall educational goals," Barty said.

The school has 270 students, from pre-schoolers to Grade 12, and 66 teachers. Of these, seven teachers are deaf.

All the groups involved with deaf and hard of hearing people—interpreters, teachers, parents—have been fighting among themselves because one method of teaching deaf people has been favoured over another.

"As long as these groups were fighting one another, government could just stand back and not take any real action," Malkowski said.

"Now, however, all of these groups have united and told the Ontario Deaf Education Review that they want options—ASL, Signed English, oralism, or auditory training—whatever is best for the individual.

"I think you're going to see a major change—provided that the Ministry of Education is willing to listen."

Failure of the educational system to openly address the needs of students with disabilities results in higher levels of illiteracy in this group, which Mona explored in several columns, including this one in 1992.

Illiteracy challenge

August 9, 1992

There is more illiteracy among people with disabilities than there is in the general population.

This is due to a number of factors, according to Ed Wadley, a literacy coordinator and trainer/consultant at Toronto's Frontier College.

"At one time, families didn't consider their severely handicapped children educatable. There was also a lack of knowledge regarding the potential of these children.

"There's still a propensity among school administrators to label disabled people, shift them aside, and give them an education—if you want to call it that—that's less than the valued population receives. Value is not attributed to people who are disabled.

"Cerebral palsy is a good example. People who are familiar with this disability know that the incidence of genius is higher here than in the general population. But because of appearances, attitudes, and assumptions, persons with cerebral palsy are often ignored or underestimated," says Wadley.

People with intellectual limitations face an even grimmer prospect because they are seldom exposed to a valued and typical education.

"We are not going to be rid of illiteracy simply by teaching people to read and write. We are going to solve it only by working within the system and eradicating attitudes which segregate, separate, and categorize. This requires energy, determination, and courage," he says.

His biggest personal frustration is that Canada is merely scratching the surface in terms of combating illiteracy. The combined initiatives in this country to reduce illiteracy have an effect on only four or five percent of the people who need it the most.

He also paints a bleak picture of the future due to the current budget cuts in education.

"What is seen as cost-saving measures today will involve more money tomorrow when we try to rectify our mistakes. We are systematically creating an underclass. The end result is that, 10 years down the road, society will be faced with higher financial, emotional, and psychological costs," he said.

Mona believed that, while criticism was necessary when warranted, so was praise when deserved. So while she relentlessly exposed the educational system's deficiencies, she was personally happy to be able to draw attention to programs and institutions that succeeded in meeting the needs of students with disabilities. She knew the good examples could also provide inspiration to others.

Develop maximum potential

May 14, 1989

It's not until persons with disabilities are seen in the community that the public recognizes that they can think, have capabilities, and possess the same human qualities as everyone else.

That's one of the many positive elements of an interesting school program for students who are intellectually delayed, says Dr. Ernie Springer.

Springer is employed by the Metro Toronto School Board and has the dual role of being principal of North York's Champlain School while also being responsible for special programs in a number of North York schools.

"The main goals of the community awareness development program are to enable the students to achieve maximum development according to their individual abilities and to prepare them to live in the community as independently as possible," explains Springer, who holds a doctorate degree in special education.

This is accomplished through a variety of school activities that help students learn how to solve problems and to communicate more effectively.

"As teachers find that students become more aware and capable, they take them out in small groups to deal with things that affect them personally," says Springer.

They learn where to find things in a supermarket and how to purchase them. They are also taught how to recognize and handle money, cross streets safely, to stand up for themselves, and not talk to strangers.

"Unless your confidence grows, you don't achieve independence," says Springer. "Confidence comes when the students start doing things they have some control over."

As long as the teacher is there, students tend to wait for the teacher to tell them what to do. However, when the teacher is not present, the students must make some decisions on their own.

"Parents have to be informed about the program," said Springer. "I feel very, very strongly about involving parents. When objectives are set for students, parents must be contacted to see what they would like to happen with their youngsters.

"When parents get involved, two things occur: they seem extremely satisfied with what the schools are doing, and their youngsters make tremendous strides over those students whose parents remain uninvolved."

It was erroneously reported in *The Sun* last month that, after two students with development disabilities who were on the program went missing recently, the entire program was discontinued. In fact, it was stopped for only one of the students and Springer will work with her parents to help restore their confidence in the program.

What happened was that the two students took one wrong direction in coming out of the subway. This happens to most people at one time or another. Disabled persons have the right to make mistakes—just like everyone else.

This school's unique

June 19, 1988

Last week I went back to high school and learned Don Mills Collegiate is the only school in North York where a consistent effort is made to make it as accessible as possible.

Therefore, it has a higher than average number of disabled students.

There are 13 physically disabled students who attend regular classes—nine come under the Metro Toronto School Board and four under the North York School Board. In addition, there are more than 30 students with learning and other disabilities who attend regular classes under the North York School Board. There is also a class of multi-handicapped students.

Barbara Garrow, a social services consultant with the North York Board, says, "The multi-handicapped students have more needs than previously acknowledged, and the challenge lies in having them take part in something the community offers, like learning how to work."

To this end, a person has been hired just to place these students in work experience programs.

"One of our students works in the dairy section of Miracle Mart every morning," says Jerry Daca, department head of the multi-handicapped class. "The Prince Hotel has been marvellous with our students, providing them with positive work experiences. Two female students are working in housekeeping and warehousing in the hotel."

Though the multi-handicapped class is a self-contained one, the students take art, gym, and other classes with the rest of the students.

However, problems do exist. Some of the students cannot work competitively in the workplace. What is needed, says Garrow, is something between a job and a sheltered workshop. She also says the housing situation is terrible.

"Usually, our people need some kind of support. They need help in monitoring their day, or some kind of supervision. But the problem with resources like the Reena Foundation and the Metro Association for Community Living is that they are limited," Garrow says.

"I have a number of parents who would like some kind of living situation outside their home for young people now, while they are still alive and able to provide support in the transition period."

According to principal Ron Bronger, the disabled students are not the only ones who benefit from integration. "It exposes our regular population to students with various disabilities. They become used to them."

Wheelchair user Charlena Mann sums it up best: "Don Mills is special because it does not treat us as special."

As well as reporting on problems and progress in the system of formal education, Mona shed light on less traditional educational programs benefiting students with disabilities, such as the following three examples.

Past can illuminate present

August 26, 1990

The Toronto Board of Education's Archaeological Resource Centre welcomes disabled students to take part in its digs.

The centre has the only program in North America designed to teach hands-on archaeology to elementary and secondary school students.

"Normally, archaeology is not offered to non-professionals—you can only get involved in it if you are taking a course at a university level," explains Carole Stimmell, the centre's information officer. "But our goal was to try to involve as many people as we could—we wanted to make it as accessible as possible to everyone," she said.

So, five years ago, students with learning disabilities began taking part in excavations.

"Students can benefit from certain aspects of the program because we have a high teacher-to-student ratio," says Stimmell. "For instance, when a student finds an artefact from the past, he or she has to map in where it was found. This way, students with learning disabilities gain skills in map-making without realizing that they're doing it."

The excavation program runs from the beginning of May until the end of October. The winter program is held in Danforth Technical School, which also houses the resource centre. In addition, there are evening programs for adults. One highlight of the winter program teaches students how to make a traditional native Canadian feast, using ground corn, beans, and squash.

"After our successful experience with learning-disabled students, we began to think of other groups who could take part in the digs because we know that there were so few field trips that special needs student could take," said Stimmell.

"We next offered the program to some groups of hearing-impaired people. The staff was taught the signing of important words and learned to speak directly and clearly to the students."

Blind students also participate in the digs. Currently, they are excavating in Trinity-Bellwoods Park, in the west end of Toronto, whose history goes back thousands of years when native groups were the only inhabitants. Also, the remains of the first brick house in the city's west end, built in 1820 and called Gore Vale, are there.

"We feel very strongly that people learn best not by seeing slides, but by having an actual experience," Stimmell says.

"Most people don't think of archaeological sites as places for disabled people. But if you're interested, we'll certainly help you try it."

Theatre troupe develops skills

May 26, 1991

A couple of weekends ago, I spent a real fun Saturday morning at Scadding Court Community Centre in downtown Toronto watching the Theatre for French Fries in action.

This consists of 18 young adults, aged 14-22, with developmental or physical disabilities. There are also other people there merely because they enjoy it.

The unusual name was chosen because an important function of the group comes during refreshment time when everyone gets together and socializes.

"The focus of the group isn't people's disabilities," says Rick Campbell, one of the three facilitators. "The focus is doing theatre."

The group began four years ago. It's part of Project Interact, a joint program of Scadding Court Community Centre and Second Look Community Arts, a popular theatre company in Toronto.

"Our first goal is to use theatre to create self-esteem and self-awareness. Then, when we develop scenes and pieces of theatre, we concentrate on important issues that concern people," says Campbell. "With this group, we are looking at dating, drugs, sex, and everything else that interests young people.

"Most of our material is improvised—we develop all our themes from scratch. A scene may wind up completely different than how it starts out. The ideas, scenes, and scripts all come from the people participating in the group," he said.

They start out the morning with relaxation exercises to awaken the body and get the creative juices flowing. On the day I was there, they performed skits around various amusing reasons for being late. This was followed by a dating scene, complete with a tender goodnight kiss.

Relatives and friends were also in the audience to bid goodbye to Campbell during the party afterwards. He and his family are returning to their native Calgary the end of May.

"Many of the people in the group are developing talent and skills as performers," he said. "This is very important because people with disabilities and, most often, people with developmental disabilities, are not recognized in creative and artistic endeavours. The experience of people with disabilities is frequently not reflected in mainstream art."

Barbara Lloyd was one of the parents in the audience and the mother of Sharon who, with Paul Smith, acted in the dating scene. Sharon and Paul have Down syndrome and have known each other— they're 16 now—since they were five months old and in an infant stimulation class at Toronto's Surrey Place Centre.

"I wish that other people would forget the label and accept and love people with disabilities for who they are," Barbara said.

So far as anyone knows, this theatre group is the only one of its kind in Metro. It's funded through a grant from the Ontario Office for Disability Issues.

Outward Bound

August 8, 1993

The important thing about an Outward Bound course is not the activities that the participants engage in nor the places that they go, but what they learn in the process about themselves and each other.

"People quickly grasp that they are capable of far more than they gave themselves credit for. We talk a great deal about perceived limits and real limits," says Philip Blackford, Outward Bound's executive director. "They also gain clarity about what they can do. The knowledge that they are able to do well in stressful situations increases their self-confidence," he added.

The Canadian Outward Bound Wilderness School was established in 1976 in Toronto. From the very beginning, its philosophy has been to accept as wide and diverse a school population as possible.

Anyone interested in taking a course must fill out a medical form. The idea is not to exclude people based on physical ability, but to ensure they are in good health. The school takes people to remote settings far away from medical treatment and they like to make sure participants are not placing themselves at risk.

"As long as people are in good physical health, their physical ability is less of an issue for us. They also need a spirit of adventure, a willingness to take on challenges, and an interest in the environment," says Blackford.

The first Outward Bound course was in Wales in 1941 for young British merchant seamen before they entered the Second World War. When they were in combat, these men were surviving at a lower rate than their older colleagues because the older men knew how to be self-reliant, develop tenacity and inner reserves, and also work together as a team.

"Our warm weather activities are canoeing expeditions, rock climbing, and white water kayaking. In the winter, we concentrate on dog-sledding, winter camping, and cross country skiing," Blackford told me.

The Access to Adventure course takes place in September, in or near Algonquin Park. The minimum age for participants is 17 and there's no upper age limit. Room for more participants is available.

Sonya Hendrickson participated in the Access course two years ago and, last year, went back as a facilitator.

"I would encourage disabled people to go on any Outward Bound course," says Hendrickson, who has osteogenesis imperfecta, a brittle bone condition. The recently graduated occupational therapist works at Toronto's East General Hospital.

Mona's delight in sharing success stories covered a wide ambit. She was especially satisfied to report on victories of those who contended, as she did herself, with cerebral palsy, as in this profile of a young woman who successfully graduated from university.

This university graduate more than makes the grade

August 10, 1997

Sarah Collinge thrives on overcoming obstacles and confronting challenges, despite the fact that she has cerebral palsy.

This young Metro Toronto woman recently graduated from London's University of Western Ontario occupational therapy program with the highest average in her class in theory and mental health courses.

"Though my disability affects everything I do, it doesn't stop me from performing anything I want. It merely means that I do some things differently. But the bottom line is, I still get them done," Collinge says.

A classmate helped her with notetaking. It was important for Collinge to find someone who took them in the same manner as she would, because it made the notes easier to study.

One of the reasons she chose Western is that it has an access van that runs all over campus for its disabled students.

"I've wanted to be an occupational therapist for a long time," she says. "I want to assist disabled people to live and not simply exist. There's more to life than that," she says.

She spent the third year of university in Nice, France—a year that she describe as one of the best in her life. It was also a most difficult and challenging year because France and Europe, in general, are older countries and do not have the architectural accessibility that we, in North America, do.

While at Western, she also completed a two-month fieldwork placement in a hospital in Bermuda. "The people with whom I worked there were great. They were advanced both in their thinking and attitude," Collinge said. However, the general public expected her to have an attendant wherever she went. "That part became a little frustrating," she admits.

At Western, Collinge was presented with the Doris Ransberry Memorial Medal—awarded annually to a student with a disability who achieves highest standing in the graduating year of any program.

Will she remain in Toronto when she starts working? "I like Toronto, but I find the winters very arduous and they get worse every year," she replies.

What advice would Collinge give to other disabled people who wish to attend university?

"It's your right to receive an education," she answers. "Disabled people have to be proactive and advocate for themselves. We must also show the non-disabled population that we possess the same likes and dislikes and goals and aims. We may go about them in a different manner, but we still achieve the same results."

– 8 –

Educational integration

Because the degree of integration of people in society continues to be a measure of how well we are overcoming segregation, early integration of students with disabilities into the school system is essential. That fact, and her own personal experience in having to attend a segregated school, are why Mona passionately advocated this cause in numerous columns.

Special Education ghettoes
December 18, 1988

A petition carrying almost 5,000 signatures has been presented to the Ontario Government asking that no child be placed in a special education class without the agreement of parents.

The petition was circulated by the Integration Action Group (IAG), an organization devoted to having children with special needs accepted into regular classrooms in their neighbourhood schools.

"The present Education Act allows children to be segregated," said IAG member Penny Gill. "We feel very strongly that this is wrong. If parents want their children in a neighbourhood school setting, they should be permitted to do so.

"However, educators will often stipulate that children have to be in a special education classroom. This has very profound, long-term effects upon the children and can cause problems that the parents are going to have to grapple with for a long time."

When a child is bussed outside his neighbourhood to a special education classroom, he remains a stranger to people who live around his home. He doesn't have a chance to make friends with the other children in his neighbourhood. This makes for lonely weekends and after-school hours.

It also means that typical students will see that children who have special needs are being segregated. This sends them a strong message that it is appropriate to do so. They are going to take that view of life into the workplace and to other residential communities. As a result, prejudices against people with special needs will be perpetuated.

"The attitude of adults who insist on segregating children with special needs is often a result of their own education because not many adults went to school with children who had special needs," Gill says. "There are a lot of decision-makers—in government and on school boards—who themselves have prejudices against people with special needs and are not even aware of it."

In 1987, Ontario's Ministry of Community and Social Services published a document called *Challenges and Opportunities* in which it stated very clearly that its policy is to help people who have special needs become a part of mainstream society. However, if the education system is not changed to allow children with special needs into regular classrooms, it will be very difficult to integrate them at a later age.

Some separate school boards, like the ones in Kitchener-Waterloo and Hamilton-Wentworth, have on their own initiative integrated children with special needs into regular classrooms.

Families are so keen on their children attending these schools that many of them either drive long distances back and forth, move to another community, or even change their religion.

It is time for educators to honestly confront their fears and prejudices, use the successes of the separate school boards as a guide, and give children with special needs and their parents the right to attend the school of their choice.

The benefit of educational integration, and the reason for Mona's heartfelt advocacy of it, is seen in the following story of Mark, whose mother worked hard to ensure he was placed in a public school.

Long fight pays off as lad blooms in school
April 30, 1989

If parents see their child as only being a disabled child, that's the way everyone else will see him.

However, if they see their child with strengths and needs like every other child, that's the way other people will view him too, says Kathy Troyer.

Troyer is the newly elected president of Ontario's Integration Action Group which held its annual meeting yesterday in Thornhill, Ontario.

Troyer, who lives in Bolton, knows what she's talking about. She has two sons, Jamie, 13, who is exceptionally gifted, and Mark, 6, who is developmentally delayed.

"Mark has a rare genetic condition called translocation of chromosome five," Troyer explains. "He has a heart condition, respiratory problems, seizures, and muscle tone difficulties. He's also non-verbal."

Mark attends a regular kindergarten class in James Bolton Public School and next September will go into Grade 1 in the same school. How did Troyer manage it?

"It took two years of hard work," she says. "I began talking to the school board a couple of years before Mark actually attended school. Whenever I went to the school open houses, Mark went with me. During the parent interviews, I always mentioned him and made it clear that he was coming."

Some of the teachers said: "No way—we're not trained, we don't have special education." Troyer's response was that they had two years in which to prepare themselves.

There were also a great many meetings with the principal and staff. Communication was a big issue so the teachers learned some of the signs that Mark uses. He goes to school with a talking computer and the teacher and class are taught how to use it by a speech pathologist.

With the assistance of a resource teacher who has a background in orthopedics, the curriculum is also adapted so that he can do it.

A neurologist at Toronto's Hospital for Sick Children drew up a list of instructions for the school on how to handle Mark's epileptic seizures. This has been a big help because someone with authority provided them with guidelines.

"When we started looking at Mark as Mark and not as a multiply-handicapped child, we got somewhere because, suddenly, everyone's focus was the same," says Troyer, "Now, there's no problem because we work as a team.

"Mark has become more independent since he's been attending school. He dresses himself and tries to verbalize a lot more now. When the other children say "hi" to him, they keep after him until he says "hi" back to them. This is very important because he is learning to interact. If he were in a segregated setting, he wouldn't be encouraged to do this because probably most of the other children would be non-verbal too."

What suggestions would she give to other parents who want their children integrated at school?

"Try to negotiate, try to work out something that you and the school can both live with."

Placing a child with disabilities into a regular school is not always the end of the struggle, though. The story Mona related in the following column shows that sometimes "integration" is only a word.

School fight is worth it

April 17, 1988

Integration—is it working for disabled children in our schools?

That's basically the question reader Debra Hartery asked when she wrote me the following letter:

"My son, Daneel, is seven and has Down syndrome. He is currently mainstreamed and the only handicapped child in his class. We had to fight

for his right to be there. The school board recommended that he attend an "integrated" school over 30 km (18 miles) from our home. We were not happy about the distance or the integration policy so we refused.

"In the integrated school, he would be with regular students only in music or gym. This is not my idea of integration.

"We have been told by one of the board's experts that mainstreaming has been a proven failure and often produces emotional problems in the child concerned. Is this true?

"I've been advised that Daneel would be in a classroom with his 'own kind' (their words) though he would be able to share an afternoon activity with other,'regular' students. However, they insist that he would do better with his 'own kind' (a term that causes instant negative feelings in me).

"The Identification, Placement and Review Committee will soon make its recommendation whether Daneel should remain where he is or go to the integrated school. Are we wrong to want Daneel to stay where he is?"

First, Mrs. Hartery, let's clear up the confusion between the terms "mainstreaming" and "integration." What many parents call integration—having their disabled child in a regular class with assistance as required—is what some educators call mainstreaming. Those school officials prefer to have "special" kids in "special-ed" classes and then call that integration.

John Laughlin, director of special education for the York Region Public Board of Education in Aurora, says: "For many youngsters with Down Syndrome, part of the day is best spent in a small class with special-ed specialists and a teaching assistant—where there's lots of individual help."

He adds, "The other half of the day should be spent with the regular class where they can be exposed to the activities that those youngsters would be involved in."

Laughlin said he has not heard of any disabled students in York Region experiencing emotional problems because of York's integration process.

The use of the expression "own kind" in Mrs. Hartery's letter bothers Phil DiFrancesco, co-ordinator of programs for special education with the Hamilton Separate School Board.

"I agree that people should be with people of their own kind," he says. "If you're six to seven years old, you should be around other six or seven year olds. That is people of your own kind."

DiFrancesco, whose board has visitors from around the world witness its success in integration, said current education literature supports "real" integration.

"Integration can be made to work or it can be made to fail. It will work if the people involved put their mind to it, if they want it to work, and if they are open to it. It will work if the kids have a sense that they belong, that their participation in the school system is valued, and that they have a right to be there."

He feels that schools are lagging behind in the integration process — there are integrated Boy Scouts and Girl Guides, integrated churches, integrated everything except integrated schools.

Mrs. Hartery, I hope this information encourages you to keep battling for Daneel's right to attend the school of your choice.

The resistance by educational authorities to integration stems from many factors. One most frequently cited is the supposed high cost of integration — a misconception that Mona did her best to lay to rest.

Inclusion costs less

April 26, 1992

It's a red herring when school boards cite high costs as a reason for not integrating students with special needs.

That's the opinion of George Flynn, superintendent of the Kitchener-Waterloo Separate School Board.

"People who didn't want to integrate throw money around as an excuse because it sells well publicly. If they think they're going to spend more money, people become upset. One of the ways not to have to do something is to tell people it's going to cost more money," says Flynn.

Inclusion actually costs less money. However, since one cannot switch overnight from one system to another, it costs more at the beginning when schools move from a segregated to an integrated system.

Inclusion is cheaper than segregation because it makes a more efficient use of people. Disabled students in an inclusive setting can be accommodated by about half the number of specialized staff found in segregated environments.

"Young people have to be in each other's presence if they're going to learn how to live in the real world later on. Students with challenging needs in ordinary classrooms take on a new and joyous life. Instead of being isolated, they become less dependent and begin to build relationships," Flynn said.

"Some school boards have difficulty with the inclusion concept because of bureaucracy, hierarchy and power. The members of the administration didn't always know about this issue, and have not taken the time or lack the interest to learn about it," he added.

A challenge is to have people understand what an inclusive community means and how the building of it will create a better world.

"It may even be our salvation. Unless we give up power and stop competing with one another, we're going to destroy ourselves," warns Flynn

Inclusion isn't only about people with special needs. It involves all types of people who have, for one reason or another, not been part of our communities.

What advice would Flynn give to parents of disabled children who are experiencing difficulties with their school boards regarding integration?

"No matter how frustrating it is or how much time it takes, don't give up. We're talking about something here that is as important as the future of your child."

A lesson on student integration

February 18, 1996

An authority on integration is challenging Brampton South MPP Tony Clement's comment in this column a few weeks ago that it can cost a yearly $100,000 to integrate a single disabled student.

"It's never cost us that kind of money," Phil DiFrancesco told me flatly.

DiFrancesco is superintendent of operations, elementary schools/ special education, for the Hamilton-Wentworth Roman Catholic Separate School Board, an acknowledged leader in integration.

"We probably integrate more special needs kids than anyone in the province. Though we've had children who require full-time nursing, the cost is nowhere near that amount," he says.

"We have been able to work out an arrangement with the Home Care Program where we pay the nurses the salaries of educational assistants for most of the day, but pay them nursing salaries when they're performing nursing functions.

"There are always creative solutions if people are interested in pursuing them," he notes.

The Hamilton Public School Board recently did an extensive study on its special education programs, as reported in *The Hamilton Spectator*. It discovered that the cost of educating an exceptional student in a self-contained (segregated) class is about $15,000. However, the cost of educating special needs students in integrated classes is only about $8,500 — almost half the cost of segregated classes.

"With modern technology, most students can be accommodated in their home area school. This cuts down on bus costs and they're in a typical classroom with 25 kids and a chance to model their behaviour on other non-disabled students," DiFrancesco points out. "There are also opportunities for peer tutoring and socialization."

The Hamilton-Wentworth Catholic Board has been integrating special needs students for about 28 years.

DiFrancesco believes that parents shouldn't have to move to another school jurisdiction to have their disabled child integrated. "The school is where their brothers, sisters, and friends are. This can provide special needs kids with an opportunity to live, grow, and blossom in their community," he says.

"It's also advantageous for regular students. We want a society that's kinder and gentler and more accepting to people who are perceived as being different.

"If people are shoved away and hidden in institutions or segregated classrooms, they never get to be part of their community. This results in a less caring society."

The struggle for educational integration was no abstract cause for Mona. The denial of it had affected her own life deeply. She shared this personal connection with readers in a series of columns about the struggle by Linda Till against the York Region Board of Education. Till sought to place her handicapped daughter Becky in a regular school, a challenge that would eventually reach the Ontario Human Rights Commission.

Segregation is no solution – columnist off base

September 24, 1989

I was upset with *Sun* education columnist Christina Blizzard for her column Sept. 19 in which she says that a severely handicapped youngster like Becky Till would be better off in a segregated school.

Becky has cerebral palsy (as I do) and was refused admission to her neighbourhood school by the York Region Board of Education.

Chris, don't be fooled by this board. They may have physically disabled children in their regular classrooms but a child with a developmental handicap is sent to a special school. This may be their idea of integration but it's certainly not mine.

Remember, this is the same school board that for years has been spending thousands of dollars of taxpayers' money in court cases fighting to keep Jaclyn Rowett, a youngster with Down syndrome, out of their regular school.

Don't be taken in either, Chris, by the myth that disabled children are better off with specially trained teachers. It is very often these same teachers who get so caught up in a child's disabilities that they cannot see his abilities.

I went to a special elementary school where all the students were handicapped. When it came time for graduating, the school told my mother that it would be impossible for me to cope in a regular high school.

Fortunately for me, my mother was a fighter. The high school right across the road from us refused me admission. However, we finally found a school within walking distance of our home that gave me a chance.

It wasn't easy but that was mainly because I was so shy and unused to the company of able-bodied students my own age. I shall always remember the teachers and principal of Central Commerce with gratitude and affection. They not only understood and encouraged my great love of reading and writing, but also practised reasonable accommodation long before anyone had even heard of it.

Chris, you point out that Becky would need extra help in the classroom. I also needed special privileges—everything from always getting a front seat so that I could hear better, to a place where I could leave my coat because of my inability to manage a locker. Nowadays, with all the resources that are available, all that's needed is a school board that possesses imagination and determination. Just look at what's been accomplished by separate school boards in Hamilton, Kitchener, and Guelph.

One of my greatest regrets is that I never had the opportunity to attend a regular elementary school. If I had, I might have been spared the nightmare of being chased down a neighbourhood street by a group of little boys, all laughing and calling me names. Children don't torment anyone they are familiar with and understand.

The final thing I would like to say to you, Chris, is integration needs bright people like you. Leadership is sorely lacking from Education Minister Sean Conway who is too cowardly to take a stand in the Becky Till-York Region battle.

Everyone benefits from integration. Disabled people reach their highest potential only when more is expected of them than they know they have to offer. Able-bodied people become better employers, fellow workers and neighbours when someone with a disability is just another person to them.

Mother fights on in school struggle

October 29, 1989

Linda Till wants everyone to know that she isn't going to stop fighting.

Yes, she's grateful to the Ontario Ministry of Community and Social Services (MCSS) for providing a tutor for her daughter Becky, disabled by cerebral palsy, but she's determined to continue her battle to get the York Region Board of Education to allow Becky to attend her neighbourhood school.

"MCSS agreed with us that she should be in an integrated placement. They have told the York Region board that, if the board lets Becky into a regular school, they would permit their funding to go with her and provide an aide support," says Till.

This is an important political decision because, as Till points out, the MCSS has made it absolutely clear for years that aide support to disabled students is the responsibility of the Ministry of Education. Obviously, however, Education Minister Sean Conway is not willing to give Becky any type of assistance or encouragement.

"We have spoken to the Catholic board in our area but there are a number of issues of concern," explains Till.

"If we move Becky to the Catholic board, would the York Public board attempt to block the human rights complaint that we have filed by claiming that they shouldn't have to respond to it because she's no longer one of their students?

"It's wrong—it's morally wrong that one should have to move and that one's own board and the minister of education should be both so unaccountable."

The Ontario Human Rights Commission has just begun investigation of the charge of discrimination that the Tills have laid against the York Region board. The parents of Jaclyn Rowett, a girl with Down syndrome, meanwhile have a court case proceeding, also against the York Region board, under the Charter of Rights.

However, the board has told the Tills publicly that they are prepared to see both the Becky and Jaclyn cases go to appeal after appeal, until the children are not in school any more.

"We had an opportunity—very reluctantly given to us a few weeks ago by the chairman of the board—to make a presentation," relates Till.

"Before we got there, two members of the media received copies of a pre-developed press release stating that the board was not budging after the information we brought forward in our presentation—and we hadn't even arrived yet, let alone made a presentation!"

The York Region board declined to comment because the case is under investigation.

Till was cheered by the recent arrival of copies of about 100 letters sent to Conway by Grades 3-8 students at St. Martin of Tours school in Stoney Creek, under the Hamilton-Wentworth Separate School Board.

Teacher "Bunny" Sawyer explained: "All I did was ... tell the children about Becky and Linda and ask them to write to the minister of education and inform him what it was like to have children with special needs in their classrooms."

When she explained about some schools not accepting disabled students, the children responded by asking her questions like: "What are they so worried about?" "What's the big deal?"

Similar questions should be asked of Conway whose cowardly refusal to get involved has shown how truly ineffectual he is.

Fighting for Becky
February 28, 1993

A precedent-setting case is going before the Ontario Human Rights Commission on March 1.

The York Region Public School Board is charged with discrimination on the basis of disability.

In 1985, Linda and King Till, who live north of Newmarket, took Becky, then 11, out of a nursing home to live with them. Becky has cerebral palsy and is, for the most part, non-verbal. They wanted Becky to attend their neighbourhood school, but faced immediate barriers.

"The York Region Public School Board not only would not allow Becky into school, they also refused to register her because they said she was not a legal resident of York Region," says Linda.

School boards are required to plan individually for the educational needs of students by an Identification, Placement and Review Committee (IPRC). But you cannot have an IPRC unless the student is registered.

"By refusing to allow Becky to register, she was not allowed to go to school anywhere for a year. When we finally obtained her legal custody, the board was then obligated to provide for her," said Linda.

Without having seen or assessed Becky, the board wanted to place her in a segregated school. It was acting on information from the nursing home and not addressing her current circumstances and environment.

The Tills finally agreed to allow Becky to try a self-contained class in a regular school. They had to provide her with a personal assistant because the board refused to meet her physical needs.

Becky was then taught at home for a time. For the past two years, she's been a student at Sacred Heart Catholic High School in Newmarket. The Tills are not Catholic, but they sent Becky there because the school has an integration policy. Her physical needs have been met with the help of an education assistant.

"Becky has a group of students around her all the time—students without any particular label, other than friends. They have learned a lot about her care and know how to communicate and dance with her. As a result, she can go to school dances without the attendance of her parents or a paid person," says Linda.

I asked Bob Cressman, the director of education for York Region, if the board will co-operate with a ruling by the commission.

"If we get an outlandish response that is entirely inappropriate, we will hire legal avenues. If it's something that's reasonable, we would consider it," he replied.

Think of what this board could accomplish if it approached integration with the same fervour and taxpayers' money that it squanders in keeping Becky and disabled students like her out of the regular school system!

Fighting the good fight

February 20, 1994

The most important aspect of taking legal action against an organization or bureaucracy for wrongdoing is that they then realize you are a force to be reckoned with and that you won't be intimidated.

"Legal action, in my opinion, is activating a process whereby one side of a conflict alleges in a legal form the breaking of the law by another side," says Linda Till.

She and her husband waged a nine-year battle with the York Region Public School Board. They charged the board with discrimination on the basis of refusing to integrate their daughter Becky, who has cerebral palsy.

The Ontario Human Rights Commission case was recently settled when the school board agreed to pay $15,000 to Becky, now 19. This school board has another similar case pending against it.

"An advantage in taking legal action is the message we send to our children: that we stand in the protection of their rights," Till said. It has had a significant impact on Becky's security and self esteem and provided an equally important lesson for our son, Jordan, who is seven and doesn't have a disability," she said.

"He now has role models: his own parents, who are prepared to stand up for their convictions."

Another advantage is that, at the end of the legal action, there may be a successful resolution to your own case and, as with the Tills, one that will affect many other people. The difficulties that you've struggled through will be lessened for those coming after you.

The disadvantages to taking legal action are that there are high financial and emotional costs. It's very stressful to battle all the time.

"There are definitely times when you are on the defensive because often the response of the other side is to counterattack," Till told me. "We also had to relive year after year of what we perceived as horrendous experiences, painful to our daughter and ourselves. In addition, we were anxious about the case's outcome.

"We tried to minimize the effect of this on our family because we stood up for a belief that many people didn't comprehend. There were many people allied with us, but others distanced themselves," said Till.

I find it appalling that Becky's case didn't begin until four years after the Tills' complaint was filed with the Human Rights Commission.

Would the Tills do it all over again?

"Yes!" was the resounding reply.

Most of Mona's columns dealt with disability topics arising in Ontario, and particularly the greater Toronto community, because this large area contained many disabled people and programs, because it was where she lived and could thus write most authoritatively about what she experienced directly, and because this was where her Sunday Sun *readers mostly lived.*

Yet scattered throughout "Disabled Today" columns was plenty of evidence that Mona was keeping her eye on the larger picture. Sometimes it was just a passing reference to developments across Canada or in the United States. Other times she devoted entire columns to situations in different parts of the country, for instance this 1994 offering on the battle for equality in New Brunswick.

New Brunswick's lessons on integration in schools
August 21, 1994

New Brunswick is the only province in Canada that has legislated integration in the school system.

To learn more, I recently interviewed Gerald Keilty, deputy minister of the New Brunswick Department of Education.

"What distinguishes New Brunswick from other jurisdictions is the strength of the legislation. It aims at inclusion and starts with the assumption that all students will attend regular classrooms in neighbourhood schools," Keilty told me.

He explained that this legislation had the backing of leaders in both government and education. There was also a strong lobby of parents and groups like the Canadian Association for Community Living.

There are factors that made it easier to mandate this legislation. New Brunswick is relatively small and has a very centralized school system, where all funding comes from the provincial government, not from school boards.

"A recent report I read states that inclusive education is a saving to the taxpayer if you measure the cost of institutionalizing students with special needs," Keilty said.

"Resources that support the students' needs are integrated into the regular school system. As a result, there is less duplication.

"Many of our regular teachers become special teachers and are able to respond to a full range of classroom needs," he observed. Keilty, himself, is a former educator and administrator.

This legislation came into effect in 1986 and it took time, perseverance, and a great deal of support to turn good teachers into better teachers.

"However, even today, some parts of the province have practices not as progressive as they are elsewhere," he admitted.

The Atlantic Provinces Special Education Authority provides services to students who are visually and hearing impaired or learning disabled. Nowadays, more visually and hearing impaired students are being educated in their neighbourhood schools.

What are features that make integration happen?

"Leadership is of paramount importance. Teachers and administrators who implement integration must have support. You also have to put your money where your mouth is and provide some financial support," Keilty replied.

– 9 –

Housing

Affordable, accessible housing is a core need of disabled people, so Mona publicized programs and provided information about buildings that would benefit individuals with special requirements. In these first two columns, from 1992 and 1994, she wrote about programs to help people with disabilities modify their homes so they could continue to dwell in them rather than moving to institutional accommodation.

Home improvements
September 27, 1992

The Ministry of Housing's Ontario Home Renewal Program helps disabled people remain in their own homes by providing them with forgivable loans for accessibility improvements.

Leona Middleton of Mississauga has a wall of accessible cupboards installed in her kitchen that match her other cupboards perfectly. "Inside the cupboards are adjustable shelves on rollers that enable me to reach items on them myself," says the wheelchair user, who fell down an elevator shaft in 1984 and who also has arthritis. A folding door that she can easily push to open was installed on a cupboard and, in addition, ramps placed wherever needed.

"I now have total independence in my own home," says Middleton, who's president of the Peel Association for Handicapped Adults.

Gail and Gary Hall live in Chatsworth, near Owen Sound. They have two sons, 15 and 17, both of whom have spinal muscular atrophy. "We had a bathroom installed with a specially designed shower stall, a counter that can be used as a change table and a sink at a convenient height so that both boys can wheel themselves under it," Gail told me.

A deck with a ramp and sliding doors was also built on the back of their house. This gives the boys an alternative exit that is not dependent on electricity, as their hydraulic lift is. "The older boy can now take a shower by himself and the younger one is able to do his own dental care because he can use the sink," she said.

As well as wheelchair accessibility aids, the program covers items like flashing lights that alert deaf people to sound.

The housing ministry also has a Low-Rise Rental Rehabilitation Program that offers landlords of apartment buildings and rooming houses forgivable loans. This encourages upgrading apartments in buildings of four storeys or less and 25 years old or more and providing better accessibility. However, few landlords have applied to the Rehabilitation Program. One reason may be that most single disabled people live in apartment buildings higher than four storeys.

Housing Minister Evelyn Gigantes says that current amendments to the Ontario Building Code would ensure accessibility features in new buildings and require them when renovations occur in existing buildings. In the non-profit and co-op sectors, which already receive government financial assistance, there will be increased funding available if accessibility provisions are made.

"We're also considering suggestions that all new units have adaptable provision like a support strip behind a bathtub wall if, in the future, somebody wants to attach a bar," says Gigantes.

Renovating with love

December 24, 1994

Randy Sora has discovered the true meaning of Christmas.

Sora is the owner of EZ Access, a Pickering design management firm begun in 1987 that specializes in the creation of barrier-free environments for physically disabled people. EZ Access co-ordinates the work involved—everything from the actual design to getting the necessary funding.

"Like other companies, it's been our tradition at Christmas to send gifts to business associates and clients. Though appreciated, this did not convey the real meaning of the season to us or those who received the gifts," Sora explains.

He knows how important it is for disabled people to have access in their homes so they can function independently and safely. Thus, the Home for the Holiday idea was born—modifying homes for needy children in time for Christmas and with no cost to the families involved.

It's based on the Habitat for Humanity concept in which homes are constructed for families who, under normal circumstances, would never be able to own their own home.

With the assistance of the Easter Seal Society, two families were chosen who were not eligible for any funding assistance for home renovations.

"The Weller family of Scarborough has a son, Derek, who is a wheelchair user as a result of Duchenne muscular dystrophy. He needed a way to navigate the entrance to their house because it involved four steps," Sora says. "The construction of a new porch and installation of a porch lift now allows Derek the freedom to enter or exit the house on his own," he said.

The second project involved the construction of a new bathroom for the Fellows family of Ajax who have a daughter, Tanya, with spina bifida. This consisted of a wheel-in shower, accessible height toilet, wheel-under vanity and a direct entrance from Tanya's bedroom to the bathroom, providing her with privacy and dignity.

"One of the criteria we have is that a family who has been chosen for this aid must contribute to the project—either in labour or volunteer work for an agency," Sora says.

Working with EZ Access on the two projects were 13 other businesses—all of whom donated their labour and supplies.

"This is only the beginning—I'd like to see more companies get involved next year," he says.

Happy Holidays, everyone!

Since individuals with disabilities require special housing to accommodate their mobility and living needs, Mona also made a point of updating her readers about the availability of such accommodation, as in these next three columns.

It's an evolution

June 21, 1992

"The evolution of Bellwoods mirrors the evolution of independent living for disabled people in Canada."

Those are the words of Claire Bryden, executive director of Bellwoods Centres for Community Living in Metro Toronto. When it opened in 1967, Bellwoods Park House was Canada's first residence for disabled adults. Now celebrating its 25th anniversary, more has changed than its name.

The original Bellwoods with its bed-sitting rooms, communal dining room and washrooms was transformed after extensive renovations in 1983 into an apartment building of 32 accessible units. This includes 14 transitional living apartments where clients stay from 12 to 18 months and learn independent living skills.

"Bellwoods Centres actually consists of four projects," says Bryden. "First, there's the Bellwoods apartment building with its own staff. The Church Street co-operative living project for multi-handicapped adults began in 1983 and is similar to a group home. Our outreach services started in 1985 and provide attendant care to persons living in their own homes. The Mimico co-op apartment building is our most recent project, beginning in 1989. Several disabled adults there receive 24-hour support services."

Bill Cane is a former Bellwoods apartment tenant who moved to the Mimico co-op after enrolling in the transitional living program. "I wanted the new challenges that more independence would bring. But one thing that I wasn't expecting was the lack of accessible buildings in the Lakeshore part of Etobicoke where I live. It's improved a great deal since then," he says.

What advice would Cane give to disabled people contemplating a similar move?

"Do a lot of soul searching, and learn the skills that I did."

Bryden told me that new ways are being considered to provide the transitional program because the present method is stressful requiring people, as it does, to move twice.

"We are also finding that our clients are becoming older and their care needs increasing. In addition, younger disabled people who require higher levels of care are entering the community. It's really difficult to provide the services they all need within the existing budget and staff framework," she observed.

Bellwoods Community Centres provides disabled people with options regarding where they live. Perhaps the feeling is best summed up by long-time tenant Jean Lauder, who says, "Bellwoods enables us to live up to our fullest potential."

Genesis of special building
August 25, 1991

North America's first apartment building for deaf-blind adults will have its ground-breaking ceremony in North York this coming Wednesday evening with Ontario Lieutenant Governor Lincoln Alexander officiating.

Sponsored by Rotary Cheshire Homes and the Toronto-Don Valley Rotary Club, it's the culmination of almost seven years of hard work. One of the reasons it took so long is that land is so expensive in Metro. With the financial assistance of the Ontario Ministry of Housing, a site has finally been chosen in the Yonge-Finch area.

In 1985, when Rotarian Yim Kocchar conceived the idea of the Great Valentine Gala, an annual money raising event, submissions were invited from groups who needed assistance with their housing projects.

"We were all moved by the presentation of Kerry Wadman, president of the Canadian National Society of Deaf-Blind Persons and deaf-blind himself," recalled Kocchar who is now chairman of Rotary Cheshire Homes.

The Toronto-based Cheshire Homes Foundation has apartment projects and group homes for disabled people throughout Ontario, and is part of a world-wide organization founded by England's World War II hero Leonard Cheshire.

"The members of Rotary Cheshire Homes and the Don Valley Rotary Club prepared the neighbourhood by going in teams to over 400 houses or apartments and speaking personally to everyone. We left them a description of our intentions, including a personal letter from a prospective tenant. We also invited them to attend a public meeting at a local church," Kocchar says.

Some of the neighbours objected to a four-storey apartment building next to them. Therefore, the building was designed so that it will be four storeys at the south end where there's another apartment building, and three stories at the north end. There will be 16 one-bedroom apartments.

One of the most asked questions is why is this building going to house only deaf-blind adults.

"We keep emphasizing that this is a sensory, barrier-free building," said Joan McIavish, property committee chair.

Everything in it will be set up in a way that can be understood by someone who can neither see nor hear—such as tactile alert systems that are felt by vibration or another sensation.

"Imagine this scenario: A deaf-blind person works all week and, when he or she goes home on Friday evening to an apartment in an ordinary building, no one may talk to this individual again until Monday morning. There is no way for this person to know what the weather is like, whether there's an earthquake coming or even if we're at war. Without knowledge, he or she can't make choices. Would you call this being integrated into a community?" asks McIavish.

In the new building, there will be staff who will act as the eyes and ears of the tenants. Communication will be done through intervention—finger spelling by an intervener on the hand of a deaf-blind person is one of many methods.

Tobias House fills gap

September 6, 1992

Though Toronto's Tobias House hasn't been open for even a year, there are already well over 100 disabled people on its waiting list.

Back in 1981, several handicapped persons needed accommodation with attendant care. An appeal was made to the Franciscan Friars for assistance and they worked with government to make it a reality.

Tobias House is located in a new apartment building in the east end of the city and is named after a priest. It supplies attendant care to 12 disabled people and will expand to 19. Affiliated with the Cheshire Homes Foundation, it received funding from Ontario's Ministry of Housing and now gets it from the province's long-term care department.*

Two non-profit groups, each with its own board of directors, are involved. Tobias House Attendant Care provides the attendant care services. The property owner is Tobias House Care for People.

---

* By 2010, Tobias House Attendant Care Inc. had grown to provide care to some 60 individuals at four locations in greater Toronto. With staff of 120, and operated by a 12-member board which includes people with disabilities and individuals named by the Franciscan Friars, the annual revenues of Tobias House now exceed $3 million.

"We will have five tenants on ventilators when our sixth floor is completed. This will show that ventilator dependent people can live in the community—they don't need to spend their lives in hospitals," says Peggy Thompson, a director on the attendant care board.

Jeff Ratz uses a ventilator at night because of his muscular dystrophy. He's already happily living in Tobias House and told me he enjoys the privacy of his own apartment after being in Bloorview Children's Hospital.

"The average hospital bed in Ontario costs $550 per day. An attendant care apartment here is $125 per day," points out Gerry Campbell, executive director of Tobias House attendant care.

With government being so strapped for money, these figures assume even greater importance when considered over a period of many years.

"The younger tenants direct their own care very intensely. However, the older people are more trusting that the attendants know what they're doing and don't mind giving up a little control," observes Campbell.

Program supervisor Andy Underwood says that attendants must be punctual. A late attendant can mean a tenant missing Wheel-Trans and not being able to go to school or work that day.

"To be successful at independent living, a person has to want to take control of their life. Tenants must also be organized and cooperative," says Underwood, a wheelchair user himself due to a spinal cord injury.

Mona was fulfilling part of her mission for "Disabled Today" by promoting the good examples of specialized accommodation offered by the Bellwoods, Cheshire, and Tobias projects, as described above.

Yet she was mindful of the dilemma in publicizing them. These relatively few projects, whether in Toronto or elsewhere across the country, could never meet the needs of all who required such accommodation, as the waiting list she mentioned attests.

Mona was thus filled with understandable hope by the plan of a commercial developer to incorporate the needs of seniors and disabled persons in its new projects. Was this an advance toward the day when the special housing needs of all might be met?

Housing project first and foremost

June 25, 1989

The Daniels Corporation has become the first private developer in Ontario to include housing to meet the special needs of disabled people and seniors in its construction plans for Lakeshore Village.

To be built on the site of the former Goodyear Tire plant in Etobicoke, this innovative development will feature 931 non-profit rental units, 5 percent of which will meet Canada Mortgage and Housing Corporation accessibility standards. As well, however, 10 percent of the project's condominiums will be built to incorporate what general manager Mitchell Cohen calls "a standard of adaptability."

"We will develop design guidelines for the condominiums that will enable these units to be easily modified or adapted to respond to the needs of people who have different kinds of disabilities," he explains.

"Over the coming years, there will be more and more people who will require assistance of different kinds. Certainly, demographics are pointing in the direction of an aging population. And as the population ages, the types of disabilities increase."

The developer wants to add to the stock of housing that is adaptable without major structural changes—like tearing down walls or knocking holes in concrete partitions. To achieve this, they are working with Toronto's Barrier Free Design Centre.

Ten percent of the condominiums will be designed in such a way to be easily adaptable to meet the individual needs of each person. For example, there will be spaces left for grab bars but no grab bars actually put in until the disabled or elderly person is actually in the condominium and can instruct where the grab bars should be most conveniently placed for them.

The non-profit rental units are eligible for funding assistance from both federal and provincial governments. As well, there will be a number of units in the development that will have rents geared to income.

"Lakeshore Village will be a community for everyone—it won't just be for people with lots of money," says Cohen.

Despite the fact that there are additional costs in making the condominiums adaptable, there are no government grants to help defray these expenses. "We're doing it because we feel it's important," he states. "It also makes more economic sense to construct adaptability into the building instead of having to retrofit later."

He points out that they, as a private sector builder, are taking the initiative by having 10 percent of the condominiums adaptable and going even further than the requirement that 5 percent of any government-sponsored development must be made accessible.

"There could probably be an attendant care facility within one of the non-profit buildings," Cohen says. "It's a possibility that we're investigating right now."

It would be wonderful indeed if other private developers would provide this type of urgently needed housing.

While specific projects such as the Daniels Corporation's enlightened Lakeshore Village offered improved housing accessibility for disabled residents, (a project which as MP for Etobicoke-Lakeshore I supported and helped steer past a couple hurdles), more generally the rights of tenants with disabilities remained a problem.

Often forced by lack of money to rent unlicensed apartments, or to lodge themselves in unregulated care facilities, many disabled individuals suffered from neglect and even abuse at the hands of their landlords or caregivers. The death at a boarding house of Joseph Kendall, a disabled man, caused Ontario's government to create a commission of inquiry. Mona made sure the issue got the attention it deserved.

A frustrating wait

March 14, 1993

Ernie Lightman is becoming impatient and frustrated.

It's been eight months since the University of Toronto professor of social policy submitted his report on unregulated residential accommodation to the Ontario NDP government—almost a year of waiting for a response and action that haven't come.

Lightman was appointed a one-man commission after the assault and death of Joseph Kendall in Cedar Glen, a boarding house near Orillia.

"The residents in Cedar Glen were not allowed to use the toilets, they had to go in buckets outside the house as if they were trained animals," Lightman told me.

Many vulnerable adults live in unregulated housing in Ontario— everything from luxury retirement homes to boarding/lodging/rest homes in which residents' only income is social assistance. These adults are largely composed of persons with psychiatric histories, developmentally disabled adults, and frail seniors.

Lightman is very critical of the lack of effective inspection services in rest homes and says there's a tendency for operators and inspectors to become too close. Indeed, one of his recommendations is that inspectors should not let operators know they are planning to visit.

"The Ministry of Health talks about a system of compliance management in nursing homes which means that they will only, as a last resort, impose a penalty or sanction on an operator. I have no problem with this idea. However, the problem is that this ministry seems to be very reluctant to go to the second stage of imposing penalties.

"In the mid-1980s, there were about 500 penalties per year imposed on nursing home operators. By 1989, this number had dropped to zero. If an operator sees there's no threat of sanctions, there's a significantly reduced need for him to fall in line," points out Lightman.

He also says that the government's plan to raise nursing homes to the same per diem rate as homes for the aged is like putting the cart before the horse. Without any quality assurance program in place, there is no way of knowing that this money is going where it should.

The Ministry of Housing has responsibility for Lightman's report.

"It will involve a number of decisions from a number of ministries. We are now working on how to bring a cabinet proposal forward," says housing minister Evelyn Gigantes.

"When you have a large group of very vulnerable people, you can't count on inspection services to provide the protection they need. This requires a combination of efforts at the community level," she said.

Getting tenants' rights

February 13, 1994

New legislation from the Ministry of Housing will give disabled people and seniors the same rights as other tenants. It's expected to be enacted into law by the Ontario legislature this spring.

Called the Residents' Rights Bill, it's based on some of the recommendations made by Ernie Lightman in his report, *Commission of Inquiry into Unregulated Residential Accommodation in Ontario.*

"I am very proud of the name of the bill. It's a statement that says tenants who have not been protected before under other legislation will now be able to exercise their rights under the Landlord and Tenant Act, Rent Control Act and the Rental Housing Protection Act," said Housing Minister Evelyn Gigantes.

These tenants will have the same security of tenure as any apartment dweller, and there will be controls on how much they pay for accommodation. As well, municipal and provincial inspectors will ensure that homes meet provincial safety and maintenance standards.

The government has coined a new term: care homes. This includes facilities that provide accommodation and a variety of services and apartments with support for disabled people. "We are going to tell municipalities through the Planning Act they do not have the power to create zones that forbid apartments in residential houses. In fact, most of Ontario is zoned against these types of apartments," Gigantes said. "Because they are illegal, this makes the tenant extremely vulnerable to eviction if he or she complains about unhealthy and unsafe conditions."

Other concerns cited in the Lightman report are being addressed through the Advocacy Act and Long-Term Care Redirection, she said.

Prof. Lightman, an economist at the University of Toronto, told me, "The most important thing in the Bill is that it extends coverage under the Landlord and Tenant Act to a large number of people. However, my report had 148 recommendations. The government is only acting on two or three."

"It was the death of a resident in Cedar Glen near Orilla that sparked the inquiry. At the end of my report, I said that the ultimate test of the government's response is whether it would prevent another Cedar Glen in the future. In terms of the appalling care, abuse, neglect, bad food and improper medication that many residents of care homes endure, this would not prevent another Cedar Glen."

Lightman noted, "But I must also point out that the problem of care homes has faced every government in Ontario for 20 years. I commend the NDP for having the concern and commitment to finally act."

– 10 –

Assisted living

Promotion of independent living for persons with disabilities was one of Mona's fundamental goals. She understood from her own life experience that, despite its challenges and frustrations, living as self-reliantly as possible gave an individual the greatest personal satisfactions in life. Beginning with this 1988 column, she returned again and again to examine both the nature of independent living and its importance.

To live a life of your own
April 26, 1988

Independent living is a popular phrase among disabled people and those working with them. It describes a lifestyle where the individual takes responsibility for his or her own decisions and actions.

It should be emphasized that independent living is in no way related to the degree of physical disability. Even severely physically disabled people can achieve this goal provided that the following two conditions are in place:

- that there exists within the community a more organized, structured level, a necessary network of support systems that the disabled person can rely upon to assist them with their physical needs; and

- that the disabled person must possess or have a desire to achieve the emotional and mental strength to cope with the many challenges that this lifestyle inevitably brings.

Opposition to this greater independence exists on many different levels.

Bill, a 28-year old man with cerebral palsy, has lived in a residence for disabled people for six years. He then decided that he wanted the fulfillment of living in an apartment building where there existed support care services for disabled persons.

Bill soon discovered that the persons most reluctant for him to make this move were his parents. They said: "We thought you were settled for a life in residence. Why do you want to give up that security for the risk-taking of this new life style?"

It is natural and understandable that parents wish to see their children—especially disabled children—settled in a reasonably happy environment. However, it is also natural for human beings to change—to aspire to different goals at different points in their life.

Another important fact that should be kept in mind is that no lifestyle—no matter how popular it is at any point in time—will find favour with all disabled people. It is therefore necessary to have a wide option of choices available and that the disabled person can be given the freedom of making his own choice.

He must do this with the full recognition that he is often "trading off" greater responsibility and effort for more independence and freedom.

A disabled man, who has been living alone for several years, recalls the battle he had with his family and friends to attain his wish.

"Everyone warned me that I was making a grave error in judgment to even attempt to live on my own," he says. "I have often wondered why it is that when able bodied people make a mistake it is regarded as a part of life. However if disabled people make an error it is treated as a catastrophe."

It is a well known fact that the country of Sweden fostered the independent living movement as early as the 1960s. They encouraged the concept of apartment living with around the clock support services called the Fokus System. A doctor, who is also disabled, summed up independent living when he said: "Life is an adventure. It is only by daring the hazards that we can experience the whole of it."

For people with disabilities, no differently than for able-bodied and mentally competent individuals, "independent living" requires some assistance because humans are not islands unto themselves. In the specific case of a person with a disability who is trying to live as independently as possible, this assistance pivots around the relationship between the disabled person and one or multiple caregivers who help the disabled person live a full life. Understandably, this relationship between client and caregiver is vitally important and often very strong, as Mona described in 1987.

Home help makes the difference
October 22, 1987

Without the help of a capable homemaker, it would be impossible for many disabled people to enjoy the independence, freedom, and dignity of living on their own.

I know—I have been a recipient of the excellent services of Senior Care for a number of years. But what kind of person would be a homemaker?

"We look for people who are committed, have a caring attitude and, above all, who can smile," says Jerry Berman, director of home services of Senior Care, formerly Co-ordinated Services to Jewish Elderly. (Don't let the name mislead you—they serve adults of all ages.)

For quite some time, Doreen Black from Senior Care has been giving me a helping hand once a week. She assists with the laundry, cleaning, and light meal preparation for the weekend when I don't receive Meals on Wheels.

"I like this job because I'm not with the same person everyday and I also go to different parts of Metro," says Black. "If anything should go wrong, I have the security agencies behind me."

Senior Care employs 90 homemakers—two of them male. The latter provide respite care for male clients and thus release family members for other tasks.

"I enjoy working with disabled people," Black says. "When I assist people who can't do things for themselves, I know that I am helping them maintain their independence in their own homes. It gives me a feeling of accomplishment."

Berman is vehemently opposed to those agencies that frequently change the homemakers they send to their clients. "The client receives a higher quality of service if she does not have to train a new homemaker every few months," he says. "It is also easier for the homemaker—she learns the individual needs of each of her clients." It is the so-called "little" things that can sometimes be the most difficult for a disabled person living alone.

"By this time, I am able to anticipate your needs," Black told me. "I know that you cannot remove tightly fitting lids. So when you buy a new container, I automatically loosen its lid.

Black never knew her grandparents and now that both her parents are also dead she feels that many of the people she sees are her family.

"When working with elderly or disabled people, a person should keep in mind that some of them need something more than someone who will do their work," she says. "They maybe lonely and isolated and need human contact like a hug and a kiss."

Berman says there is currently difficulty in recruiting new homemakers, as a result of the stricter immigration laws of the federal government. Another reason is the low unemployment rate in Metro.

Unfortunately, as Mona described in this 1995 column, the relationship between disabled clients and their caregivers was not always an easy one.

Best judge of our needs
August 20, 1995

Few things are more frustrating to a disabled person than asking a caregiver for help and being told, "You don't need it!"

A friend of mine who has cerebral palsy lives in an apartment project where there is 24-hour attendant care. Her fingernails must be kept very short because if they are not, the jerky, uncoordinated movements of her hands will cause her to scratch herself.

"Most of my attendants are understanding and they file my nails weekly. But there are one or two who look at my nails and then tell me they don't need filing," my friend says.

Who knows better what a disabled person requires—the disabled individual who asks for help, or the person who is being paid to give it?

I know there are lazy disabled people who take advantage of caregivers by requesting aid with functions they are capable of handling by themselves. I also realize that due to cutbacks, most caregivers are coping with extra demands on their time, patience, and energy.

However, as another disabled person said to me: "If it's a question of a caregiver not having enough time to do something I ask of them, they should say so and we could try to work out a compromise. But I become very irritated if someone tells me I don't need something done when I know that I do."

Many handicapped people live alone. Therefore, if they are refused assistance by a caregiver, there is no one else they can ask for aid.

To live on one's own with a disability requires a great deal of determination. Negative attitudes by caregivers can weaken the strongest resolve and leave the individual feeling extremely vulnerable. Every time a disabled person is refused needed assistance, it threatens their continued ability to live alone.

Sometimes, it's the so-called little things that can cause the most annoyance. A fellow who is on an Outreach Program told me about the following incident: "One morning my attendant was in a considerable hurry because he had overslept. He did up the buttons on my shirt the wrong way. When I pointed this out to him, he did not wish to take the time to correct his error. As a result, I felt very uncomfortable the entire day."

For people who care about presenting a neat, pleasing appearance, it can be upsetting to have a caregiver who is sloppy or careless.

This conflict could be avoided if caregivers would follow what my nurse from the Victorian Order of Nurses, Judy Kidd, once said to me: "I treat my clients as I would wish to be treated were I in their shoes."

While problems with caregivers sometimes result from a clashing of incompatible temperaments, Mona knew such difficulties could not just be expediently fobbed off on personality issues. Such difficulties often arose from deeper causes, and were but the surface manifestations of structural problems in the homecare program.

Becoming a nightmare

October 2, 1994

A long cherished dream is becoming an unending nightmare for some disabled people living in apartment projects with 24-hour attendant care.

Enza Lupo, peer advocate at the Centre for Independent Living in Toronto, explains the concerns of people in these government funded projects that are operated by service providers: "One of the main difficulties is they cannot get the amount of time they require from their attendants. Because they are also often not represented on the project's board of directors, their views are never expressed or their anxieties understood."

Some projects do include consumers as much as possible in the decision-making process. However, it's where this isn't done that such problems as the following arise.

Many disabled women do not feel comfortable when male attendants assist them with such personal functions as bathing and going to the bathroom.

When one woman requested only female attendants to do her personal hygiene, the service provider's reply was, "In hospitals, you get whoever is available."

The consumer responded: "This is not a hospital—it's my home."

A reasonable solution was reached only after the consumer threatened to take the matter to the Ontario Human Rights Commission.

"Since women with disabilities are very vulnerable, there's always a risk of sexual harassment and abuse in these cases," Lupo points out.

Consumers should keep documentation of both their complaints and the responses they receive. If necessary, they should also contact their nearest Ontario Ministry of Health Long Term Care area office.

The Ontario Federation for Cerebral Palsy has 25 apartment projects under its umbrella. Clarence Meyers, the organization's executive director, says, "In a very large percentage of the projects in this province, it is the administrative staff and the health ministry that have the power.

"Recently, there has been an increase in efforts to control as people within the Community and Social Services and Health ministries see the possibility of their power going to District Health Councils."

Meyers believes consumers should get more clout by forming a group and obtaining legal advice. Even then, he admits it will be difficult.

"Government, boards of directors, and especially administrators are all afraid of power in the hands of consumers," he said.

It is not fear so much as an inability to recognize that, despite our limitations, we disabled people can lead productive lives of self-determination and worth.

Another source of problems with homecare services, which Mona brought to light frequently, occurs when governments devise programs which treat the needs of disabled persons and seniors as if they were identical.

Long-term care plan under fire
January 26, 1992

You know there's something seriously wrong with a new Ontario NDP consultation paper when three provincial disability groups are all critical of it.

"Redirection of Long-Term Care and Support Services in Ontario" describes a shift in emphasis from institutions to community-based services for disabled people and seniors. The document was collaborated on by the ministries of Community and Social Services, Health, and Citizenship.

A big concern is the coupling of elderly and disabled people.

"There is a strong likelihood that people with disabilities will end up under-serviced because of the large numbers of elderly persons," points out Art Montague, executive director of the Cheshire Homes Foundation.

"The disabled consumer is going to be fitted into programs for seniors rather than the other way around," predicts Clarence Meyers, executive director of the Ontario Federation for Cerebral Palsy (OFCP).

Younger people with disabilities are interested in education, employment, and the same variety of social activities that any individual in the same age group has. Most elderly persons, however, are retired and already have solid social networks of families and friends.

"Many young disabled people have spent the better part of their lives in institutions. There's a need for them to build their lives and grow. With the emphasis on services and housing for seniors, their fates will be lost in the shuffle," says Montague.

While the OFCP and Cheshire have these misgivings, another group is disturbed about something else.

"Our major concern is the obvious exclusion of people with developmental handicaps in the stated definition of disabilities," says Barbara Thornber, executive director of the Ontario Association for Community Living.

The government plans to establish 40 new service coordination agencies across Ontario that will act as single points of access for consumers requiring services. These agencies will assess the needs of the individual, provide information, advice and referral services, and then purchase the services.

"These agencies will hold a tremendous amount of power in deciding the future of both the consumer and service provider. If an agency did not wish to deal with a particular service provider, it could be squeezed out of business," warns Meyers.

Independent choice is going to be removed from consumer control—many of the major decisions in life will be made by the agencies.

The paper does state that, if a consumer disagrees with an agency, a process will be introduced to review decisions. It also mentions that the Advocacy Act will provide advocates for vulnerable people.

"Like other people, persons with disabilities wish to have choices. They want options about how they choose to live their lives," says Montague. "People should have an opportunity to take a risk once in a while. Unless they have that right and the chance to exercise it, they don't have independence."

There's one item in the paper that Cheshire finds exciting: A pilot project in which disabled people would receive direct funding from government to hire their own attendants.

The minister of citizenship with responsibility for disability and senior issues, Elaine Ziemba, says that it's been traditional to place elderly and disabled people together because many of their requirements are the same.

"We don't want to take away people's freedom, we want to offer them more choices. If a service coordination agency were set up within a board of directors and was accountable to that board, it could work well," she said.

A solution to the ongoing problem of single-format homecare services not meeting the particular needs of a disparate population of disabled persons is "direct funding." With this approach, as Mona noted in the preceding column, instead of the government paying directly for care-giver services, funding goes to those in need who themselves then hire suitable care providers, as needed. Mona endorsed the freedom of choice allowed by this approach.

Program supporting independence gets the OK
June 13, 1999

It's a success story!

Ontario's government-funded Direct Funding Program, or Self-Managed Attendant Care, is now a permanent plan and will expand over the next three years to serve another 600 people throughout the province.

"It's the only program of its kind in Canada that is government-legislated and operated by consumers," says program manager Ian Parker.

As its name implies, Self-Managed Attendant Care is directed by the client or consumer. The money flows directly to the consumer, and he or she must manage their own attendants.

The two-year pilot project began in 1994 and was designed for 100 people. However, users needed more hours of care than was originally estimated. Therefore, the pilot project ended up serving a fewer 78 people.

An evaluation of the pilot project done by the Roeher Institute was extremely positive. The consumers appreciated the greater control, while the attendants enjoyed better relations with the consumers. The evaluation also found that consumers involved in the project needed less hospital and Community Care Access Centre services.

"Our program costs only two-thirds as much as the outreach attendant services do per hour and half the amount per hour of supportive housing programs," Parker says.

"Consumers advertise, interview, and hire their own attendants and are compensated financially for advertising and bookkeeping costs. The rest of the money is spent only when the attendant is performing their tasks.

"If, for example, you need a person to sleep overnight mainly for security reasons, you can use some type of a flat-rate arrangement in your private home. You would not pay them for eight hours at the full cost per hour," he points out.

However, supportive housing, or Support Service Living Units, would have to pay their staff the full hourly rate. The wage rate is set by looking at the provincial average for attendants, which currently is $13 per hour.

"The Centre for Independent Living in Toronto handles the program's administration while the Ontario Network of Independent Living Centrés helps enormously with the interviews to select persons who wish to become candidates for the program," Parker says.

Of course level of funding, as always, remained an issue.

It just doesn't add up
June 26, 1994

The Ontario government does not understand simple arithmetic.

Placing a disabled child for respite care in Metro's Bloorview Hospital costs them about $600 per day. Yet, the child could remain at home for a fraction of this cost with an expansion of one of the government's own programs.

The Special Services at Home (SSAH) Family Alliance was organized in November 1993 to fight this and other injustices. It's composed of families in Ontario who already receive or urgently need this service.

More than 9,000 families use SSAH. The Ministry of Community and Social Services (MCSS) provides a yearly $3,000 for each user family to hire a support worker who helps the disabled person reach their highest potential and avoid placement in hospitals or institutions.

"SSAH has an annual budget of $26 million—only 3 per cent of the Developmental Services operating budget," notes Rev. Myroslaw Tataryn, SSAH's press liaison. "During 1992-93, Schedule 1 and 2 institutions received more than $347 million for 3,300 persons. SSAH serves almost three times that number of people at a fraction of the budget," he points out.

The yearly cost for each resident living in a government funded and operated Schedule 1 facility was more than $107,000. A Schedule 2 government-funded facility, operated by a community board of directors, costs over $77,000 per resident a year.

"Much of the SSAH funding is channelled through agencies or treatment centres and some of them take off 20 to 30 percent for their so-called administration fees," says Tataryn. "This is totally abhorrent."

Brian Low, director of the Developmental Services Branch of MCSS, explained that sometimes it was necessary to place a child in an expensive respite care setting when no other option was available and the family was in a crisis situation. "In the last seven years, we have provided opportunities for over 1,000 people to leave our facilities and move to the community," Low says.

"We need to ensure that, wherever possible, resources are being used to support services for the individual and not going to administration fees. We're following up on this."

He also told me the government is looking at making these support services portable if the family moves to another community, as long as the services are not already available in the second community.

"What we need to do is look at those characteristics of SSAH that make it effective and how to integrate those elements in our other service areas. We're not looking at the reduction of funding, but the best use of the available funds," Low says.

Despite the positive innovation of direct funding, the 1990s saw enormous cutbacks in social services and radical restructuring of the organizations designed to provide those services, generally in the name of efficiency, but brought on because of government deficits. Mona recognized the need for change, but worried, along with other individuals with disabilities, that the changes endangered the level of services for those in need.

Restructuring long-term care
June 19, 1994

The main reason Ontario's long-term care system needs to be reformed is that it is highly fragmented. It's very difficult for a consumer to access the services he or she needs. Also, it's not cost-effective," says David Wright.

Wright is the executive director of Toronto's Visiting Homemakers Association and chairman of the Long-term Care Steering Committee of the Metropolitan Toronto District Health Council.

District Health Councils have been established throughout Ontario by the Ministry of Health to act as local planners, advisors and facilitators. Major plans affecting disabled people and seniors are under way to restructure the long-term care sector in Metropolitan Toronto.

"Many people argue that consolidating about 150 organizations into 15 or 20 will not be, by itself, cost-effective," says Wright.

"However, a centralized authority or Multiple Service Agency (MSA) will be a better, more accessible system because it's going to be created within one's local community. Furthermore, the MSA is designed by and for that area and will presumably be unique," says Wright.

A major concern to disabled people is that an MSA may lead to one or two organizations in a geographical area gaining a monopoly in the provision of services and thus eliminate the choices previously available.

"We're looking at a time very soon when cost and structure are going to be severely threatened. The existing level of current programs must be protected and with any luck, improved," says Wright.

He predicts a series of groups will be formed as precursors to MSAs. Some organizations will disappear into this new group and some may remain independent.

North Toronto is a geographical area that has done a competent job of getting its local service providers, consumers, and planners together to talk about the shape of a possible MSA.

"If they wish, disabled people will be provided with an envelope of dollars to purchase their own services. They also have the option of going with MSA," Wright says.

Individualized funding is the choice of a small but very vocal group of disabled people. Most of us, however, do not want the work and responsibilities of hiring, firing, and bookkeeping this would entail.

Government solutions to problems tend to cost taxpayers more money and end up being of less benefit to people they are supposedly helping.

Worried about long-term care

February 25, 1996

I'm uneasy about the Ontario Conservative government's plans for long-term care reforms, unveiled recently by the Ministry of Health.

Community long-term care involves about 1,000 agencies across the province and includes such services as nursing, therapy, and homemaking that are used mainly by disabled people and seniors.

The government will reduce 74 existing Home Care and Placement Co-ordination Programs to 43 Community Care Access Centres (CCACs).

CCACs will help consumers decide what services they need and when community care is no longer appropriate, arrange for admission into a long-term care facility of the consumer's choice.

These services will be purchased from not-for-profit and profit-making agencies, in competition with each other.

Despite government assurances of developing a transition plan for not-for-profit agencies and other providers and their emphasis on "highest quality, best price," I am concerned that their biggest priority will be saving money. As a result, consumers may not receive the quantity or quality of service they require.

"Under previous governments, the not-for-profit agencies often had preferential status in working with Home Care Programs," explains Michael Scheinert, executive director of Senior Care, one of the largest multi-service agencies in Ontario. They serve adults of all ages.

"With the current government, we'll have to compete much more with commercial agencies that will strive for larger contracts with CCACs," says Scheinert. "Costs for services are going to have to come down, especially where there are unions with collective agreements like we have. We've been able to raise the level of pay and benefits for home service workers.

"Commercial agencies generally hire their homemakers at much lower wages with reduced benefits and therefore, reduced costs. This will create serious problems for not-for-profit agencies that must reduce costs significantly and yet maintain the quality of care," he points out.

Competition isn't always a bad thing. Some agencies may benefit from a little shaking up. But I fear consumers will be the real losers because it could also drive the worthwhile ones out of business.

Attendant services for disabled people will be independent of CCACs, whose boards are going to be composed of consumers and community members. However, there is no mention of an appeal process in case of a disagreement between the consumer and a CCAC.

Accessibility

Mona knew the quest to live independently required improving facilities to accommodate special needs, so kept a clear and constant focus on issues surrounding "accessibility."

Designed for better living
November 12, 1989

The new guidelines of the Ontario Human Rights Code for people with disabilities have one very important change.

In the old code, the phrase "reasonable accommodation" was used. The new Guidelines for Assessing Accommodation Requirements for Persons With Disabilities talk about "accommodation, short of undue hardship" and that's a significant difference.

"It used to be that you had to do everything that was reasonable to accommodate," explains Catherine Frazee, chief commissioner of the Ontario Human Rights Commission.

"The employer, service provider, and landlord might invest some money or effort but they also had a right not to be interfered with. The 'reasonable' part of the 'reasonable accommodation' phrase tended to weaken the right of the disabled person.

"Now, we're going with accommodation, period, short of undue hardship. This means that the standards, expectations, and responsibility are much higher than they used to be."

Undue hardship is defined in two categories: cost so high that it alters the essential nature of the business or enterprise or affects its viability; and cases where the safety risk created by accommodating the disabled person would outweigh the benefit of providing equality.

The first article of the guidelines is aptly expressed: "The needs of persons with disabilities must be accommodated in a manner which most respects their dignity, if to do so does not create undue hardship."

The phrase "respects their dignity" means acting in a manner that recognizes the privacy, confidentiality, comfort, autonomy, and self-esteem of disabled people, which maximizes their integration and promotes their full participation in society.

"You can imagine how my eyes lit up when I saw the phrase about maximizing integration," says Orville Endicott, legal counsel for the Canada Association for Community Living.

"Our main objective is for people with disabilities to be part of the mainstream of society and not a sub-society that is totally dependant on the munificence of the majority."

Endicott pointed out that it was under the Human Rights Code that the Till family was charging the York Region Board of Education with discrimination for refusing to allow daughter Becky, who has cerebral palsy, to attend her neighbourhood school.

Frazee expresses hope that company decision makers, store owners, managers and other people become aware of what is expected of them and that they do it before the situation escalates into a complaint. She also feels it is essential that people with disabilities are empowered with a clear understanding of their rights.

"I believe that attitudes of people are the major handicap that disabled persons have to deal with," says Endicott. "What human rights laws, and 'accommodation' guidelines in particular, achieve is that they require people to do the things they would do if they had the right attitude."

The indignities to disabled individuals caused by the lack of accessibility was brought home in Mona's 1994 column about the experiences of the renowned Beryl Potter.

Let's maintain dignity

March 6, 1994

Disabled rights activist Beryl Potter hasn't been making headlines lately—all because she's been fighting a private battle so many disabled women face.

"My problems began almost five years ago—at first, I thought it was indigestion. There was a constant pressure in my stomach and vagina. I had pressure sores and skin irritation," the feisty activist explains.

Potter has been a wheelchair user since 1965 when she had the accident that caused her to become a triple amputee—both legs and one arm were gone.

"Finally, I went to see a woman gynecologist at a downtown Toronto hospital. However, I couldn't get up on the examining table. No one in the hospital could help me, including the six nurses who were in the cubicle, because they are not taught how to lift a person without legs.

"I had to lie down and slide forward in my wheelchair so the doctor could examine me and do a Pap test. I was most embarrassed because the nurses all stood around watching me. Neither the doctor nor the nurses seemed to realize the indignity of the situation. Disabled people have feelings. We are not on public display," Potter said.

Swelling worsened her condition and this caused bladder problems and excruciating pain.

She then saw Dr. Paul McCleary, chief of obstetrics and gynaecology at Wellesley Hospital. As the clinic had more space, she went there.

"I couldn't believe it—there was a wheelchair-accessible examining table that could be dropped to the level of my wheelchair. I rolled over onto it and then it was pumped up to its proper height," says Potter.

Finally, she was able to have the examination all women are supposed to have every year. The doctor said that hers was a chronic condition caused by sitting in her wheelchair so much and recommended some salve to help it.

McCleary told me special female procedure chairs have been ordered for Wellesley. They have a button that is pushed to make them go down or come up. The side of these chairs drops away so that a woman can transfer smoothly between her chair and the hospital chair.

"The other thing that's exciting is that we're opening a new 18-room birthing centre here shortly. One of these rooms is wheelchair-accessible with a bigger than usual washroom and shower.

"We sometimes forget that not everybody has two arms and two legs and that some people cannot walk. What we should be doing is considering how to make conditions easier for everyone. It doesn't cost anything to be caring," he observes.

An avid reader all her life, Mona was happy to acknowledge the success of the Toronto library system in providing access to all citizens.

More than books at amalgamated libraries
October 25, 1998

A wealth of disability-related services awaits you at Toronto Public Libraries.

Metro Toronto's amalgamation has resulted in its libraries being divided into four regions: the south region, comprising the libraries in the old city of Toronto; the east region, joining the libraries in Scarborough and East York; the west region, combining the libraries of Etobicoke with York, and the north region, containing the libraries in North York.

To learn more, I spoke to Susan Back, manager of community services in the north region.

"The Home Library Service, available across the city, delivers books to anyone with a physical disability that prevents them from coming into the library. To receive this service, contact your local library," Back said.

If there's a group of people in a seniors' apartment building or nursing home who cannot get to the library, the library deposits a number of books in both places. Volumes are changed regularly.

There are also Talking Books for persons with visual impairment. In addition, large print books can be borrowed from all libraries.

Back continues: "A Centre for People with Disabilities at the Toronto Reference Library has a great deal of specialized equipment. One of these is a personal reader machine with a voice that reads the text of a book to a blind person. The Centre also carries disability-related information," she said.

The Public Library Directory for Metropolitan Toronto (it's an old directory) provides a map and chart that notes the accessible libraries. It's available at local libraries.

"We have an adult literacy program for people in the north region that has students with physical disabilities. We also have people who are developmentally delayed and learning to read," Back explained.

"This program is conducted by volunteers. We do an assessment and it depends upon the disability whether we can help them," she said.

For children who can use the phone, there is a dial-a-story program in several languages.

The north region library is collaborating with the Canadian Council on Rehabilitation and Work to help disabled people write resumés. The resumés are then placed on the wide area employment network on the Internet for prospective employers.

Mona also felt the North York Performing Arts Centre was an institution whose support of disabled people deserved to be celebrated for the good example it provided.

Gem of accessibility

June 5, 1994

I don't understand it.

The unique accessibility of the new North York Performing Arts Centre has gone largely unnoticed by the media. If fact, *The Sun*'s art critic, Lisa Balfour Bowen, was the only one to even briefly comment on it when she described the centre's art gallery.

I recently toured this beautiful building, accompanied by Marjorie Platt, past chairman of the North York Advisory Committee for People with Disabilities, and Glenn Garwood, the centre's executive manager.

The building is on a site that slopes from the back of the theatre to the front. To avoid steps, this slope has been absorbed into the building. The front and back doors, at different heights, are thus both level with streets.

A counter at the box office has been lowered to make it accessible to wheelchair users. There is also a theatre floor plan to enable disabled people to select their seats.

"The large lobby connects the lobbies of all three theatres. One of its main features is a graceful, gently sloping ramp that is integrated into the lobby's design," Garwood points out.

"Disabled persons are not the only ones who find this ramp useful. Others use it as an overview or for some people-watching, while many people find it handy to meander up to another level," he observes.

There is also an elevator that is deep enough to comfortably accommodate a scooter or wheelchair.

Platt uses a scooter. As well, she is a physiotherapist. This combination makes her own experience and advice invaluable.

"There are spaces for wheelchairs in different parts of the theatres and this, unlike most theatres, provides disabled people with a variety of ticket prices," she said.

A regret of Garwood's is that the gift shop—because its location had to be changed at the last moment—is reached by stairs. However, this has been partially compensated for by accessible kiosks.

"If accessibility is a basic objective from the very beginning, construction expenses are not higher. It's the retrofitting or having to go back after plans have been developed that costs a lot of money.

"At the beginning, we put the 25 building designers in a room with members of the North York Committee, all of whom have different disabilities. This was very important because designers tend to think only of wheelchair access," he said.

It should be mandatory for architecture students to visit the North York Performing Arts Centre to see real accessibility created with the input of disabled people themselves, instead of so-called experts.

While buildings and some institutions were becoming more accessible, Mona felt most consumer products were not very disabled-friendly at all. In 1994 she took Canadian manufacturers to task over their lack of consideration for a valuable market segment.

Make 'em accessible

July 31, 1994

Most Canadian manufacturers, industrial designers, and packagers are completely ignoring one very lucrative market.

There are an estimated 4.2 million Canadians whose physical disabilities make it difficult or impossible for them to perform such everyday tasks as opening a tube of toothpaste, using a can opener, or doing up and undoing buttons.

Yet they are not even considered when these products are designed.

We also have an increasingly aging population, some of whom will develop ailments that make their hands weaker or more infirm.

I have to leave a tube of toothpaste uncapped because I can't turn the cap to close it. While in Florida a couple of years ago, I noticed the American version of the same toothpaste had a cap that merely required one finger to open or close it. When I suggested this cap to the Canadian manufacturer, they weren't interested. It needn't be this way.

Arthritis News recently had a story about McNeil Consumer Products, makers of Tylenol Extra Strength, that have a new, easy-to-open cap. Naturally, precautions must be taken if there are small children around.

There are can openers that can be operated by one hand. However, what are people to do if they have problems using both hands?

Buttons are the most troublesome—their doing up and undoing. Zippers with attached pulls are better, but they can get stuck.

Please don't suggest Velcro as a substitute for buttons! It requires two steady hands so that both sides will be pressed together evenly. Another nuisance is that it catches on other garments unless it's closed.

Several years ago, I had a pant suit with a belt whose clasp shut magnetically. Why couldn't this idea be used instead of buttons?

How about it, manufacturers and designers? I've given you some ideas and you can think of others to make your products accessible to greater numbers of consumers.

While Mona knew that educating the public about the need to improve accessibility, she understood that for this to happen, her own voice alone was not enough. As she writes here, the greatest changes would happen when people with disabilities spoke up for themselves.

Great games but...

July 26, 1987

"The 1987 games were the best ones that I have ever participated in!"

"Everything was so well organized—it left the athletes free to concentrate on the competitions."

These were just some of the many enthusiastic comments that were made about the Ontario Games for the Physically Disabled held last weekend in North York.

Despite 30-degree temperatures, there were more records broken at these games than ever before.

It was wonderful to see the large crowds that attended the various events. They were not only the relatives and friends of competing athletes, but also individuals who came to cheer the athletes in their endeavours or assist in other ways.

However, not everything was ideal. There were many spectators in wheelchairs and people often stood in front of them, unthinkingly blocking their view. "When a person is a wheelchair user, he or she cannot move to a better seat when someone decides to stand right in front of him," says Frances Hill, herself a wheelchair user.

It must be remembered that crowds, by their very nature, are informal and spontaneous. It is very natural for them to stand up when something exciting occurs. However, it can also be pointed out to them that their actions may interfere with the enjoyment of other people in the audience. A tactfully worded request over the PA system would have helped immeasurably. It would also have made the crowd aware of another need of disabled people.

The question is: Whose responsibility was it to see that this was done—the authorities involved with other games or disabled people themselves?

I believe that we disabled people have to begin taking more responsibility for the way we are treated. Instead of expecting other people to instinctively respond to our difficulties, we must learn to make both our wishes and our needs known in an effective manner.

"We have to show able-bodied people how to help us," says Betty Lindsey, chair of the North York Physically Disabled.

We have to take more control over our lives. This was really brought home to me a couple of weeks ago at North York's "Courage Parade" to display the billboard art advertising the games.

Before setting out on the tour, we gathered at the North York City Hall. A city hall staff person told me "not to bother" getting out of the car to go into city hall. I waited there for 40 minutes. It was only afterwards that I discovered that Mayor Mel Lastman had been hosting a reception during this time and that I should have been there.

The staff person, it was explained to me later, thought it would be easier for me not to get out of the car. However, she should not have made this decision on my behalf.

That decision was mine to make.

If disabled people are truly to become a part of the mainstream of life, we must learn to be assertive by recognizing that everyone has rights and responsibilities.

One of ours is that we speak up—loud and clear—on our own behalf.

– 12 –

Assistive devices

The goal of independent living for persons with disabilities is more readily achieved as the assistive devices available to persons with special needs are improved and increased. While regularly urging manufacturers to better tailor their products to the needs of disabled people, Mona also made sure her readers knew about the products and services that were already available.

Design display is a treat

August 6, 1989

You will never forgive yourself if you miss the *Designs for Independent Living* exhibit at The Power Plant, Harbourfront's art gallery.

The show features a wide variety of products designed to help disabled people and seniors cope with the many challenges of living independently. It was organized by New York's Museum of Modern Art. Products shown—everything from wheelchairs to baby bottles—were created by a collaboration of industrial designers, medical professionals, and users.

The warm and vibrant use of colour transforms even mundane wheelchairs into mobility aids as striking and sleek as sports cars. With large wheels in bright shades of yellow or red and remarkably lightweight and portable, they are designed for racing and other athletic activities.

"The main purpose of these products is to make them useful to people with disabilities and, at the same time, attractive to able-bodied persons. This encourages the entire integration process," says Barbara Fischer, curator of The Power Plant.

A breadboard and knife from Sweden have proven so popular that they are now being manufactured for the mass market—thus proving, once again, that items that make life easier for handicapped people often benefit the general population.

For children, there are tumble forms—made from moulded foam with flexible upholstery—that can be arranged in many different ways to help with their posture and exercises. The vivid colours are a recognition of the fact that children enjoy therapeutic devices that are also fun to use.

No one is too young to benefit from this ingenious technology. On display is a baby bottle with a hole in the middle to enable an infant with limited use of its hands an easier grasp. This could also help a parent who is disabled.

One very versatile product has a dual function. "The Rollator" is a walker that converts to a chair—just the thing when one is waiting for Wheel-Trans!

Other innovative items include a newspaper holder, unbreakable mugs, plates and bowls that discourage spilling, and devices to help people who are visually or hearing impaired. There's even a hand prosthesis that looks astonishingly real.

The *Sun's* travel writer, Jane Stokes, went with me to this exhibit and said she is amazed and impressed at how much has already been done to meet the needs of disabled people. "It's important for everyone to be aware of the new technology for it keeps handicapped people functioning in the mainstream of life," she said.

Most of the items in this show came from Sweden, as well as from the U.S., England and Denmark. It's on the second floor. On the first floor is a small exhibition of items for people with disabilities made by students at the Ontario College of Art and the University of Toronto.

This exhibit stresses that, with the right technology, disabled people can be active participants in every aspect of daily living. It also shows that eye-appealing assistive devices enhance the abilities of the person using them.

Hi-tech aids can make life so much easier
March 28, 1999

The Assistive Technology Clinic improves the quality of life for disabled people through modern technology.

It's a service of Sunnybrook and Women's College Health Sciences Centre and is located at the Sunnybrook Centre for Independent Living in Toronto under the direction of occupational therapist Pearl Gryfe.

Gryfe recalls: "We came into being in 1994 in response to the critical need for technological services for people with amyotrophic lateral sclerosis (ALS) or Lou Gehrig's disease."

The ALS Society of Toronto helps fund the clinic, with the Assistive Devices Program (ADP) of the Ministry of Health providing matching grants. Despite the additional financial assistance of community agencies and the Sunnybrook Foundation, which recently received a donation to provide this service to persons with multiple sclerosis, funding remains a continuing challenge.

An interdisciplinary team including occupational, physical and speech therapists and technologists now serves other disabilities as well.

Gryfe continues: "As technology advances, the tools available to people with disabilities become very powerful and extremely complex. Power wheelchairs, computers to write and speak with, and operating your TV, VCR and lights, blinds, doors and phones—one can do all this, with the touch of a switch or the blink of an eye.

"But how do you access this technology and who will train you once you have obtained it? These are the reasons our clinic was started."

They also work with seating for wheelchair users, augmentative communication, and environmental controls. The Sunnybrook team assesses the client and prescribes the appropriate technology that will accommodate their disability and teach them how to use it.

Of equal importance, they consult and listen to their clients and are always open to new ideas. They understand that the right equipment not only enhances the client's ability to function but also permits him or her to remain in their own home.

"First and foremost, we help to give people independence. This, in turn, provides them with the opportunity to lead satisfying lives by enabling them to get out, work, socialize, and be included," Gryfe says.

Mona also made sure her readers were aware of advances rendering communications devices more accessible.

Dial "I" for independence

December 4, 1994

It's what my nephew, Michael, calls the "ongoing saga of Mona and Bell Canada." Unlike many other stories, however, mine has a happy ending.

Almost two years ago, I suddenly began having trouble using my telephone. I could not complete my dialling without a recorded message coming on the line telling me to please hang up and try my call again.

The phone not only allows me to keep in touch with family and friends, but I also use it to conduct most of my interviews for this column.

I contacted the Bell Telecommunication Centre for Special Needs here in Toronto and they suggested I replace my old rotary dial phone with one having large push buttons and that I also install speed dialling.

This helped a little but I was still using operators to place most of my calls and missed my former independence in using the phone. So, back I went to the Special Needs Centre.

Shayna Maislin, the centre's manager, explained that as a result of inter-digital timing, 20 seconds were now allowed for dialling a number. Any change would affect the entire North American telephone network.

When Maislin contacted her U.S. counterpart, she learned they too are experiencing this problem and are looking at some solutions for 1995.

"I then met with our network services people who suggested the new Vista 200 phone because it has two important features: On-hook dialling, which means you do not have to lift the receiver to dial the number. This bypasses the problem with the 20 seconds. It also has the availability of 10 programmable numbers," she told me.

In addition, the Vista 200 has a redial key—handy when one is trying to get through to busy numbers like Wheel-Trans.

I was elated when, for the first time in my life, I dialled a 10-digit number by myself.

Currently, 75 percent of the centre's customers are hearing impaired. I'm in that category and the Vista 200 has a volume control. If needed, a portable Walker 10 amplifier can increase the volume.

"We must be more proactive. Whoever develops a product has to consider everyone—not just non-disabled people—but disabled and seniors as well," stresses Maislin.

I am extremely grateful to Bell Canada for giving me what I value most: my independence.

Keyboard to widen the world— Sound helps users see 'n' learn
February 17, 1991

A new and revolutionary phonetic computer keyboard is enabling many disabled people to develop word processing and language skills they never believed possible.

A brainchild of blind computer programmer Erol Hembroff and court reporter Maggie Dodd, both of Vancouver, the Boswell keyboard is the first of its kind in the world.

"Originally, Maggie and Erol wanted something that would allow blind people to take notes faster—particularly those who had trouble with Braille. Then they realized it could help other handicapped people as well," explains Ron Craig, president of Vancouver-based Boswell International Technologies, which makes the keyboard.

The unusual thing about this keyboard is that it produces syllables instead of individual letters.

There are only 46 phonetic sounds in the entire English language. The Boswell keyboard has 24 phonetic keys, a speech synthesizer, and software. When a user pushes a key or a combination of keys to create one syllable, two other things happen simultaneously: a voice chip in the machine repeats the sound on the speaker (or the headphones), and the software writes the correct spelling on the screen.

Touching the keys, seeing the word on the screen, and hearing it pronounced all at the same time provides an unique learning experience to those who are visually impaired or learning disabled.

"When we speak, we use phonetics, not letters," says Craig. "Boswell does the same thing.

"This removes an obstacle for someone, for example, with dyslexia who can't handle letters but can cope with sound. When they type, they don't have to think about how anything is spelled. They just put in the sound, the same as in speech. It's an equalizer for the print handicapped," he said.

In March, his company will place several Boswells into the Enabler Program for disabled students attending California community colleges, and one at Toronto's Hugh MacMillan Rehabilitation Centre.

It takes about 50 hours to learn where all the sounds are on a Boswell, the same amount of time it takes to learn an average keyboard.

"Once we get our operators up to the speed of 150 words per minute, we are confident that Boswell will also provide low cost closed captioning for deaf people on everything from city council meetings to TV," predicts Craig.

The Boswell keyboard requires an average amount of dexterity to operate. It is lightweight and portable and can store up to 200 pages of written text. One could use Boswell all week and then put the contents in a standard computer for editing.

A Boswell costs $3,000. Company officials are coming to Ontario soon to discuss this province's Assistive Devices Program in the hope that Boswell will qualify for 75 percent funding.

As well as helping disabled people, Boswell can assist those who are illiterate or learning English as a second language.

The Boswell keyboard is named after James Boswell, the seventeenth-century writer and biographer of Dr. Samuel Johnson, who compiled the first English dictionary.

Mona likewise promoted improvements in the design and availability of wheelchairs and scooters.

Hot wheels!

June 28, 1992

Forget the gloom and doom recession stories! Today, I'm going to introduce you to a disabled young man who has a new and successful wheelchair manufacturing business in Toronto.

The unique aspect of his wheelchairs is that they are individually made to suit the person.

John McRoberts became a quadraplegic at the age of 18 in a diving accident at Lake Erie in 1981. "I had an injury that would allow me to become independent if I worked hard enough. So, that's what I set as my goal—the regaining of my physical independence," he told me.

"What fuelled me was watching other people who either gave up or won the race. I made my choice very early: I wanted to be one of the winners."

As a student at Toronto's Northern Vocational secondary school, he was very interested in machine shop and welding. Now, however, he lacked the physical ability to do that type of work.

"One day in 1983, I was sitting on a couch at home with my wheelchair beside me. Suddenly, I realized that wheelchair is never going to leave my side no matter where I go. That was a real eye-opener for me. It made me recognize how important my wheelchair was," he said.

He was always dissatisfied with the wheelchairs that were available. They would not allow him to get close to anything because his feet stuck out in front.

"Every time I turned around, I bumped into a doorway. I felt and looked disabled," he says.

With the assistance of a $15,000 Ontario government New Venture loan, which he matched dollar for dollar, he began his own wheelchair manufacturing business.

Wheelin Designs became incorporated in 1988 and is approved for funding under the Assistive Devices Program. A motorcycle shop in Toronto, Ontario Honda, manufactures the wheelchairs and a friend, also a quadriplegic, sews the upholstery.

Wheelin Designs is currently experiencing its best year so far.

"After my injury, I was constantly told that I couldn't do this and I couldn't do that. However, I learned that my mind is a very powerful motivating force. As a result, my philosophy now is: It's not what I can't do, but what I can do, that's important," McRoberts said.

He's a second-hand saviour

July 9, 1995

James McKellar does all the accounting, most of the repairs, and the deliveries in his Burlington business, the ReMed Foundation, with the assistance of only one volunteer.

ReMed is a non-profit group, begun in 1993, that recently became the only used health care vendor in Ontario on a six-month trial basis with the Ministry of Health.

Necessary repairs are made to used wheelchairs, scooters, and walkers. The person donating the equipment receives a tax receipt.

"The Assistive Devices Program (ADP) pays 75 percent of the cost of a new piece of equipment while the client pays the other 25 percent. With used equipment, however, ADP pays 75 percent of the client's portion while the client pays the other 25 percent. For example, if the client's portion of a new wheelchair is $800, the ADP would pay $600 for a used wheelchair, while the client pays only $200," explains McKellar, ReMed's executive director.

ReMed also donates health care equipment to third world countries.

"A young St. Catharines girl needed a reclining power chair that cost $22,000 along with special seating. She could not afford a new one.

"My lawyer in Toronto, Bernie Gluckstein, heard about it and paid for a renovated one we had in stock. The girl was just ecstatic when we gave it to her," McKellar relates.

ReMed has two trucks and a trailer to pick up the equipment. An almost-new minivan was donated to them by the late Ralph Cooper's family in Burlington. Cooper was disabled.

In 1976, McKellar designed and manufactured the first ambulance buses in the world. He was an ambulance driver-attendant at the time.

He receives around 200 calls a week from people who require used equipment, mainly wheelchairs. This is because people are being sent home from hospitals earlier and more people want to have their family member at home rather than in the hospital.

"If we had the money and manpower, we could definitely help more people. I need someone to answer the phones, another individual to help with the repairs and a person to look after the deliveries," he says.

ReMed urgently needs used wheelchairs. Since it receives no funding, donations of money would also be welcome.

"You can't put a price tag on selling a wheelchair to someone at a very low price and seeing the smile on their face," says McKellar.

Such assistive devices as just described allow individuals with disabilities to lead richer, more integrated lives by better connecting with the world around them. In this 1990 column Mona explained how sometimes these new links were especially noteworthy, as when one program to produce assistive devices allowed a group of prisoners to better connect with the disabled.

Unlikely partners help out the kids
September 30, 1990

A unique partnership has come into existence between Toronto's Hugh MacMillan Rehabilitation Centre and, of all places, Kingston Penitentiary.

"A year ago my son, who is a mechanical engineer, was doing summer work with an office in Ottawa called Corcan, a marketing company of Corrections Canada. They transfer products for manufacture into penitentiaries across the country," explains Mickey Milner, vice-president of research and development at the centre.

"We shared the annual report of our engineering department with the people at Corcan for the purpose of seeing whether they could manufacture some of our products in a more economical manner than we can."

After visits to each other's facilities, the Centre and Kingston Penitentiary decided that the inmates would begin the development of some prototypes of devices that make life easier for disabled youngsters.

One of these is a special desk for wheelchair users so that they can easily use computers without leaving their chairs. Another is training wheels that could be included on bicycles to help handicapped children maintain their stability. Standing braces for youngsters with spina bifida is another product the inmates are working on.

"It's a very exciting program because we, at the Centre, are concerned with one type of rehabilitation and Corrections Canada is involved with a different type of rehabilitation. As a result, we have rehabilitation people helping other rehabilitation people," observes Milner.

Michael Elkins, the regional administrator of industrial and agricultural programs for Correctional Services, agrees with Milner.

"We're always looking for marriages between our organization and organizations that deal with similar issues," he says. "People who perceive themselves as being disadvantaged often want to help other people whom they also consider to be disadvantaged."

The work is being done in a combination sheet metal and tool-and-die shop in the Collins Bay facility. The inmates there are generally in their mid-20s and they're a rough group, many having a history with drugs and violence.

One of the inmates in the shop is a wheelchair user. Like most federal departments, the penal institutions in Kingston have been made accessible.

"When Mickey and his staff put on a slide show for the offenders who are working in the shop, it was much the same sort of revelation to them," says Elkins.

"You can see it in their faces and in the way they do their work now that it really makes a difference because they know that what they're producing is going to help disabled children."

In addition to the work they are doing for the centre, the penitentiary manufactures a line of office furnishings, computer work stations, and modular shelving. Though they can't sell their products directly to the private sector, they can sell them to any level of government and registered, non-profit groups.

— 13 —

Transportation

Right up there with housing, the issue of transportation is crucially important to people with disabilities, which is why Mona reported on public transit in all its forms, including various alternatives.

In the first column below, though, Mona dealt not only with the transit infrastructure, but with the human component of getting around town, to underscore why one's ability to travel is key to independent living.

Travelling can boost self-worth

February 16, 1992

"I've seen very few programs that are making such a difference to a person's life, freedom, and feeling of self-worth," says David Pitt, central regional director of the Metro Toronto Association for Community Living (MTACL).

He's talking about a travel training program for adults with developmental disabilities. The one-year pilot project was funded by a private foundation with a one-time grant. It has had to be discontinued because of lack of money.

"At the simplest level, travel training means the ability to get from where you live to your place of employment or recreation on your own, without having to be driven or using a taxi," he explains.

"One month, you're dependent on other people to make arrangements for you. A while later, you are in charge of getting from one place to another. You decide when, where, and why you are going. You are in control of these factors—all of which are key components in self-worth," he said.

There are people with developmental handicaps who have job skills, but become disoriented or confused when travelling. Even though they have the ability to do the job and can make a contribution, they are doomed to spend their lives on social assistance because they are unable to travel independently.

There are other people who may not be able to cope with competitive employment, but who could handle supported training on the job, where they are like apprentices. However, even this opportunity is closed to them when they cannot come and go on their own. This, in turn, significantly restricts their options for the future.

"A person may not be able to find a job, but can still be capable of a rich, social life with many friends," Pitt points out.

"If they can travel by themselves, they can get to the social experience or meet a friend. If they are unable to get out on their own, all they can do is sit at home and watch television. This creates incredible frustration, both for them and their families."

Individuals who are developmentally handicapped are no different from other people in their learning experience. Some learn slowly, others swiftly. There are people who can be travel trained in 10 days, while others take up to 60 days. The average is between 30 and 45 days.

Even if a person is unable to read, he or she can still be taught to travel independently. It is more risky and difficult, but it is still possible. The training must be highly specific and probably involves one or two routes.

"We make a distinction of travel training, route training, and pedestrian training," says Pitt.

"Travel training is the ability to use several modes of travel—bus, subway and pedestrian—and to travel to different locations.

"Route training teaches an individual to go from one place to another. If that route changes, the person needs to be trained again on the new route.

"Pedestrian training gives instructions on how to use the streets safely and to obey the rules of crosswalks and street lights," he said.

Some developmentally handicapped adults can use the bus or subway, but need to be instructed in appropriate behaviour such as not talking excessively to strangers or hanging over subway platforms.

A very important aspect of the program is the volunteer assistance MTACL receives from Metro Police and the TTC. They provide demonstrations on how to transfer from a bus to a subway and what to do if help is needed—the basics that most people take for granted.

Though a proposal for financial assistance was made to the Ontario Ministry of Community and Social Services, they do not have the money to make this an ongoing program.

Since the 1970s, most public transit systems have operated a special service for passengers with disabilities. In Toronto, where Mona lived and wrote her column, the municipal transit commission's service, known as "Wheel-Trans," is Ontario's largest such system. Mona was a close follower of Wheel-Trans' progress and problems, both as a user of the service and one who appeared before transportation committees to advise and advocate for improvements. She devoted many columns to Wheel-Trans, examining its service, its funding issues, and the politics associated with it.

Transit enters new era

August 19, 1990

Wheel-Trans is on the brink of one of the most exciting times in its 15-year history.

That's the opinion of manager Bob Evans as he outlines a "family of services" developed by the TTC to improve transit for disabled people in Metro.

"We now have four taxi companies for ambulatory disabled people: Able-Atlantic, Diamond, Beck and Royal-A-Kwik," Evans said.

"The expanded criteria (on who can use Wheel-Trans) have brought more ambulatory passengers onto the buses and, as a result, we have not been able to accommodate wheelchair users. I'm hoping that, by this time next year, the Orion 11 buses will be almost exclusively for wheelchair users."

Evans stressed that in the contracts the TTC has with taxi companies, the drivers must provide assistance from the door to the taxi and then from the taxi to the door.

"We also have an indication of support for the community bus concept which will have at least one route implemented within the next year," he predicts.

A community bus will travel on a fixed schedule. It will serve residences for disabled and link them with medical, shopping and recreational facilities within a specific area. It will also provide spontaneous travel, with the driver getting out of his or her seat to help riders on and off the bus. Eventually, these buses will feed accessible, key subway stations as well.

Metro's disabled community can also look forward to "kneeling" buses, elevators being installed in some subway stations, and more Orion 11s.

Evans was gratified by the large number of people at the recent public meetings to discuss Wheel-Trans.

"The biggest issue is that people want a ride," Evans said. "It doesn't matter which type of vehicle it is, just as long as a ride is available. At the present time, there is not enough service out there to meet the needs of the community. The riders also feel that four days is too long an advance time to have to book a ride."

Sometimes two people who live in the same area request rides that will take them to and from the same destination at the same time. One of them may get the ride, the other may not.

"The public's perception is that we are weak in the scheduling of rides," Evans admits. "As a result, consultants are doing an exhaustive review of the entire scheduling system. With the volume of rides that we're now facing because of the expanded eligibility, we need a much more sophisticated system."

Consultants are mapping out a five-year plan for Wheel-Trans, including the costs associated with improving the system.

Transit system in peril

January 20, 1991

Unless the provincial government tightens the eligibility criteria of Wheel-Trans, costs are going to continue to soar and the disabled people who need this service the most will be denied access to it.

Shortly before the Liberals lost the election last year, they expanded the criteria for persons who are eligible to use specialized transit services in Ontario. Up to then, only people who were unable to board conventional transit vehicles could use special systems like Wheel-Trans.

The expanded criteria, however, opened up use of special transit vehicles to persons unable to walk 175 metres (approximately three city blocks).

But the Liberals did not provide more funding for Wheel-Trans to meet the resulting increased demand for its services. Only government can be so asinine and lacking in foresight.

Now, many people cannot get rides, and the system continues to grow with more than 500 new persons each month applying for ridership on Wheel-Trans.

"Our community committee expressed concern with the expansion of the eligibility criteria when the province proposed it," Bob Evans, manager of Wheel-Trans, told me. "Wheel-Trans is the largest system in Ontario and, because of this, it is most adversely affected by the criteria change."

Its ridership five years ago was 55 percent wheelchair user and 45 percent ambulatory. This has now completely reversed, due to the expansion of the eligibility criteria, and the ridership is now composed of 55 percent ambulatory and 45 percent are people using wheelchairs.

"Wheel-Trans has a large number of questionable riders now — people who don't need it," charges disabled rights activist Beryl Potter, who has a special interest in transportation.

"If they can't get a ride with Wheel-Trans, some persons are seen getting on a regular TTC bus. To them, special transit is a convenience, not a necessity.

"Also, nursing homes should use their own vehicles, wherever possible, and leave Wheel-Trans for people who have no other transportation option," Potter says.

Many disabled people were appalled when the *Sun* recently reported Metro Chairman Alan Tonks as advocating a cut of more than

$1 million from the Wheel-Trans budget and saying that handicapped people have to get along with less service.

"I don't want to cut $1 million from the Wheel-Trans budget," Tonks now says, "I'm not going to say I was misquoted, but what I did say is that was one of the possibilities we would be looking at.

"We're also going to find out if the NDP government would be willing to change the formula of funding. Right now, the province and Metro share the cost of Wheel-Trans on a 50-50 basis. Even a shift of 5 percent would make a big difference," he said.

To relieve the pressure on Wheel-Trans, there should be more community buses like the one now on Bathurst St., old buses should be replaced by ones that kneel or have low floors, and all key subway stations should be made accessible.

"Without an adequate transportation system, disabled people cannot take advantage of employment equity or educational opportunities and integration becomes a word without a meaning," says Potter.

Activist rips TTC proposals

July 28, 1991

Canada's most famous disabled rights activist has sharply criticized a report that calls for increased funding from the province to make 22 key stations in Metro's subway system accessible to wheelchair users in five years instead of the proposed 10.

"We're in tough economic times—we can't ask for pie in the sky. The money just isn't there!" said Beryl Potter, in response to the report, *Action for Access*, which was presented to the TTC last Tuesday. Potters' special interest and expertise are in transportation for disabled people and seniors.

Now, the report itself is the subject of a second report in which TTC staff will do a study on its 49 recommendations.

"We're recommending that the Ontario NDP government increase its level of funding from 75 percent to 90 percent to make some of the subway stations accessible," says Bob Evans, manager of Wheel-Trans and chairman of the committee that produced the report.

"What the key station concept will do is enable us to develop community bus routes that will feed the accessible subway stations," Evans says.

The community bus route on Bathurst St. has been such a success that there will be four added routes in the fall.

The report calls for the introduction of accessible taxis in Metro. An accessible taxi costs $35,000 to $40,000. The provincial government has just doubled the amount of its grant from $5,000 to $10,000 to taxi owners who wish to make their cabs accessible. The committee also recommends that drivers of these cabs should be given special training.

Wheel-Trans already uses seven taxi companies for its ambulatory riders: Able-Atlantic, Beck, Co-op, Diamond, Kingsboro, Kipling, and Royal.

"We are developing, with the Ontario Urban Transit Association, a taxi driver training package that will enable us to train the taxi companies' trainers so that they can, in turn, train their employees. We recognize this is a big issue," says Evans.

He credits the use of taxis with an all-time low in the number of rides that Wheel-Trans had to reject.

I have used these taxis for almost two years and found that most drivers are helpful. Unfortunately, I have also occasionally encountered drivers who are downright rude and give assistance very reluctantly.

The Orion 11 bus fleet will be expanded by 11 new buses this fall and six will be added to the community bus service.

Beryl Potter, however, is not impressed.

"I am shocked that they would order more Orions." she told me. "They're not cost effective—you often see them running around Metro with only one or two riders.

"The conventional system should be made more accessible for ambulatory disabled people with such things as audio-visual equipment, enforced courtesy seating, and better lighting.

"Even with an entirely accessible system, disabled people will still need the door-to-door service during the bad weather months of winter," she said.

TTC service cuts, fare increases unjustified

November 19, 1995

I question the financial necessity that caused the TTC to reduce contracted taxis for ambulatory Wheel-Trans riders and raise fares when they obviously have enough money to give some of their staff generous salary increases.

If they were truly interested in cutting costs, they would take another look at the manner in which they operate Wheel-Trans.

Brian Crow is president of the Ontario Motor Coach Association, an organization representing 1,200 bus companies.

"Savings occur when the operation of the service is contracted out. If it costs less to operate the service through competitive bidding, more rides could be provided," he points out.

"In 1987, when Wheel-Trans buses were contracted out, the cost was $23.39 per trip. By 1993, under the TTC, the cost had doubled to $46.01 for each trip.

"With the help of the Consumers Price Index of Statistics Canada, we calculated that if the private contractor had continued to operate Wheel-Trans, the cost in 1993 would have been slightly over $29.00.

"The TTC spent $52 million more on Wheel-Trans buses in this period of time than the contractor would have if that arrangement had been retained.

"In addition, the contracted out service could have provided 1.9 million more trips for the same money spent by the TTC," Crow states.

He also notes that the Wheel-Trans administrative staff increased by a giant 341 percent when TTC took it over. However, the number of drivers went up by only 15 percent.

Several Wheel-Trans riders have signed an Ontario Human Rights Commission complaint against the TTC for depriving them of rides.

Paulene Pasieka is the lawyer for the TTC in this matter and she told me: "We are in the midst of litigation and this somewhat changes parameters."

"Factually, we're not in a position to verify some of the information you have. Some of the questions you ask are quite sophisticated and they require a considerable degree of analysis."

"This is a little frustrating, especially when your information may be from parties who could have their own interests. It's very easy for individuals to calculate figures in a way that benefits their position," she observes.

Nonetheless, the TTC has shown a callous disregard of its responsibilities by depriving disabled people and seniors of essential rides and yet providing themselves with handsome salary increases.

My criticism of the TTC does not extend to Wheel-Trans manager Bob Evans or his staff, for whom I have a high regard.

Along with profiling policy issues of urban transit, Mona let readers know about various transportation options for disabled individuals wishing to travel between cities and towns.

Fancy a trip for fun?
Bus tour service caters to the disabled
July 21, 1991

If you're disabled and enjoy travelling by bus, I have good news for you.

The new Handicapped Charter & Tour Services of Metropolitan Toronto arranges everything from one-day outings to Niagara Falls and the Stratford Festival to longer trips through the U.S.

"This is something I've wanted to do all my life," says Bill Alcock, the company's founder-driver.

"To the best of my knowledge, I'm the only person in Canada who is doing this."

The former TTC driver quit his job four years ago so that he could work for one highway coach company and then another to obtain the experience of driving a highway coach and to learn about touring.

"Our first trip was May 11 to Florida," recalls Alcock. "Our 19 passengers had a great time and the experience taught us a lot. I suspect that, during the first year, we will be learning about what we can and cannot do.

"Our Florida trip was for 14 days and took three days of travel each way. Every day, there were 10 hours of driving time, plus three or four rest stops.

"This made it into a 14-hour day and everyone became tired. In the future, we will take four days going and coming back."

Alcock has what's called a mini-coach. He installed a lift and a larger than usual washroom with handrails.

The bus can handle up to three wheelchair users and 16 ambulatory passengers, or one wheelchair user and 20 ambulatory passengers. A trailer carries the wheelchairs of those people who are able to transfer on and off their chairs.

"At this point, we have to accept the word of the proprietors regarding the accessibility of our overnight stopovers," Alcock says.

"We question them very thoroughly, but we were disappointed in a couple of places and won't go back there again."

This will cease to be a concern when he is able to personally visit each of the destinations beforehand to make certain they are accessible. He's already done this with a trip that's scheduled for November to Kentucky.

All of you country music fans won't want to miss a trip to Nashville coming up the end of September. Other excursions are planned for Alabama and Louisiana.

Alcock is also hoping to take a group to Buffalo the first weekend of December, for shopping and to attend the Festival of Lights in Niagara Falls.

"If the interest was there, I would take more trips in Canada," he says.

Alcock also invites groups of disabled people in smaller localities to charter his bus and take them on shopping excursions to Toronto or other places.

"The Port Perry Nursing Home has chartered the bus to take residents to Florida for two weeks in January, 1992. The disabled people and seniors in the nursing home are having fund-raising events all summer to finance the trip," he said.

Another Florida excursion will be offered in 1992.

His fares compare favourably with other bus tours. People who need attendants are asked to bring their own at full fare. Efforts are being made to get subsidies for attendants, but this may take an indefinite time.

Have bus, will travel

July 23, 1995

The number of disabled North Americans who travel is increasing four times faster than the general travelling population, according to the American Society of Travel Agents.

This interesting fact was in the informative magazine *Disability Today*.

Greyhound Lines of Canada is keeping abreast of the times and has made 10 of its coaches wheelchair accessible with government financial assistance. Coaches can also be lowered 3 ½ inches to make it easier to mount the steps.

I was invited to see one of these coaches at Greyhound's property on Lakeshore Blvd. in Toronto by John Coombs, Regional Manager of Safety and Driver Development for Greyhound Lines in Ontario.

"Lifts have been installed that can hold up to 450 pounds and wheelchairs that are no wider than 32 inches.

"There are two side by side positions for wheelchairs on the coach. The seats that the wheelchairs replace can be moved back and forth, so if no wheelchair users are scheduled on a trip the seats are left in their regular place," Coombs pointed out.

Wheelchairs are anchored securely to the floor and the individuals in them must wear a lap belt.

Instead of having an accessible washroom on the coach, Greyhound ensures adequate stops are made at accessible washrooms during the trip.

Stu Pettigrew is a driving instructor with Greyhound's Eastern Division and teacher of their disability sensitivity awareness program which all drivers are required to take.

"We have guests with disabilities give talks to the drivers. They enjoy driving the accessibility coaches and being able to help," he told me.

"Teaching the program has made me more sensitive to the needs of others both on the job and at home," he said.

If a disabled person requires lifting or other special aids, he or she must have an assistant, who can then travel free.

Schedules are available that note which coaches are wheelchair accessible. But you still must phone in advance of making your trip to ensure wheelchair-accessible service.

I'm interested in learning more about accessible travel. Cruise ships, trains, planes, hotels and motels, as well as travel agents, are invited to send me information on this subject.

Just good train-ing
July 12, 1992

I have a new love in my life—travelling by train.

Recently, I went by Via Rail from Toronto to Montreal, where I spent the night at the Queen Elizabeth Hotel, and then came home. The idea was to see how accessible this trip would be for a disabled person.

Via likes to have 48 hours notice of passengers with special needs. I can walk but I use a wheelchair for long distances. At Union Station, a friendly Redcap and I used wheelchair lifts to bypass all the steps.

"We have a strong commitment to providing our customers having special needs with the most accessible, comfortable, and complete rail service possible," says Dianne Graham, senior officer of public affairs for Via Ontario.

"Toronto's Union Station has just had its first escalator installed and we hope to have two more by the end of 1992. We also make our washrooms accessible whenever we can."

Via has wheelchair tie-down areas in many of its trains, including the transcontinental ones to the West. Its trains to the Maritimes will have them by the end of 1992. Personal attendants of disabled people can travel free. I found the food delicious and service excellent.

Montreal's Central Station connects to Place Ville Marie shopping centre and the beautiful Queen Elizabeth Hotel.

"We have 11 rooms that are designed specially for disabled people. Some of the TV channels have signers for persons who are deaf," said Caroline Des Rosiers, the hotel's director of public relations.

To make it easier for me to handle the security card that opened my door, Denis Poirier, at the front desk, punched a hole in its top and attached a key ring to it. The hotel takes care of the needs of all its guests.

I still had some difficulties. Poirier, however, offered helpful suggestions until, at last, I was able to open the door on my own.

"I feel happy too because I have assisted you to gain your independence," he told me.

One complaint, however. On the way home, I asked an older Via staff to have my meat cut up and he said, "You shouldn't be travelling alone. You need an attendant."

I was able to assure him that, with a little help, I was fine on my own.

From the moment that Via's Benoit Dulong helped me off the train in Montreal, I was warmed by the friendliness and compassion of its people. Regrettably, I am not bilingual. However, I discovered there that a cheerful smile and pleasant manners are understood in any language.

For individuals with disabilities who drive their own vehicles, Mona emphasized the services available for driving instruction, as well as particular issues associated with driving and the disabled.

On the road to good driving

August 25, 1996

It's all a question of attitude, says Carl Wiese, driving rehabilitation specialist at Metro Toronto's Bloorview-Hugh MacMillan Centre.

When he teaches non-disabled people to drive, the question they are most concerned about is: "How quickly can I get my license?"

However, the Hugh MacMillan students want to know: "How can I become a better driver?"

They are also more courteous and willing to share the road and compromise, he notes.

"I help special needs people learn how to drive either for the first time or teach persons who have become disabled how to drive again, using such equipment as hand controls," Wiese says.

"When people have a problem, they realize they must do their best and so they try harder."

"The students must be at least 16 years old. My oldest student was 92. We get many people in their 60s, 70s and 80s. In several cases, they've had strokes and have to learn to drive again with the aid of special devices," he tells me.

The student must first undergo a two-hour assessment conducted by occupational therapists who have specialized in driving. If he passes, the student becomes a candidate for driving lessons.

Some people need only a few lessons, while others require several months of training.

"The biggest problem disabled drivers face is people who think that anyone with a handicap should not be driving. This is so unjust, because most disabled drivers become better than the average driver," he says.

Another problem is people who selfishly and illegally continue to use handicapped parking permits belonging to disabled relatives who are now dead. They do not seem to care that they are depriving handicapped people of their rightful parking spaces.

To prevent this from happening, the Ministry of Transportation could make these permits renewable on a yearly basis in the same manner as car licenses.

Persons who thoughtlessly park close to a van with a ramp, thus effectively blocking a wheelchair user from entering the van, can be another headache.

Work

The difficulty many people with disabilities have finding employment, let alone satisfying and financially rewarding work, causes immense frustration. To address this, Mona promoted the value of individuals with disabilities as workers and publicized programs available to help disabled workers find employment.

A "step" in the right direction
July 17, 1988

After graduating from high school most students have the option of finding jobs or continuing their education. This is not the case for young adults with developmental disabilities.

Scott Lawson, co-ordinator of North York division of Metro Toronto Association for Community Living, believes that many of these young adults end up in segregated work situations.

"Sheltered workshops have been like a life sentence for most people because there's no other option," he says.

This is why Lawson began a year ago to develop a new endeavour for North York called the Supported Training and Employment Program (STEP).

"In its broadest concept, STEP will finally give individuals a choice," Lawson says.

"STEP is going to take individuals through a systematic approach to employment. It will include the finding of jobs, advocating for them on the job site, teaching and training of job skills, helping them to be more socially acceptable, and the teaching of appropriate interaction with people. A job coach will take them through this whole process as required, and will be available to them for three or four months."

Sharon Kelly, a teacher at the Metro separate school board's Madonna High School, which is an integrated school in Downsview for students age 14 to 21, agrees there is a great need for STEP.

"Other municipalities have training programs or co-operative education," Kelly says. "In Downsview, there's nothing for disabled students to go to unless they have a job."

A proposal for STEP funding has been made to the Ontario Ministry of Community and Social Services and a presentation will be made to the ministry in the fall.

By having a unique follow-up policy for its 12 clients, STEP will take the time limit away from how long people can be served. It will find out what happens to its clients after two years on the job: Do they want new jobs? Do they need new job skills? How can their jobs be replaced if they lose them."

Gus Leuschemer is the assistant director of Daybreak, a L'Arche community in Richmond Hill, begun by Jean Vanier for people with a wide range of ability levels. Leuschemer, like Sharon Kelly, is a member of the STEP board of directors.

"Work is a part of life—it can facilitate the feeling of belonging and participation," he says.

"Attitudes are changing. There is a growing awareness that people who are different, whatever the label is, not only have the right to participate but can enrich the workplace and culture."

Not only does real pay for real work help a person's self-esteem, but it can also transform him from a social assistance recipient to taxpayer and consumer.

Opening the doors to co-op learning
May 6, 1990

Every student—no matter what his or her disability is—should have an opportunity to participate in a co-operative education program.

That's the view of Terry Miller, who is the co-ordinator of career and co-operative education for the Dufferin-Peel Separate School Board.

Co-op education is a non-traditional way of teaching and learning. A student in a regular co-op program chooses a career that he or she is interested in and then contracts with the business, firm, or agency to spend 15 weeks, four days a week, at the job placement learning about the work.

"We have a special needs co-op for students who are either physically, mentally or emotionally handicapped," Miller explains.

He admits that it's more difficult to find a placement for disabled students because of the supports that they require. Despite this, however, they have been successful with their program, which is only four years old.

The work experience is concentrated into shorter periods of time and spread out for about a year for mentally handicapped students. They learn new job techniques in a certain sequence and this is reinforced by school work as well.

"We have to spend a great deal more time monitoring or helping at the job site. The student may also need the aid of a teaching assistant for a while until he can do the work on his own," Miller says.

Most of the physically disabled students can take part in the regular co-ops and can also spend longer periods of time on the work site.

Generally, the students are 16 years old and enrolled in one of the board's high schools. Miller estimates there are 20 to 30 students currently in the work experience program.

"Physically disabled students can do almost any type of work, as long as they can get around and it doesn't impinge on their handicap.

"We have had mentally handicapped students working in nursing homes, as clerks in food stores, in the printing department at our board office, and in the cafeteria.

"Many employers are very open to the idea of work experience programs as long as you explain to them beforehand what the student can and cannot do," he said.

The disabled students are given the same certificate upon completion of the program as the other students receive.

"What we're trying to do is help the students plot their future," Miller said.

"If you look at a student as a student—despite the problems he or she may have—every student needs the same approach in terms of career planning. You have to do that or else you're going to have to look after people for the rest of their lives. I don't think that's very good for the students, the parents, the school system, or the country."

An equal chance to build Big Macs
August 20, 1989

John Alden has had disabled employees in his McDonald's restaurant since he first opened in September 1982.

"My son, Mark, who has spina bifida, was the start of everything I've done for disabled people," says Alden, whose restaurant is located at the Canadian Forces Base in Borden. "Because of our experiences since he was born in 1966, I've always been involved with handicapped people—either directly or indirectly."

Though Mark now lives in Metro Toronto, where he is employed as a switchboard operator at Queen's Park, his father continues to hire people with a variety of mental or physical disabilities.

During a job interview with an applicant, they're treated the same as any other applicant — with one exception.

"I tell them that I'm experienced with disabled people and I'd like to know about their disability. This enables me to assess what their abilities are — what they can do and what I think they're able to handle," explains Alden.

He informs the rest of his staff when a person with a physical disability will be joining their ranks, because the handicap is an obvious one. However, with a person who has a developmental disability, he tells only the manager and the person who is going to train him.

"The two young gentlemen I have working for me now are slow learners within the school system. However, at McDonald's, their disability is not as evident because we can teach them ... very easily.

"We treat them all the same as anyone else, whether they're disabled physically or mentally," he says. Both his able-bodied and disabled employees benefit from this hiring practice.

For disabled people, it means being accepted as part of the group. They think: I'm the same as my friends at school now. I have a job at McDonald's. As for his able-bodied employees, they become knowledgeable about disabled people. Soon, Alden says, they don't even notice the disability.

He has this advice for other employers who may feel a little apprehensive about employing disabled people: "You have to give yourself a chance to find out what the strengths and limitations are of people with disabilities. You may have to make a minor change, such as buying a swivelling bar stool to give an individual more freedom of movement, or make the cut in the counter a little wider so that a person in a wheelchair can get through to the back room."

McDonald's does not keep records of how many disabled employees they have.

"Our hiring practice for many, many years has been to treat able-bodied and disabled people equally. Therefore, it's never been a policy of ours to segregate in one column or another an able-bodied or disabled person," says Maureen Kitts, their director of public relations.

However, they do have an excellent, new film that shows several of their handicapped employees in action. Just under 15 minutes in length, its title reflects the positive attitude of McDonald's: "Yes, We Can!"

Network issues a challenge

December 6, 1987

CTV wants to hire disabled people—yet when the private television network placed an ad in a Toronto daily, it received only one response.

CTV needs five people to work as captioners—to provide captioning or subtitles for spoken words on TV that more than a million Canadians having hearing problems would benefit from.

To place an ad specifically requesting disabled applicants, CTV had to ask for special exemption from the Ontario Human Rights Commission. "The ad is discriminatory because it states we don't want anyone but disabled people," says Fergus Griffin, CTV's personal coordinator. However, the commission gave permission to run the ad, considering it a positive step in the hiring of disabled people.

The positions call for a 40-hour work week in the evenings. Peter O'Neill, vice-president of finance, told me that it is a policy of CTV to offer taxi service to its female employees if they have to work after 7 p.m.

Among the qualifications needed are an excellent command of English and typing word-processing skills. These skills are not easily found in even able-bodied persons. The yearly salary is $18, 000 to $24, 000. However, this is open to negotiation—dependent upon the applicant's qualifications and current salaries being made for similar positions. Regrettably, the control room is not wheelchair accessible.

Griffin denied being discouraged by the lack of response to the ad. "We were told that part of the reason for this was that many disabled people had lost their motivation because of having so many doors slammed in their face."

He added, "Another reason is that some disabled people are receiving pensions."

That makes me ask again: When is the Ontario government going to wake up and realize that its asinine limitations on someone's earnings if he or she is still receiving a disability pension seriously penalizes disabled people and destroys their initiative?

"When we first began our program of hiring disabled people, I thought we were going to have them beating down our doors," says Griffin. "The more I got into the program, however, the more I realized we had to do more than place ads in the paper. That is why we started our outreach program of going to different agencies who work with disabled people. We wanted to make them aware of the job opportunities that are available."

One of the disillusioning things he has learned is that there is a real lack of co-ordination among the various organizations working for disabled people. He also felt that the organizations did not work well together.

"We are issuing a challenge to the disabled community," says O'Neill. "CTV had job opportunities but disabled people and their organizations are going to have to meet us halfway."

O'Neill said that when he wanted a particular staff position filled, he told Griffin to contact a specialized agency dealing with that type of position. However, there is no such agency like this for disabled people.

They also agreed that a challenge for television itself would be to show disabled people in the mainstream of life.

CTV is determined to have disabled people in its workforce. The broadcaster's representatives assured me that they will base their selection on the person's qualifications to do the job—not the person who has a disability easiest on the eye.

Bankers learning quickly

July 14, 1991

Before the Ontario NDP government brings in its employment equity legislation, I hope it will learn something from the experience of the Canadian Bankers Association.

The CBA represents the interests of all the chartered banks in Canada and speaks with one industry voice on issues of importance.

Like other federally regulated industries that have 100 or more employees, the banks came under the federal government's Employment Equity Act in 1986. The purpose of the act is to ensure equality of opportunity in the workplace for four designated groups: women, aboriginal people, visible minorities, and people with disabilities.

"There has been a great deal of criticism of the banks since the act came into effect," admits Nancy Leamen, CBA's director of human resources policy.

"After the first survey of our employees in 1987, the banks were disappointed because it indicated that the representation of people with disabilities was very low."

There were three major things the banks realized they must do if they wished to improve the numbers of disabled people in their workforce.

They discovered very early that their recruiting methods had to change because they were not attracting applicants through the traditional methods of business school placements or newspaper advertisements. It became apparent that they would have to go out and look for applicants.

They also realized they needed the help of agencies and organizations that worked with disabled people in order to find the candidates they wanted. Their third discovery was that, even when they found applicants, they were not job-ready—they had no skills for acceptance into the job-entry level.

"Therefore, we became involved in establishing bridge training programs that span the gap by providing individuals with basic skills they need to be job ready," Leamen said.

In 1984, even before employment equity became law, four banks began aiding Toronto's Alternative Computer Training. Nearly 20 graduates with disabilities from this program are full-time employees with the banks.

Another bank is helping with the Ontario March of Dimes Microcomputer Application Training Program at George Brown College, while another is working with the Canadian National Institute for the Blind to obtain bank work for visually impaired people. There are programs like these across Canada.

"What we have found, in every case, is that we're working with small numbers of people," observes Leamen.

Government's punitive rules on how much disabled people can earn and still retain their disability allowance, lack of transportation, and insufficient education are all inhibitive factors in handicapped people seeking and keeping jobs.

"The banks have also accepted that their employees need training to overcome their fears, misconceptions, and lack of comfort around disabled people," says Leamen.

"The most common myth about people with disabilities is that they can't take part in daily life as we know it.

"We've had a series of seminars called Windmills, co-sponsored with the Canadian Council of Rehabilitation and Work, that teach our employees how faulty these feelings are and shows them how to see the abilities in disabled people," she said.

"We are committed to the success of employment equity," Leamen says.

Breaking down barriers

August 29, 1993

Some of the biggest barriers to employment of disabled people are caused by federal, provincial, and territorial governments.

It's a fact that's made clear in the 241-page book, *On Target? Canada's Employment-Related Programs for Persons with Disabilities* published by The Roeher Institute.

"This was a cross-disability study, undertaken because a recent Statistics Canada survey showed that only 40 percent of people with disabilities are employed and a number of these are in sheltered workshops. The survey also found that more than 50 percent of disabled people had annual incomes below $10,000," explains Roeher researcher, Michael Bach.

Though there are various government-sponsored education and training programs across Canada, disabled people can't always use them because training sites are inaccessible or training material is not available in alternative formats. Also, a provincial government counsellor can deny funding if a person's vocational goal is deemed unrealistic.

On the federal level, persons can be excluded from training if they can't prove they will be independently employable or do not display motivation for finding a job.

It took researchers two years to wind their way through the maze of disability-related employment programs.

"People don't have an entitlement to have their disability-related needs, such as portable attendant care and assistive devices, provided.

"The underlying problem is we've been very reluctant to give people with disabilities power to make their own choices about what they require and how they're going to use it," observes Bach.

Exclusion from education has also prevented disabled people from taking part in the labour force.

"People with disabilities have to rely on social assistance because so few get into the labour market. But there are many disincentives to them finding a job. They have disability-related expenses that would not be covered by a salary. Also, what they can earn is so low and reductions in social assistance so high that it often doesn't pay to work.

"We've assumed that people with severe disabilities cannot work. But these people have their success stories too," Bach notes.

Removing job barriers
September 4, 1994

Employment equity became law in Ontario on September 1. It's aimed at removing the barriers to employment for four groups: disabled people, women, racial minorities, and aboriginal people.

The United Way of Greater Toronto has already met or exceeded the guidelines in employing members of these three groups.

"However, the hiring of people with disabilities has presented us with the most difficulty," says Robin Cardozo, the United Way's Director of Finance and Human Resources.

During their fall campaign, temporary data entry positions are filled very successfully by, for example, people who are hearing impaired. The Canadian Hearing Society acts as a helpful resource.

However, almost all of their permanent, full-time jobs require a combination of visual and hearing skills—such as being able to respond to a donor's telephone inquiry by checking a computer screen.

"We have considered changing job descriptions but have not yet given it careful thought," says Cardozo.

"I understand there are new types of telephones and computers that are of assistance to people with hearing or visual problems, but we are concerned about the cost of this equipment," he says.

They will study the available equipment and then include some of it in their 1995 budget if the cost is reasonable.

"We realize our gains have been modest and are determined to take a leadership role in this area," he said.

Ontario Employment Equity Commissioner Juanita Westmoreland-Traore has three suggestions for the hiring and retention of disabled people: changing some of the job descriptions, job sharing, and making part-time work available.

"The majority of accommodations required to adapt a workplace for a disabled person cost under $500. Some funding is available from the Ministry of Community and Social Services that provides wage subsidies and assistance with adaptations," she told me.

"We are preparing a document that will outline issues for employing persons with disabilities and suggestions of how to address those concerns.

"It will be part of the guidelines and available before the end of September."

Deaf help police
July 24, 1988

People with impaired hearing make good workers because they aren't distracted by noises around them in the office.

That's one discovery Metro Police have made since they began hiring their first deaf employees two years ago. The force now has 10 such individuals performing a variety of civilian jobs.

"We had to learn sign language so we could communicate and train them in their jobs," says Doug MacKay, a supervisor in the record bureau. "Arrangements were made through the Canadian Hearing Society for an instructor to come here and teach us."

MacKay believes he was chosen to learn sign language because at the beginning he was very opposed to the idea.

"One of the first hearing impaired women we hired was placed with me and I became very frustrated trying to show her things without being able to communicate with her," MacKay says now.

"I have changed completely since I have taken that course. I now understand that they are regular people—they just cannot hear."

MacKay wasn't the only one who had negative feelings initially about learning how to sign. Judy Sandford, another supervisor, says: "When these courses first became available, I wasn't really interested. I was kind of scared because I didn't know how to communicate.

"I asked to attend and see what it was like. Now I just love it! It is a totally different language to learn."

Before Stanford and MacKay learned how to sign, any communication they had with their hearing impaired employees had to be written down. This was unsatisfactory and frustrating for both parties.

"Learning to sign is like learning French so that when you go to Quebec, you can communicate with the people," says MacKay. "It's a second language skill."

What knowledge have they gained from working with deaf people?

"A lot of people think, as I did, that they are deaf *and dumb*," says MacKay. "They are not—they are just like you and me."

With Stanford and MacKay interpreting, I then spoke to three hearing impaired employees: Edith Harte, Ellen Robinson, and Joanne Armory. All three like their jobs and find it very helpful that their supervisors can sign.

Robinson drives her own car and I asked if it had been difficult for her to obtain her driver's license.

"Driving instructors like deaf drivers because they pay more attention to the road," she said.

Susan Lewis, Metro Police Employment Equity Adviser says, "We have a wide range of civilian positions having entirely different physical demands. What we're hoping to do is open up our jobs to anyone who can meet the physical requirements."

The police are commended for their fine hiring initiative. I hope that other employers will follow their example.

– 15 –
Sport and recreation

As individuals with disabilities succeed in leading fuller, more independent lives, they find themselves participating in activities once considered off-limits, including sports and active recreational pursuits. Seeking always to push back the dark edges of misunderstanding, Mona shone the spotlight on these new ways disabled individuals were leading, or trying to lead, more active lives in the arena of sports.

Open up leisure activities
July 23, 1989

We have a very narrow definition of recreation and leisure in our society. In a broad sense, it could be defined as being able to make choices, feeling free, and exercising one's ability to be creative.

That's the opinion of Deborah Gold, a consultant in recreation and leisure at The G. Allan Rocher Institute, an arm of the Canadian Association for Community Living. Her position was made possible by a grant from Fitness and Amateur Sport Canada.

"We need to strengthen parents so that they can ask for access to recreational programs for children with disabilities. And not only access, but the support within these programs that will make them a success," she says.

"For example, staff training equips staff to feel good about integration and realize that they have problem-solving skills. It also enables them to meet someone with a disability by having a disabled person speak to the group about people deserving to be included and the importance of designing programs that are inclusive rather than exclusive."

A child who is unable to move quickly often isn't allowed to participate in games like soccer and basketball. Instead of this, ways should be found to include the individual in the activity.

Staff who are trained in how to include disabled children might say to the other children: "This young person is a part of our program and we need to find a way to adapt this game so that he can play. What are some ideas that you have?"

That is what is meant by support—staff and children are able to deal with the situation.

"Sometimes, a child will need somebody with him to make him become a part of the group and the parent may be asked to find a support person. However, this is really the responsibility of the people providing the program," Gold states.

The City of York has three integration facilitators. As well as making certain that the child with a disability is a part of the group, the facilitator does any extra teaching that may be needed and also supports the leader and other children in the program.

"Parents must be included in the planning of all recreation programs and children should be made to feel welcome," she stresses.

For adults, however, Gold feels that recreational programs are inappropriate.

"People need to be given the opportunity to make real choices about their leisure. The Kitchener Parks and Recreation Department and Community Living Mississauga provide a support person to go out with an adult who has a disability and assist them to become involved in the leisure activity of their choice—like learning how to use the bus so they can get about on their own, taking swimming lessons, or going out to dinner. These activities, rather than programming people, help them become more connected to their community."

Ski centre caters to everyone

January 14, 1990

The North York Ski Centre is one of the only ski schools in Canada with an integrated ski program for people with or without disabilities.

Fear and self-doubt are some of the challenges that skiers with disabilities share with able-bodied skiers, says Michael Laflamme, the centre's assistant director. Other concerns include whether there is equipment available to meet their needs, and if instructors have the knowledge and expertise to help them.

For skiers who need special equipment, the following are available:

- Outriggers: These are similar to ski poles with a short ski on the end of it. They are like modified crutches and are, in fact, used by people who ordinarily walk with crutches. They allow students who have a disability in their lower bodies to transfer their weight to their arms.

- Ski bras: Yes, you read it correctly! Either a piece of rope or metal is attached to the tip of the skis to prevent them from crossing or going separate ways.

- Tethers: These are ropes that are fastened around the skiers and held onto at the other end by other skiers for the purpose of controlling the speed of disabled skiers.

There is more interest in disabled skiing due largely to organizations like the Ontario Handicapped Skiing Association and the Canadian Association of Disabled Skiing, says Laflamme. "Also, downhill skiing for disabled skiers has now become part of the Olympics."

Lessons for students start at the age of five. Private lessons are given to children under this age. There is no upper age limit.

The school teaches all types of ambulatory handicapped people. Students are hearing impaired or brain injured and have polio, cerebral palsy, or developmental disabilities.

"I haven't taught blind people yet but I'm up for the challenge!" Laflamme says.

The Centre, located in Earl Bales Park at Bathurst and Sheppard, will be open until March 16.

How does skiing help the self-esteem of disabled people?

"For children, it's something to talk about when they go back to school. They feel like one of the gang because everyone else skies," says Laflamme."For adults, it's something for them to look forward to on the weekend. Downhill skiing allows people who have mobility problems to enjoy the gliding sensation and experience other movement. This sport keeps them in the mainstream."

Satisfaction fills their sails

July 9, 1989

Sailing a boat offers disabled people a feeling of accomplishment because they can, through their own abilities, literally propel themselves forward.

That's the opinion of Christine Carter, head instructor at the Independence Afloat Sailing School. The school, which was begun 10 years ago with the ongoing financial help of the Central Toronto branch of the Lions Club, now has six boats and 60 students in different programs over the summer months of July and August.

"Students have to be at least 10 years old—after that, there's no age limit," says Carter. "They have a wide range of physical and mental disabilities.

"We do our swim tests at the Hugh MacMillian Medical Centre. The students don't have to actually swim. We prefer that they be able to roll themselves over to their back from their front. But mostly they have to feel comfortable in the water. If they panic while they're in the pool, they fail the test."

When the weather is bad, they stay on shore and learn sailing knots and theory, visit the Science Centre, or play games. Sailing theory is information about what makes your boat go besides just the wind, and how to trim your boat and make it do what you want. Basically it's teaching sailing on land, so the day is never wasted.

"The program has day and evening sessions," explains Carter. "The day sessions run for two weeks, five days a week from 9 a.m. to 4 p.m. The evening sessions last one month and take place Monday and Wednesday evenings from 6 to 9 p.m. The course costs $100 for two weeks or one month. There are some limited bursaries available from the Lions Club.

"The July evening program is full," says Carter. "However, we can still accommodate students for the July day program and both the day and evening programs in August."

All of the students, even the ones who are severely disabled, learn something. They derive a great feeling of achievement because it's been done on their own.

Carter assures apprehensive parents that students and instructors must wear life jackets in the boats and on the docks at all times.

Instructors are with the students constantly and they have never had a mishap.

"We have some able-bodied students—most of them are siblings of the disabled students," she says. "We also have an instructor who wears two artificial legs."

One of her first exposures to disabled people was when she taught a child with Down syndrome basic gymnastics. If left a lasting impression upon her because he enjoyed it so much. Carter, who is 22, wants to become a school teacher and integrate handicapped and able-bodied students.

What advice would she give to a disabled person who wanted to learn to sail but was afraid he couldn't handle it?

"Go for it! Give it a try!"

Disabled martial their talents

December 11, 1988

Disabled people and martial arts? If you think the two don't go together—think again!

"Anybody can do martial arts—no matter how disabled or what age they are," says Ron Yamanaka, owner and instructor of the Yamanaka School of Martial Arts in Scarborough. "I have taught grandmothers in their 60s who walk in here with a cane."

Yamanaka introduced me to one of his star students, Brian Opekan, who describes his disabilities as "I'm blind and I'm kind of crippled— my left leg has a very bad limp." Now 41, he has been taking jujitsu for a little over two years after being injured in a 1996 shooting accident.

"At first, I took martial arts for my leg muscles. Now, however, it is a part of my life. Most people think that it is only macho guys who take it. That is not so. Martial arts gives one a feeling of accomplishment— it makes one feel whole."

Opekan used to take lessons two or three times per week. Now that he is training for the Masters demonstration next June, he practises four or five times a week. "For the Masters demonstration, we have coming from Japan, living national treasures," explains Yamanaka. "They are the greatest teachers of martial arts of all time—they're in their 70s and 80s. It's their first trip to Canada and they'll be in Toronto and Ottawa for one week in June.

"We are very proud of the fact that Brian is going to do a demonstration for them."

Martial arts began in China about 4,000 years ago. Now of course the Japanese are the acknowledged world leaders in this field.

The school teaches judo—grappling and learning how to fall so as to not hurt oneself and how to throw people properly; aikido—a beautiful, totally non-violent art where one uses the strength of one's opponent against him; and jujitsu—grappling, locking joints, and throwing. All police instructors in Ontario have been trained in this art at Yamanaka's school.

Yamanaka has been teaching for 29 years in eight countries all over the world.

"Martial arts people do not think in terms of violence. They think only of bettering themselves—through learning a positive mental attitude and how to think in a more peaceful way and of bettering people around them," says Yamanaka.

If step one was featuring the sports programs available to persons with disabilities, step two was promoting new devices that would enable participation in ways never before imagined possible.

New chair flips, flops 'n' jumps
August 21, 1988

A few days ago, I saw an amazing new wheelchair demonstrated by Gord Dowton, its inventor, and Jeremy Ein. This chair can turn somersaults, flip over, and stretch up so that its occupant is almost in a standing position.

"I was watching a wheelchair basketball game on TV and realized that something more dynamic than conventional wheelchairs was needed for athletic activities," says Dowton, who teaches movement at the Toronto Dance Theatre. This chair allows you to propel yourself with either both hands or one hand on the ground. There is not much danger in falling."

The chair has two hydraulic cylinders—one at the back and one at the knees with fluid acid running between them. By leaning back, you drive hydraulic fluid to the cylinder at the knees and this makes the knees extend. To hold the back up, you reverse the process by leaning forward. This returns the chair to its original position.

Dowton calls his chair the "Techno-jump spider" after the jumping spider that jumps, not with muscles, but with the fluid in its body.

Ein, who has a malformation of his spinal cord but can walk, is enthusiastic. "I can pick up an apple from the floor with my teeth while I am in a roll over position in the chair," he says.

Dowton, who has worked for five years to bring the chair to its present stage, told me that it has been tried and approved by many disabled people. One of the many things they like about it is its portability. Dowton is now looking for a manufacturer.

The Techno-jump spider is not meant to take the place of a conventional wheelchair. Instead, it will offer an alternate form of movement and give wheelchair athletes greater mobility in sports.

The chair was displayed at the Ontario Science Centre as a part of the "Sport" exhibition.

"We want to make the community aware of the tremendous progress made in disabled sports," said Thom Jenkins, the Science Centre's communication officer.

Like a community billboard, Mona used her column to draw attention to sporting events featuring disabled athletes.

Let the games begin!
July 12, 1987

For almost a year, the City of North York has promoted the twelfth Ontario Games for the Physically Disabled, with everything from a formal gala to colourful billboard art. Sheila White is Mayor Mel Lastman's community resource co-ordinator and vice-chair of protocol and special events for the games. By participating in preparations for the games, she has learned that disabled people want to be a part of our community and do not want to be viewed as separate.

White says, "When I was younger, I was taught not to stare at someone in a wheelchair. What I should have been told is to interact with this person—he or she is really no different from you and me."

The committee members—all disabled—have been volunteering their services in shopping malls throughout North York in booths publicizing the games. As well, a visually impaired member of the committee is advertising the games on his ham radio and urging everyone to come.

"Disabled people have been reluctant to help themselves," says Betty Lindsey, another organizer of the games. "Many of them are too passive." "How do other people know to come over and speak to me if I don't smile and act friendly? We cannot always expect able-bodied people to make the first overtures."

Two hundred and thirty athletes from all over Ontario will be competing at the games. Two hundred volunteers have been working on the games thus far and another 600 to 700 will be involved in the games themselves.

"A delightful surprise has been the amount of resources—both human and financial—that have been committed to this event," says Laura Garton, co-ordinator of the games.

The North York Board of Education's physical education teachers have disabled youngsters in their classes whose involvement they will now be able to encourage in future games.

Betty Lindsey, Laura Garton and Sheila White are grateful to Rick Hansen and hope that when the games are over, people will realize that there are other types of disabilities and people inside these disabilities are intelligent, loving, capable people.

In the name of the Duke and Duchess of York, who will be honoured visitors, the city will present a gift of automatic doors for the North York City Hall to improve accessibility.

White said she would like to see disabled sports integrated into the mainstream of able-bodied sporting events.

"Differences don't separate us—differences are what make us whole. When you put all the pieces together, you have wonderful symmetry."

Mona did everything she could through her column to celebrate achievements of disabled athletes, a telling counterpoint to how news media largely ignored the thrilling efforts of these Canadian athletes and the trophy-winning successes of these sweaty amd smiling sports figures.

Athletes neglected by media

April 16, 1989

In Metro, we have a 27-year-old athlete who has won two gold medals in two World Cycling Championships for Canada in 1986 and 1988. Chances are you've never heard his name.

Dean Dwyer won his honours at the Paralympic Games—the disabled equivalent of the Olympics that take place right after the Olympic Games.

Sports have always played a major role in Dwyer's life. They really did until 1979 when he crashed his motorcycle going 190 km/h (120 mph) near Peterborough. He was in a coma for three weeks and his left side was paralyzed. "It was a difficult transition—accepting the fact that I was disabled," Dwyer recalls. "Once I did that, I became interested in sports for disabled people.

By 1982, he was training six hours a day. Then, he competed in the 1984 Paralympics in New York City where he won two silver medals for cycling.

"Disabled sports are not accepted on the same level as able-bodied sports," said Dwyer. "People look at us in a different way, as if we were competing on a lower level. However, people like Rick Hansen, Terry Fox, and Steve Fonyo are real eye-openers and help to break down barriers in the way people think. They make viewers realize that, though a person is disabled, he or she can accomplish a great deal in sports. This helps to change the public's perspective. Able-bodied athletes give the best of what they have and we give the best of what we have."

Dwyer won a gold medal in the 1986 World Cycling Championships in Belgium. Last year, he won another gold in Seoul, for the 60-km world bicycle race.

The Seoul games attracted 20,000 spectators every day, and 100,000 for the opening and closing games. There were special daily segments in the Seoul newspaper, and everyone knew what was going on. Wherever a disabled athlete went in uniform, he or she was treated with respect. The children were especially incredible. They didn't see the disability, not even when athletes in electric wheelchairs signed autographs with pens held in their mouths.

"In Canada, the smaller the town, the bigger the news story it was," says Doug Wilton, executive director of Sports for Disabled, Ontario.

Unfortunately, it was really lost in Metro. These athletes were neglected by the media.

"People need to look beyond the disability—it's the same in education and employment. You have to be able to see the individuals and what they are able to accomplish."

Once, even Dwyer's parents didn't know he had won until he phoned home and told them. If he had been an able-bodied athlete, the media would have broadcast the news far and wide.

Sports have not only brought Dwyer medals. He met his fiancée last year at the eastern Canadian championships in Quebec and they plan on marrying soon.

Turnbull, athlete, honoured

February 10, 1991

Barbara Turnbull will be one of the three disabled Canadians to receive the King Clancy Award next Friday, at the Seventh Great

Valentine Gala presented by the Canadian Foundation for Physically Disabled Persons.

Turnbull, who became a quadriplegic as a teenager after she was senselessly shot in a variety store hold-up a few years ago, has just graduated from a journalism course at Arizona State University.

"At Arizona State, they didn't know anything about me so I was just like any other person there," Turnbull explains. "I also wanted to get away from the Toronto winter weather and go somewhere new."

I asked her how she was able to go about her life without any bitterness or self-pity over the events that put her in a wheelchair. "They are just wasted emotions," was her simple and eloquent reply.

She's worked at the Toronto *Star* for the past two summers and enjoys newspaper writing. What is her advice to other newly disabled people? "Do whatever you want to do—whether it's going back to school or working—and not something because you merely feel you should," she said.

Another King Clancy Award winner, André Viger, has been Canada's most successful wheelchair athlete since he began competing in wheelchair racing in 1979. Viger suffered spinal cord damage in1972 after a car accident in which his best friend fell asleep at the wheel. He lives in Sherbrook, Que., where he works as a jeweller. In 1985, he was named Quebec's Athlete-of-the-Year and he also received the Sport Excellence Award from the government of Canada. Viger has won all the major wheelchair racing events and has been dubbed King of the Road. "Rick Hansen is my biggest inspiration," he says. "Neither Rick nor I can change the world, but we can educate everyone about the capabilities of disabled people."

A posthumous King Clancy Award goes to one-legged marathon runner Terry Fox, who died of cancer in June 1981, just one month short of his 23rd birthday. Terry had been an athlete all his life, his mother Betty told me on the phone from the Fox home in Vancouver. When he was first told he was going lose his leg to cancer, he said "I've always tried hard, but now I'm going to try harder." After he got his artificial limb, he had to learn to run all over again. "When he told people he wanted to run across Canada to raise money for cancer research so that the hurting would stop, nobody who knew Terry well was surprised," Betty recalled.

"Its a wonderful feeling to know Canadians still have him on their list of highly regarded people. My husband and I are very proud and honoured to have been a part of raising someone who means so much to other people," she said.

– 16 –

Getting away

If work and physical activity are part of a balanced life, so apparently is relaxation. Vacationing is promoted for experiencing different cultures, seeing new places, allowing one's batteries to recharge, and gaining perspective on one's life. With vacationing difficult for people with disabilities, Mona addressed accessibility issues of transportation and accommodation when travelling.

A great place to unwind
December 13, 1987

It's an adventure—go with a light heart and enjoy it! This is one of the prerequisites given by Toronto travel consultant Barbara Hancock for having a great holiday.

According to Hancock, who used to be a special education teacher, more disabled people are becoming aware that they can travel. "This has resulted in making airports and other facilities conscious of accessibility," she says.

Her first recommendation is to find a travel agent who is familiar with your special needs. "It is important that the agent knows all the relevant facts about your disability beforehand in order to obtain the necessary assistance and accommodation that you require," she advises.

Both Canadian Airlines and Air Canada offer a half-price fare to attendants of disabled people who have letters from their doctors stating that this help is necessary. Hancock feels it would be wise—especially with the current strike at Air Canada—to check with other airlines, bus lines and railways to discover their policy in this respect. Pre-boarding assistance is also offered by most carriers.

One of my favourite winter holidays is a visit to St. Petersburg beach in Florida. The airport at Tampa is beautifully accessible, and from there, it is only about 40 km (35 miles) to "St. Pete's Beach."

"Our main features are sunshine and the beach—we provide a very relaxing and family-oriented vacation," says St. Petersburg Beach mayor Ron Mckenny.

Florida state law makes it mandatory for new buildings to be accessible to disabled people. Older buildings, if they are renovated, must also be made accessible. All sidewalks have curb cuts.

St. Pete's Beach has about 10,000 permanent residents and can handle another 11,000 temporary ones. The police take a dim view of anyone taking a parking space reserved for the disabled.

"They hand out five citations a week at $100 each, which is a great many considering the size of our city," McKenny told me. In Ontario, most fines for this offence are $25 and the law itself is not strictly enforced in Metro.

McKenny has his own unique way of dealing with these offenders. If he sees a car pull into a designated parking space and person jump out and goes into a store while someone else waits in the car, he'll walk over and say to the individual: "Can I help you?"

"What do you mean?" the person in the car usually responds.

"I notice that you are parked in a disabled parking zone and I thought I could be of assistance," the mayor replies.

This little exchange succeeds in embarrassing the guilty parties so much that they never make the same error again!

Permanent residents and disabled guests of the city are both entitled to Meals on Wheels. It is hoped that a volunteer transportation service will also soon become a reality.

Mona loved Florida for vacationing, in common with many Canadian travellers, including those with disabilities. The Sun *dispatched Mona, without protest, to research a number of Florida destinations to see what they offered for those with disabilities.*

Special feature

Sunday Sun's Mona Winberg looks at facilities for disabled travellers

February 11, 1990

When the "Travel in the Sun" section asked me to go to Florida on my own and then write an article about travel and disabled people, I was excited, but nervous too.

I've been writing the "Disabled Today" column in the *Sunday Sun* for more than three years and am handicapped myself due to cerebral palsy. This means that I do not have good use of my hands and I'm also speech and hearing impaired.

My greatest concern was eating in strange restaurants by myself. Even at home, I am very shy and self-conscious about doing this.

The Odyssey International flight for the early morning had been booked for me by Thomson Vacations. While the driver from Airline Travellers limousine was taking out my luggage, my hearing aid suddenly went dead.

"I can't hear!" I said to him in a panic.

In my excitement, I had accidentally pulled out my hearing aid chord. The driver put it back in as calmly and matter-of-factly as if this task was included in his job description.

Thomson had arranged for me to get a wheelchair at the airport. Though I can walk, it's easier to use a chair for long distances. Along with a wheelchair, it is necessary that the flight attendant be aware I am a person with special needs. This should be arranged before departure.

The flight was most enjoyable, thanks to the thoughtfulness of the Odyssey staff. When Wardair merged with Canadian Airlines, some of Wardair's top people went to Odyssey.

When we landed at Tampa, I asked that a phone call be placed to the "limo"—a large vehicle with steps, that takes people to St. Petersburg and Clearwater in Pinellas County.

The Sirata Beach Resort was my home the first week—it has three handicapped suites and elevators. I stayed at the Colonial Gateway Inn the second week, an older resort with no wheelchair accessible washrooms in its units.

The handicapped suites at the Sirata are wheelchair accessible and include a living room, a kitchen, and bedroom. I thought this too much space for a single person; however Lenne Nicklaus-Bell, the Sirata's manager, said the suites are usually occupied by families who are travelling with a disabled member, not just for a disabled person alone.

At Colonial Gateway Inn, where the rooms aren't equipped for disabled guests, manager Bud Zipin said there's a number of things to consider in making changes.

"The cost of renovating suites isn't really the problem," said Zipin. "We just wouldn't know where to begin."

It would be difficult, he said, to provide accessible rooms to please everyone who asked, because people would want different views— from ocean view to poolside.

Another problem is that different disabilities require different facilities. For instance, the needs of seeing-impaired people are different from mine. It is difficult to outfit a room which would cater to all.

I would like to hear from readers, hotel managers and members of the travel industry with their ideas and solutions on providing facilities for different types of disabilities.

Both of these resorts in St. Petersburg Beach have accessible restaurants.

At the Sirata Sands, a restaurant near the Sirata Beach Resort, I found this two-level restaurant outfitted with an elevator for disabled people. I was told by one of the staff that in Florida it is mandatory for restaurants with more than one floor to have an elevator for disabled people.

The Colonial serves its meals buffet style, which caused me much initial worry. However, the staff at both resorts included some of the finest people I have ever met and, as soon as they got to know me, they were quick to help—either with carrying a plate of food to a table or unlocking a room door.

Not only were they generous in helping me, but after the first couple of days they reached a point where they could anticipate my needs—and then I didn't have to ask for help. For example, I cannot pick up cutlery from the table, I need to have it placed in my hand. They became accustomed to doing this for me as if it was a part of their job.

Accessibility is important, but even more essential is the right attitude. With the right attitude, anything is possible. Without it, all the accessibility in the world cannot make up for an unpleasant encounter.

At the Colonial, I encountered problems with the light switches and the door key. I went down to the front desk to ask for assistance. I received help getting into my room and an appointment was made for a maintenance man to come to my room first thing the next morning to see what he could do.

He arrived promptly the next morning and rigged the lights to make them easier for me. The problem with the door, however, wasn't so easily solved. I experienced problems getting the key to turn in the lock. But when the maintenance man had trouble with the door as well, I didn't feel so bad. Despite his efforts, we couldn't get the door adjusted to the point where I could open it. However, the kind staff and my fellow guests helped me whenever I needed it.

Always remember that if you encounter problems with the facilities in your room or in the dining room, ask for help. Go in person to the front desk and politely explain what assistance you require. Hotel staff are there to ensure their guests have an enjoyable stay. Both Nicklaus-Bell of the Sirata and Zipin at the Colonial told me they want to be informed about people with special needs.

Travelling alone isn't for everyone, but it certainly allows you to get to know a great many people. It is usually up to you to make the first overture. Once a contact has been established, I've found most people ready to offer a helping hand and enjoyable company.

All of the delightful attractions I saw in the Pinellas were accessible. So was the Salvador Dali museum (which was built in St. Petersburg after the *Wall Street Journal* headlined a story about efforts to find a permanent home for the artist's work: "U.S. Art World Dilly-Dallies Over Dali.")

In the lush and fertile Sunken Gardens, a brightly coloured macaw bird said "hello" to me. But I also ran into a problem at Sunken Gardens, when meeting with one of the owners for an interview. Upon seeing me he callously asked how I was going to take notes. I informed him that I carried a tape recorder for taking notes.

Despite this initial misunderstanding, the interview did proceed very well after that. It was a reminder to me that it's unrealistic of disabled people to think that everyone will be nice all the time. Some people only see the disability, not the ability.

An enjoyable stop was made at Great Explorations, a hands-on museum. It's a real fun place for all ages.

The beautiful Don Cesar luxury hotel was a treat for me; my sandals almost disappeared in the thick broadloom! It has one wheelchair accessible room and is going to renovate another one.

The Pinellas Suncoast has made inroads with its services for disabled people.

"A television crew from the BBC series, *The Travel Show Guide*, did two different TV specials on the Pinellas Suncoast and they said that this area has as accessible facilities for disabled people as any resort area they have been to," Lee Daniel, the Public Relations Director of the Pinellas Tourist Development Council, told me.

You can be as active or as lazy as you want in the Pinellas. You can go to all the attractions I just mentioned, or walk along the cleanest, sandiest beaches I've ever seen. I know of no more beautiful thing than to view the sunset off the Gulf of Mexico.

Mona also provided readers with information on the accessibility of various hotels closer to home, including a number in Toronto.

Hotels open their doors

June 26, 1988

It is one of the Ontario Fire Marshal's requirements that hotels keep records of any disabilities of guests, such as a hearing impairment, to make sure hotel staff are aware of it so that in case of an emergency the staff could go to their rooms and help them.

This is one of the many interesting facts I discovered during an informal survey of five Toronto hotels and their accessibility.

The Royal York Hotel has six rooms for handicapped people that include easy access to washrooms. Light switches are at wheelchair height and are the type you can push up or down. For wheelchair users, there is a lift to get into the hotel. This can be avoided if you have your own car and go in through the underground garage.

The King Edward Hotel has a ramp into its east entrance at 22 Leader Lane. Albert Kofri, the friendly concierge, says keys are easily turned in the locks of the rooms designated for the handicapped. "We are quite used to disabled people coming and staying with us." There are no steps in the dining room, and telephones with volume control for hearing impaired are located in the public booths.

The Sheraton Centre Hotel has 20 guest rooms specially designed for disabled people. Regular light switches that one pushes up or down are placed in a lower position, as are locks in the doors.

Though the 30-year-old Westbury hotel has ramps into its main building, it does not have wheelchair accessible rooms.

On the other hand, the Radisson-Don Valley Hotel has recently renovated to make its premises accessible. The front entrance now has a ramp leading up to a push button door, and there is another ramp leading into the main lobby. Paul McCabe, guest services manager, says there are two new wheelchair accessible rooms on the first floor and a power lift that takes a wheelchair user past the six steps leading up to the rooms. In the rooms themselves are hooks in the ceiling for someone who uses a pulley or other device switches for persons who do not have good use of their hands.

It would also be more convenient for a hearing impaired person to use a telephone with volume controls in their own room instead of having to go out to use public telephones.

Top marks for hotel that really takes care

September 2, 1990

I recently spent a night at Toronto's beautiful Four Seasons Hotel on Avenue Rd. to check out its facilities for disabled guests.

This hotel is the flagship of the proudly Canadian-based company with headquarters in Toronto and 23 properties in Canada, the U.S., and England.

There are two rooms specially designed for handicapped people— one is a bedroom, the other is a Four Seasons suite consisting of living room, bedroom, and bathroom. I stayed in the latter.

Among its many special features were two peepholes in the entry door, one at an average height, the other a convenient height for wheelchair users.

There were also lower closets with hangers one could lift out entirely, instead of struggling to separate the lower part and then fit it together again. One of the closets even contained a wheelchair accessible safe!

The bathroom was spacious, with a higher vanity, lower towel bar, adjustable shower-head, and conveniently placed grab bars.

There are fire alarm strobe lights for deaf people. In addition, the Four Seasons is the first hotel in the city to provide the Digital Display System, a portable telecommunications device that plugs into guest room telephones and allows deaf people to communicate with other DDS users. I had my own portable telephone amplifier, but when I tried to use it, it was only to discover that its battery was dead.

I had neglected an important rule of travelling when one is disabled: Before you set out, make certain that your assistive devices are in good working condition. When my inability to use the phone was explained to the front desk, staff helpfully offered to write down any telephone messages I received and then, if necessary, relay any back to the callers from me.

I suggested to Cherry Kam, the hotel's director of public relations, that it would be easier for disabled people with limited hand co-ordination if door knobs in the accessible rooms were replaced by levers. In place of their current lamps that are turned off and on by a tiny knob, I also recommended that they get "Touch Me" lamps that can be touched almost anywhere to perform the same function.

Sun travel writer Jane Stokes and I had dinner in The Café, and the next morning my nephew Michael Winberg joined me for breakfast there. In both cases, the staff spoke to each of us individually instead of, as sometimes happens, only directing their comments to my able-bodied companions while making me feel invisible.

"When we have new staff come on board, we give them orientation training in how to cater to guests with special needs," Kam told me. "The Four Seasons philosophy emphasizes the three "Ps" — people, product and profit. However, we would never sacrifice the first two for the third."

Other features that I appreciated were elevator doors that did not close too rapidly, and that chimed when arriving at one's floor. This helped direct me to the one I wanted. There are also ramps, wherever necessary, in public areas.

It is no wonder that, with this fine attention to the comfort of all their guests, the Four Seasons Toronto was recently named the best hotel in Canada and the eighth best in North America by *Condé Nast Traveller* magazine.

The Four Seasons Toronto provides an enjoyable experience in having one's needs anticipated, sometimes even before one recognizes them oneself.

Mona liked to hold out visions for people with disabilities to aspire to. One version of this was to feature information about tourist destinations and travel options.

Special care cruise
February 14, 1993

All aboard! Horizon Holidays in Toronto is launching its first Special Care Holidays trip with a week long Caribbean cruise for people who have a respiratory illness.

The cruise is the brainchild of Toronto respirologist Dr. Avi Perl who, along with a registered respiratory therapist and an intensive care nurse, will accompany the trip. As well, arrangements have been made to have oxygen available on Air Canada and the ship itself.

"At every port of call, our local transportation agents will make certain that those guests with a respiratory illness will be made comfortable, so that they enjoy the same degree of mobility they do at home," says Stephen Burnett, Horizon's vice-president of planning and development.

The ship *Westerdam* will stop at ports whose very names conjure up visions of sun-bleached beaches, sparkling blue waters and fun-filled days and nights: San Juan, Tortola, St. Thomas, and Nassau.

"You can be as busy or as lazy as you wish on a holiday like this," points out Burnett. "If you don't want to get off at every port, the ship itself has much to occupy you.

"On board is both an excellent library of books and a good selection of videos. There are movies every day and a show each evening. Also, such daily activities as discussion groups, lectures, games, and card playing are available. The controlled environment of a cruise allows a traveller with a physical challenge to dictate the pace of their holiday."

The cost of this Special Care cruise is a little higher than a regular cruise. But travellers receive more, too. A night has been added at Toronto airport's Bristol Place Hotel before the trip begins. The stay includes dinner and a get-acquainted reception, along with breakfast the next morning before flying to Miami. Accompanying the tourists will be a professional Horizon tour escort as well as the medical team.

"We can accommodate about 30 people—a small and intimate group. It's a magic number because everyone has an opportunity to meet five or six other mini-groups, understand their experiences, and take home an additional richness to their lives," Burnett says.

There is limited single accommodation. However, an individual could, if willing, share a cabin with another person. At this time, they are regrettably not equipped to take persons who cannot walk.

Bon voyage!

– 17 –

Fighting abuse and neglect

It would be pleasing to think that, while the quality of life for people with disabilities could yet be improved, at least the grosser forms of abuse and discrimination experienced by disabled individuals in earlier days no longer exist. But the two are not necessarily linked. Progress definitely has been made, but Mona provided reminders that abuse and neglect, sometimes with fatal consequences, remain endemic.

Ignorance of Down is appalling

March 20, 1988

Just over a year ago, a newborn baby died in a Montreal Children's hospital after being deprived of food and water for almost two weeks by hospital authorities.

The baby had Down syndrome and was born with a part of his esophagus missing, a condition that is correctable by surgery. In language so ignorant it is mind boggling, the coroner's report stated that the Down syndrome was a "cause of death." People with Down syndrome have varying degrees of intellectual handicap, but it is hardly a life-threatening condition.

This is followed by the equally uninformed statement: "The presence of Down syndrome was another element (in the decision not to operate) since mongolism implies a quasi-vegetative life or severely diminished quality of life."

Such an appalling lack of knowledge would be offensive on the part of anyone. However, for a coroner, it is inexcusable.

I know two people with Down syndrome—one is an actor, and the other recently had a showing of watercolours at the Mississauga Public Library. Would the Quebec coroner like to say that these people live semi-vegetative lives? Such a medieval attitude is both disgraceful and dangerous.

"The Canadian Pediatrics Society has adopted a policy that says the suspicion of knowledge that the individual may have a handicapping condition is basically irrelevant to treatment decisions that relate strictly to physical conditions," says Orville Endicott, legal counsel for the Canadian Association for Community Living (CACL), which first exposed the Montreal case.

In 1974, an article in the *Journal of Pediatric Surgery* reported that 50 children with Down syndrome and duodenal atresia were brought to Toronto's Hospital for Sick Children over a 20-year period beginning in 1952. Duodenal atresia is a condition where food cannot leave the stomach to go to the intestines and is correctable by surgery (like the Montreal baby's esophageal atresia). Of those 50 babies, 27, or more than half, were allowed to die because their parents refused to give permission for the life-saving surgery.

Dr. Abbyann Lynch, director of London's Westminster Institute for Ethics and Human Values and the ethicist for the Hospital for Sick Children in Toronto, believes such a shocking situation could not occur today.

"Society has really changed its outlook towards persons with a disability and physicians are doing what society says is the right thing to do," Lynch said. "My sense is that any hospital today — where individuals said we're not going to provide treatment to a baby that has Down syndrome and duodenal atresia would be in serious trouble."

The CACL has failed to convince Quebec Justice Minister Herbert Marx to take action in the Montreal baby's case. However, a group in Hull who works with developmentally handicapped people has issued a complaint to the Quebec Human Rights Commission and asked it to investigate.

Let us never forget the potential of people we think should be allowed to die because they were born with a handicap.

Over 20 years ago, a baby in Dublin, Ireland, was almost asphyxiated at birth. He grew up so severely disabled by cerebral palsy that his mother has to hold his head with a unicorn stick. Yet Christy Nolan recently won Britain's top literary prize for his autobiographical novel *Under the Eye of the Clock*. In his acceptance speech (read by his mother) Nolan said: "Imagine all that would have been missed if the doctors had not revived me."

Yes, and think of what the world would have missed, as well.

Mona urged people with disabilities to speak out for themselves. While such personal advocacy was another aspect of self-reliance, a darker reason Mona preached for disabled people to come forward "as their own best advocates" was the inexcusable silence of those who had a duty to advocate for the interests and issues of disabled people.

No more Brantford tragedies

December 16, 1990

The most appalling aspect of the 15 deaths of developmentally handicapped people at Brantwood over a two-year period is that apparently no one from either the institution itself or the community of Brantford, where the facility is located, raised any concerns about this matter.

The situation may still have gone unreported if Ontario's auditor hadn't begun asking questions.

"We are told that the 15 people at Brantwood died from pneumonia, aspiration, malnutrition, dehydration, and other causes. It's not the number of deaths, although it's significantly high, but what qualified people are saying they died from that concerns me," Flora Nicholson said.

"There's a board of directors, staff, parents, volunteers, an advocacy group and yet no one in that community noticed that anything was wrong."

Nicholson was the administrator of Rygiel Home in Hamilton for 18 years. She retired a few months ago. Rygiel is funded by the Ontario government and is, like Brantwood, a "schedule two operation," explains Nicholson.

"This means that it's smaller, usually community-based, and operated by a board of directors. The schedule one facilities, like the Orillia regional centre, are run by the government and their employees are civil servants," she said.

Nicholson feels that the best type of supervision for a facility is provided by a community board because the people live in the area and wouldn't be involved if they weren't interested. "It's horrifying that these conditions at Brantwood could have existed, if, in fact, they did, without anyone advocating for the young people. To me, that's the tragedy. We really are our brother's keeper, whether we like it or not," she says.

Nicholson notes that the NDP government has a moratorium on the move to community living.

"Obviously, having people gathered in large groups doesn't necessarily mean they are safe or less fearful," she observes. "I'm not saying you can't get neglect in a community living program. However, in smaller, community-based operations, there's more likely to be bonding and a better understanding of the needs of the individual."

In a related move, the minister of citizenship, Elaine Ziemba, who has responsibility for disabled persons and senior citizens, has appointed a commissioner, Ernie Lightman, to enquire into unregulated residential facilities. He will also provide a census of vulnerable adults living in these facilities in Ontario.

"My first priority is to find out everything I can about the two areas I have to make recommendations on: boarding homes, many of which house ex-psychiatric patients, and unregulated rest and retirement homes, which are largely used by seniors. In both these areas, there is virtually no protection for the client," said Lightman, who's an economist in the faculty of social work at the University of Toronto. He's been given six months to do the job.

There is one question we all should be asking ourselves: If this could happen at Brantwood, what is going on at the other institutions in Ontario?

What's full story in young deaths?

October 13, 1991

Patrick Worth, who's the past president of People First of Ontario, a group of disabled self-advocates, says the full story isn't coming out in two controversial inquests.*

One involves 15 deaths that occurred over a two-year period at Brantwood, a residence for developmentally handicapped young adults in Brantford. The other concerns 30 deaths at the Christopher Robin Home for Disabled Children in Ajax, Ontario, between 1986 and 1990.

People First has been restrained from participating as fully as it wants in the two inquests.

The inquests are concentrating on four deaths at Brantwood and 15 at Christopher Robin because it was felt these deaths are representative of the others.

"The death of any person cannot be called representative of the deaths of other human beings—not if we truly believe all people are unique individuals," says Barbara Thornber, of the parents' advocacy group the Ontario Association for Community Living (OACL).

When the Christopher Robin inquest began, People First was represented by lawyers from the Advocacy Resource Centre for the Handicapped who tried, unsuccessfully, to get a more active role. Also, they were denied access to medical records of the children who died. Then a lawyer for family members of two children who died at Christopher Robin requested, and was denied, access to the medical

---

* On October 9, 1991 the Ontario Superior Court of Justice rendered its verdict in the Brantwood case. Because of the nature of the deaths of individuals with disabilities, and the inquest into those deaths, the case was one in which many parties became or sought to become involved as intervenors. At issue then was the nature of an inquest. The court clarified that in law, notwithstanding the emerging public interest in jury recommendations of a modern Ontario inquest, an inquest is not a royal commission inquiry, nor is it a trial, public platform, campaign, lobby, or crusade. When it came to the right of a coroner to restrict participation of intervenors in an inquest, the court ruled that, if an intervenor's direct and substantial interest extends to the facts surrounding the individual deaths being investigated, then such intervenor should have the same rights as other parties. If their direct and substantial interest is limited to the social and preventative functions involved in the potential jury recommendations, however, then their rights of cross-examination and participation should be correspondingly limited to the extent it can be done fairly. It remained open to a coroner, said the Court, to distinguish between degrees of direct interest by the various parties to an inquest, and to limit the participation of each intervenor to the issues of fact vital to their particular interest, the question in each case being whether that can be done fairly.

records. When he applied to court for a review of that decision, the Christopher Robin inquest was adjourned.

When the Brantwood inquest began, lawyer Tim Gilbert represented People First, OACL, and the Canadian Disability Rights Council. As in the Christopher Robin inquest, access to the medical records was denied. Gilbert applied to court to review the decision, and the inquest was adjourned.

"The two applications were joined together. The Ontario divisional court dismissed the application and stated it was up to the coroner to decide what level of participation people are given," said Gilbert, who asked for an adjournment of the inquest to allow an appeal, but that request was refused by the coroner.

This is not the first time conditions at Brantwood have raised concerns.

"In 1986, a parent of a son at Brantwood became concerned about his care. An OACL staff person visited the residence and then prepared a 14-page report about problems with feeding, nutrition, and the day-to-day activities of this person that had implications for all the residents. This report was sent to the Brantwood board of directors and the area representative of the Ministry of Community and Social Services. However, we don't have any record of whether anything was done," Gilbert said.

The lawyer for the government, Leah Price, has refused to comment on the current Brantwood case.

Even supposedly therapeutic treatments can sometimes amount to abuse. Shock therapy, a form of treatment long popular with the medical establishment for psychiatric patients, is extremely painful and damaging. Its supporters claim, even so, that the therapy is effective in curbing self-destructive behaviour, so that its benefits outweigh the drawbacks. Mona's perspective on this was from a different angle.

Program reveals shocking reality

December 3, 1989

If you were the parent of a man who had to be tied to his bed with a football helmet on his head to prevent him from hurting himself, wouldn't you long for an alternative way to work with him?

The controversial "gentle teaching" method of American John Magee, described on this Tuesday's CBC *Man Alive* program, offers this alternative to people with mental handicaps.

Magee was sponsored on a six-month tour of Canada last summer by the Canadian Association for Community Living.

"Gentle teaching is a lot of common sense based on a very compassionate understanding of the needs of the person who is presenting some challenging behaviours," says Cameron Crawford, assistant director of the G. Allan Roeher Institute.

A scene at the self-injurious behaviour unit at the Southwestern Regional Centre near Chatham describes the various self-inflicted injuries of the residents. It is not for those with queasy stomachs.

There are various ways of discouraging this type of behaviour and most of them use the reward and punishment logic. One of the most aversive (defined as procedures unacceptable for non-handicapped) is the electric cattle prod.

"The theory is that repeated shocking—when the behaviour manifests itself—will be so aversive that, over time, the individual will come to associate the shocking with the behaviour and will stop doing it," says Crawford.

"Even animals would not be subjected to that conditioning as often ... people would cringe.

"The aggressive and destructive behaviours that the individual might manifest are very often a symptom of the acute anguish he or she is experiencing."

He points out that the aim of the person using "gentle teaching" is to establish a relationship and a reciprocal bond with the individual who is presenting challenging behaviours.

The TV program centres on two families, each with a child who has self-injurious behaviours. Tammy's family had to institutionalize her at one point, but after a week spent in a workshop with Magee her behaviour improved and she blossomed with the love and warmth he exudes.

"When Tammy was institutionalized, it cost over $40,000 a year to look after her," says Michael Gerard, a CBC producer who worked on the "Gentle Teaching" show and got to know the people involved.

"No one begrudges it, no one says we shouldn't be spending it if she needs it. Most people are saying that it's a good idea to get these persons back in the community and to close those big institutions because they dehumanize.

"Now, look at the situation of Tammy's mother Sheila, who has three younger children and is getting no assistance. Can you imagine how exhausted she is? She can't get money to hire people to work with Tammy a few hours each day. Tammy also needs at least two people to take her out. How that family survives, I have no idea. They desperately need help."

Is government deinstitutionalizing people because it's the right thing to do? *Man Alive* raises this and other provocative questions with its engrossing production of "Gentle Teaching." Don't miss it!

Shock fight setback

July 16, 1995

Supporters of the abolition of electric shock treatment on people with severe behavioural problems received a setback recently.

In Ontario both *The Consent to Treatment Act* and *The Substitute Decisions Act* state that no substitute consent can be given to the use of electric shock for purposes of aversive conditioning. This is shock delivered to the skin in sufficient intensity to make it painful.

"It is applied after unwanted behaviour, such as aggressiveness toward others or oneself, on the theory that punishment will reduce the probability the same behaviour will be engaged in again in the short term," explains Orville Endicott, legal counsel for the Canadian Association for Community Living.

A case brought by two sets of parents was scheduled for Ontario's Divisional Court in September. The parents wanted the court to order that shock treatments continue.

If it's withdrawn from use on their sons, the parents claim, they will inevitably do such harm to themselves that their "security of the person" will be threatened.

However, the case has been indefinitely postponed and a judge has issued an interim ruling allowing shock treatments in these two cases.

"We feel shock treatment is inhumane. Though it may be effective in stopping people from injuring themselves, it probably also causes them to withdraw into themselves, to be unable to relate to other people in constructive ways or begin to develop a concept of who they are. That includes being someone who doesn't have to be punished," says Endicott.

"Somehow, one can't help believing their behaviour is the behaviour of a person who feels they must be punished. If you use punishment to try and stop that behaviour, our argument is that it reinforces the belief they need to be punished."

Some persons think people engage in self-destructive behaviour as a way of saying: "Come and attend to me and my needs. Show me how much you care about me."

The Southwest Regional Centre near Chatham is the only facility in Ontario allowed to administer shock treatment.

Worried about shock therapy law

January 14, 1996

An old evil is resurfacing in Ontario, now that *The Advocacy Act* and *The Consent to Treatment Act* are being repealed.*

This legislation of the previous NDP government made it unlawful to administer aversive shock therapy to someone without his or her informed consent. It effectively abolished the practice.

"I, as a parent, can have my son declared mentally incompetent— it's not difficult to do. Then, I have the right to say he should have shock therapy. As his guardian, I have authority over him and he has no say in it," explains Nancy Stone, president of the Ontario Association for Community Living (OACL).

Shock is probably the most blatant of the aversive therapies. Southwestern Regional Centre, halfway between London and Windsor, is the only place where it's still being done on developmentally handicapped people.

In shock therapy, straps, wires and a battery pack are strapped to an individual's legs. The staff person has a remote control device. Every time the individual engages in unacceptable behaviour, like banging his head, the staff person pushes a button on the remote control to deliver a shock to the individual's legs. The theory is that it eliminates this type of behaviour.

Proponents of the therapy say it's one of the only treatments that prevents these people from seriously hurting themselves. "Of course it does, because the person is being punished," says Stone.

"My sense is that he's begging for something when he's banging his head," she continues. "The first step in a positive approach would be to find out what this person is trying to tell us. Is he bored? Does he want some attention? Then, you look at achieving the things he wants," she says.

---

* Both statutes were repealed on March 29, 1996. Subsequent enactments, such as The Provincial Advocate for Children and Youth Act in 2007, have returned to the subject, at least in part.

Some of these people were being given shocks 30, 40 and 50 times per day before the NDP brought in its legislation. Yet they did without it while it was banned for more than a year.

Disabled individuals are abused in many ways. Beyond this issue of whether to classify shocks administered to institutionalized patients as a form of abuse, Mona shone the searchlight of "Disabled Today" into even darker corners where individuals with mental disabilities are subjected to general abuse and neglect, in some institutions to rapes and beatings.

Controversial care points to abuse

April 18, 1999

"People are being abused there. They're being raped. They're being drugged. They're being beaten," says Diane Richler, executive vice-president of the Canadian Association for Community Living (CACL).

She's referring to a recent report on Quebec's Hôpital Rivière des Prairies in Laval. Though it is a psychiatric hospital, 150 people with an intellectual disability like Down Syndrome, not a psychiatric disorder, are being kept there.

Abuse wears many different faces. In Ontario this past winter, a developmentally disabled man, who is also blind and has epilepsy, lost seven fingers to frostbite after being left outside the group home where he lived. Police have charged four former employees of the home with failing to provide the necessities of life to a person under their care.

A similar incident occurred two winters ago in which a man lost a foot.

George Svetkoff of Toronto has a 25-year-old daughter, Kelly, who is both developmentally and physically disabled. She lives with another disabled woman in an apartment where they receive assistance from a non-profit agency.

Svetkoff has worked as a front-line staff person and also served on an agency's volunteer board of directors. He knows from firsthand experience about a number of controversial practices. He points to the male staff who sometime provide personal hygiene for female residents, many of whom are nonverbal and can't express their aversion to this practice.

He also speaks about staff who can be so ignorant of the medication they are dispensing that they blame a resident's weight gain on over-eating, instead of realizing it is a side-effect of the medication. In addition, Svetkoff says no one questions the honesty of agencies that have full control over the $112 monthly comfort allowance provided by government to people living in group homes and institutions.

"People who live in these places are regarded as asexual, but it's worse than that," Svetkoff said. "It's as if they were looked upon as non-persons." Svetkoff feels that the boards of directors of institutions and group homes should get more involved in their supervision.

David Pitt, regional director of the Toronto Association for Community Living, said that efforts were made to match residents with the same-sex staff wherever possible, but that it was too costly to double-shift in group homes—that is, provide one male staff for male residents and one female staff for female residents.

In the health care system, Pitt said, it is not uncommon to have a male nurse caring for females.

Keith Powell, executive director of the Ontario Association for Community Living (OACL), said there's a risk in getting boards or government more involved in the operation of group homes and institutions. "It's too easy to just parachute in and think you have the answer, point out something that's being done wrong, and then you're gone again."

He continues: "OACL and the Ontario Federation for Cerebral Palsy have founded a non-profit organization called Accreditation Ontario. It identifies standards which we are training other organizations to meet and self-administer."

These standards cover everything from quality of life to freedom of choice and are available from the OACL in Toronto.

Standards are helpful, but what do you do with people who cannot see any reason to improve or change, and a government that doesn't care?

Diane Richler of CACL says that the Shadley Commission had exposed the horrors of the Quebec hospital in 1986, yet nothing had changed 13 years later.

"When their executive director retired, we knew a very good person for the job. However, the board refused to hire him because of his commitment to the rights of people who have a disability.

"Unfortunately, the board is very much influenced by the staff who are there now. Instead of the board ordering the staff around, the staff is ordering the board around," she said.

Quebec's Health and Social Services Minister Pauline Marois said that the recommendations of the latest expose will be put into action.

Critics in Quebec and elsewhere say they've heard that promise many times before.

"It was a year ago that Canada won an international human rights award for its treatment of people who have a disability," Richler said. "But the reality is that it's no easier to live here if you have a disability than anywhere else. Often, it's harder."

– 18 –

The tragedy of Tracy Latimer

The case of Robert Latimer, who was convicted of murdering his 12-year-old daughter Tracy, supposedly because of the pain she was suffering as a result of her cerebral palsy, remains controversial in Canada to this day.

Mona was intensely affected by the killing of helpless Tracy by one on whom she depended, the one who had the most control over her well-being, her father. As someone suffering from cerebral palsy herself, and whose own life had been allowed to develop to its potential because her mother refused to accept society's polite arrangement for the equivalent of a mercy killing ("put her in an institution and forget you ever had her"), Mona identified strongly with Tracy. She took the issue seriously. She discussed it with her closest in-laws. She addressed it with people she encountered at the United Way and the Toronto Sun. She grew increasingly concerned when she saw how public opinion was becoming sympathetic to the plight of the perpetrator rather than the victim. And through it all, she wrote these columns on Tracy's death and the trials of her father.

Tragedy avoidable
November 20, 1994

Robert Latimer is both the victim and the criminal in a tragedy that all of Canada is talking about. The Saskatchewan farmer was found guilty of second-degree murder a few days ago in the death of his 12-year-old daughter Tracy, who had cerebral palsy.

I do not know the Latimer family, but I can imagine the desperation that drove him to commit such an irrevocable act.

His family were probably not given the supports they needed to cope with Tracy's degree of disability. It's likely they were isolated from other families in similar circumstances. Families gain strength from each other by sharing information and their ups and downs. Most doctors know very little about cerebral palsy. So they may have painted an unduly black picture of Tracy's future. Latimer was also like many other parents—he did not want to institutionalize his daughter. But it need not have ended with a child dead and her father going to prison.

Let me tell you a similar story. This one, however, has a different ending.

Stan Woronko of Richmond Hill is provincial chairman of the Special Services at Home (SSAH) Family Alliance, a group of parents with disabled children.

His wife has cancer and has been made more ill by chemotherapy. They need 60 hours of support per week to help with their daughter Katherine, 23, who is developmentally disabled and has a mild form of cerebral palsy. She requires help with all the activities of daily living and is nonverbal.

With typical buck-passing, Woronko was directed by the Ministry of Community and Social Services (MCSS) to go to his local Association for Community Living for funding.

It took six months of fighting with government before, a year ago, MCSS finally provided individualized funding of $40,000 per year that flows through an agency to the Woronkos.

"My experience with the Family Alliance has been that many families do not get the support they need to cope with the demands on their time, pressure on finances, and mental anxieties. People can only do and take so much. Eventually, they break down," Woronko said.

The average amount received by a family in Ontario through SSAH is $2,500 per year. Yet the average funding for an individual served by an agency is a yearly $30,000—12 times more per capita than families get.

"The government has said they are closing institutions, but this is happening very slowly. The number of beds in institutions has been decreasing and yet in the last two years, the costs for the large institutions have risen from $100 per person per year to $110.

"It is also more cost-effective to support families in their natural environment than to pay for bricks and mortar and establish bureaucracies.

"Parents, siblings and close relatives are the ones who provide the real qualities in a person's life. No matter how severely disabled a person is, he or she knows when they're loved," he said.

There are two tragedies in the Latimer case. The first one is that Robert Latimer did not know there are other options. With a program like the SSAH to provide support, he could have continued to keep Tracy at home.

The second tragedy is, of course, that Tracy was not given a voice when her father decided to end her life. I believe that very few disabled people would choose suicide despite what "experts" and others may say about the quality of our lives.

I have been writing the "Disabled Today" column in *The Sunday Sun* for eight years. I have cerebral palsy and a hearing impairment for which I wear an unusual hearing aid. My disability has affected mainly my speech and hands. I do all my typing very slowly with one finger.

When I was born more than 45 years ago, the leading Toronto paediatrician said, "Mother, this child will never walk and she'll never talk. She'll be nothing but a human vegetable. The best thing you can do is put her in an institution and forget you ever had her."

Whereupon my mother drew herself up to all of her 4-feet-10 and replied: "Doctor, I suggest you try doing that to one of your children." Then, she stalked out of his office.

Years later, she told me she thought that, even if all I was able to do was to look up at the stars at night and appreciate their beauty, surely that would be better than if I had never lived.

Eventually, I did learn to walk and talk and received a good education.

I spent some time in a sheltered workshop where I did the payroll. But I was always interested in writing and became editor of the newsletter of the Canadian Cerebral Palsy Association and then editor of the Ontario Federation for Cerebral Palsy newsletter.

My mother constantly urged me to be independent so I would not be a burden to anyone when she was gone.

My father died when I was a child and my mother has been gone for several years. I have had the grief of the deaths of my older brothers and sister.

But I am lucky to have two lovely sisters-in-law and a fine brother-in-law who keep in contact, and great nephews and nieces. I love them all dearly.

Without the services I receive from Senior Care (which despite its name serves adults of all ages) and the Victorian Order of Nurses (VON), Metro Toronto branch, I could not live independently in the community.

I'm on the boards of the United Way of Greater Toronto and the Metro branch of VON.

I feel that life is a precious gift, given not only to the beautiful and the brilliant, but to people of all appearances and capabilities. Disabled people don't wish for your pity. All we want is the freedom to live, love, and make a contribution.

Life is precious for all
December 18, 1994

One element has been conspicuously missing from media coverage of the tragedies of handicapped children being killed by their parents: very few disabled people have been asked to comment on it.

Paul Young is president of People First of Canada, a group of developmentally handicapped self-advocates. Young also has cerebral palsy. From his home in Sydney, N.S., he gives his opinion on the Tracy Latimer case: "I am sad that neither the politicians nor the general public recognize that Tracy was a person. She had the right to live, just like anyone else," he said.

The federal and provincial governments do not have the proper supports in place. For an individual to live as regular a life as possible in the community, it's necessary to have respite care, medication, transportation, and attendant services.

"There are some people who think we are not the same as everyone else because we may look or do things differently. But we are the same—we want to be needed, earn our own way, and be as independent as we can," Young declares.

He attended a segregated school for four or five years. Then he was in a sheltered workshop for 12 years. Until his parents died, he was unable to look after himself.

"I am now 50 years old, married, own a home, drive a car, and work for CBC Radio as a technician," Young said. "We deserve the same chances that other people get. Whether we're mildly or severely disabled, we have a right to everything that life has to offer."

"This is not another case of euthanasia," he stresses. "People like Sue Rodriguez made a clear, conscious choice. What choice did Tracy have? Or other people like Tracy—what choice will they have? Persons with mental disabilities are the most controlled people in the world," he said.

Tracy, who had cerebral palsy, is described by *Globe and Mail* columnist Margaret Wente as being "horribly disabled." My dictionary defines the word "horrible" as causing physical fear, disgust, or moral repulsion.

If this is how we appear to you, Ms. Wente, we disabled people have an even more formidable job of education than we thought. We must haul people's attitudes out of the Middle Ages into more enlightened times.

Unfortunately, not all disabilities are as easy on the eyes as that of Rick Hansen's. We are given no choice in this matter.

But you, Ms. Wente, are in a unique position. You can either help as we strive for greater acceptance, or place obstacles in our way—all in the language you choose to use.

What's at stake

March 5, 1995

The Council of Canadians with Disabilities (CCD) is one of three groups that have been granted intervener status in the Latimer case before the Saskatchewan Court of Appeal. Robert Latimer was convicted recently for second-degree murder of his daughter, Tracy Latimer, who had cerebral palsy.

"If the court and the public say that it is acceptable for Latimer to kill a person simply because the individual has a disability, that is a clear violation of the constitutional rights of people with disabilities to equal protection and benefit of the law under the Canadian Charter of Rights and Freedoms," says Hugh Scher. Scher, a Toronto constitutional lawyer who has a visual impairment, serves on the CCD's national committee on human rights.

The media has stressed that Tracy was in a great deal of pain and couldn't function well. But doctors felt that with an operation to fix her dislocated hip, much of the pain she was reportedly experiencing could be removed. In her brief life, Tracy very much enjoyed music, participating with her classmates at school, and laughing with her friends.

According to her teacher, she was a joy to be with.

"This case lays bare one of the biggest problems disabled people have: the way in which we are perceived by the public. The public regards Tracy Latimer only as having been severely a disabled girl without recognizing the happiness she brought to the lives of many people," Scher says.

There are thousands of people with mental and other disabilities in Canada who lead meaningful lives and contribute to society.

"CCD says the law should be upheld. The law states that where a second-degree murder conviction is rendered, there's a mandatory 10-year minimum sentence. If Latimer is given a lighter sentence, it will show people with disabilities that the law regards their lives as being of a lesser value," Scher warns.

It will also be a mockery of the struggles of the Special Services at Home Family Alliance, fighting to permit disabled sons and daughters to be raised in the loving environment of their own homes.

It will turn the recent Ontario Court of Appeal school integration victory of the Eaton Family over the Brant Community School Board of Education into a meaningless one.

It will make the efforts of disabled adults—striving to live with independence and dignity in the community—seem worthless and futile.

A dangerous precedent

May 14, 1995

The death of Tracy Latimer at the hands of her father and the public response to it signals a very grave danger.

"It has very strong parallels to the shift in attitude evident in the early months of Hitler's regime in Germany. About 30,000 people with disabilities were exterminated during the Nazi regime. However, the first 8,000 of these were voluntarily taken to the authorities by their families. If we allow those voices in support of Robert Latimer to go unchecked, we leave ourselves open to the very same kind of dynamic that led to those 8,000 deaths."

This warning is voiced by Catherine Frazee, a vice chair of the Workers Compensation Appeals Tribunal, who was previously the Chief Commissioner at the Ontario Human Rights Commission. She is also a lawyer and a wheelchair user.

People have failed to view Robert Latimer's act as the crime and murder that it is. The story has been so distorted he is like a folk hero. The March issue of *Saturday Night*, a reputable Canadian news magazine, had an absolutely outlandish account of the Tracy Latimer story. The words used to describe her were "grotesque" and "helpless." There was a total emphasis on the distortions of her body.

"Language like this completely undermines our humanity and likens us to aberrations of nature," charges Frazee.

"Instead of her spinal fusion surgery being described as the miracle of medical science it is, it was described in language that was meant to horrify and portray it as mutilation, which it is not.

Latimer's original 10-year prison sentence is now before the Saskatchewan Court of Appeal. Tracy's pain has been perhaps enlarged and magnified as a smokescreen by people who can't face the reality of disability.

"Cosmetically, some people with disabilities meet the general standard of normality better. We are a society that is influenced by image, form, and exterior appearance. Tracy had cerebral palsy. Given the media's emphasis on her pain, spasms, and uncontrollable body movements, everyone zeros in to this too," Frazee notes.

To ensure that amendments are not made to the Criminal Code that would allow for a lesser sentence for this type of crime, you should write to Canada's Minister of Justice, Allan Rock, in Ottawa. You are also encouraged to write to the Council of Canadians with Disabilities (CCD), the advocacy group who intervened in the Saskatchewan Court of Appeal.

Latimer case under review

December 15, 1996

The Robert Latimer case came to Canada's Supreme Court recently, and the court is being asked to acquit him. Approximately three years ago, the Saskatchewan farmer admitted killing his 12-year-old daughter, Tracy, who had cerebral palsy. He claimed this was an act of mercy because Tracy was suffering and it was what she would have wanted him to do if she could have spoken.

Charged with first degree murder and subsequently convicted on a lesser charge of second-degree murder, he was sentenced to 10 years in prison. In fact, he has spent only one or two days in jail since his arrest. Latimer has been defended throughout by lawyer Mark Brayford.

"I'm sure that Brayford depicted Tracy as having been severely disabled. I'm equally certain he used words that I would not want to repeat to describe her state of humanity," says Catherine Frazee.

Frazee is a spokesperson for the Council of Canadians with Disabilities (CCD) and she attended the Supreme Court hearing.

She says, "There were mistakes made by the Crown attorney's office and the police at the time of Latimer's arrest. Prospective jurors were asked their view on euthanasia. Questions like these are considered improper for the selection of a jury, particularly in a trial of this nature."

As a result, the Crown conceded that Latimer is entitled to a new trial. It is expected, therefore, that the Supreme Court ruling will be the same.

Frazee adds, "They will also rule on the admissibility of his confession. There were, perhaps, improper ways in how the police obtained it and his lawyer is asking the Supreme Court to rule that his confession is inadmissible evidence."

Latimer, however, denies killing his daughter.

"We at the CCD are very concerned that no message has yet been sent to the Canadian public whether this type of act is tolerable. As a result children with disabilities are vulnerable to the misguided, erroneous actions of their parents and others. More plea bargaining may take place and the charge against Latimer could be reduced to manslaughter with a suspended sentence."

At time of writing, the Supreme Court has not yet announced its ruling.

I and others who have cerebral palsy feel the reason Tracy's pain has been so emphasized is to justify her father's actions. He deprived her of a future in which she could have been the recipient of new medical and therapeutic skills, the enjoyment of fresh experiences and friends and, above all, an ability to love and be loved.

Father's love can work wonders

October 19, 1997

"Robert Latimer should receive the appropriate sentence for first-degree murder," declares Victor Gascom, a Metro Toronto father.

Latimer killed his 12-year-old daughter, Tracy, who had cerebral palsy.

The Saskatchewan farmer is having a second trial, starting the end of this month. At his first trial, three years ago, he was convicted of second-degree murder and sentenced to 10 years in jail.

In fact, he has spent only one or two days in prison. He's getting another trial because of errors made at his first.

Now, I'd like you to meet another father: Victor Gascom.

Gascom, who's single, adopted Bill, then eight years old, 10 years ago. Bill has cerebral palsy, uses a wheelchair, and is nonverbal.

Regular *Sunday Sun* readers may remember that I wrote about them at that time. Bill is now fully integrated in high school.

"When I first met Bill, I was taken aback—I had never met anyone so severely disabled," recalls Victor.

His friend Michael worked at a group home where Bill lived. At Christmas, all the children were invited out except Bill. Michael took Bill home for a week to the apartment he shared with Victor.

"On Christmas morning, we placed all his gifts around him. We wound up a musical toy and it woke him up with a big smile on his face. It melted my heart," says Victor.

"When it came time for Bill to go home, all I could see was this little boy going to a place where he wasn't loved.

"My love for him grew and I found it unbearable that he lived at the group home all week and I would see him only on the weekend. So, I adopted him," he says.

Bill's disability is very similar to Tracy Latimer's. However, unlike Tracy, whose life was cut short, Bill is being encouraged to reach his highest potential.

"I am constantly urging people to stop looking only at Bill's disability. He's a human being with the same rights and ability to enjoy life as anyone else," Victor says.

"When a father kills his own child, it defeats the battles most parents wage to have their children included.

"The pain that Tracy is supposed to have had has been blown out of all proportion. It's (Latimer's) only defence and is being used as a licence to kill.

"Children are supposed to outlive their parents. Now, I'm afraid of dying before Bill does—I don't want to leave him to the wolves," he says.

Lessons in love and courage can enrich us all

October 26, 1997

Tomorrow, Robert Latimer's second trial begins. He's getting another trial because several errors were made at his first.

For many Canadians, however, the guilty verdict at Latimer's second-degree murder trial should stand.

"What Latimer did was wrong," states Carol Eaton flatly.

"As a parent of a child with very similar disabilities to Tracy, I know our daughter, Emily, has life in her, joy in her, and gifts to give.

"Taking another person's life is murder. He should go to jail in the same way anyone who commits a murder goes to jail.

"There's no reason to show compassion to a man who took the life of a person just because that individual had a disability.

"From what I have read about the case, it seems to me he wasn't as much concerned with whether she was suffering as he was about not having to deal with her.

"I have the distinct impression he did not fully value his daughter. He saw her as that little crippled kid who lives with us and in terms of the extra work she caused.

"He didn't see her for who Tracy, the inside person, was," Carol says.

Carol and her husband Clayton, who live near Brantford, took their battle to have Emily integrated in public school to Canada's Supreme Court. In an example of how out of touch with the times the Court is, it ruled against them.

Despite this temporary setback, Emily is doing very well in an integrated Roman Catholic school.

Carol feels the first Latimer trial taught us all a lesson.

"As parents and persons with disabilities, we need to do much more to educate the public.

"Tracy was not a garbage heap—she was a human being with thoughts, feelings, needs and wishes like we all have. When I see television news clips of her sitting in her wheelchair laughing and hear that she loved music, I know there was a real person in there," she says.

She hopes the second trial will generate more positive awareness of people with disabilities.

"My heart goes out to all parents who are coping with children who have severe disabilities," Carol says. "I know what it's like—I know how much assistance there is and how much there isn't.

"I urge them to hang in—our children are worth it. With our support, they can become deserving citizens. We will feel our work has been worth it, every second of it," she says.

Father knows best?

June 4, 2000

Few murder cases in Canada's history have been so dangerously misleading as the Robert Latimer one.

In October 1993, the Saskatchewan farmer killed his 12-year-old daughter, Tracy, who had cerebral palsy. After two trials and various appeals, the case is going to Canada's Supreme Court on June 14.

A Voice Unheard: The Latimer Case and People with Disabilities is a meticulously researched book by Ruth Enns who speaks from her own experiences with disability resulting from polio and glaucoma. Her book shows how a little-understood disability, plus a biased media that accepted without question virtually everything it was told, has led to a distorted view of the case.

Public support for assisted suicide was high in October 1993. Sue Rodriguez, who had the steadily deteriorating condition amyotrophic lateral sclerosis (ALS or Lou Gehrig's disease), had just lost her bid for a physician-aided death.

It was in this sympathetic climate for so-called mercy killing that Latimer killed his severely disabled eldest child by placing her in his truck and turning on the gas until she died of carbon monoxide poisoning. After initially lying, Latimer later confessed his crime to the RCMP.

Like many children with cerebral palsy, Tracy had had several surgeries, some more successful than others.

She was slated for another surgery before her murder. Despite the doctor's assurance that this surgery could help Tracy, Laura Latimer, Tracy's mother, told her husband she wished for a Jack Kevorkian, the U.S. advocate of assisted suicide who was receiving much publicity at that time.

"In his confession Latimer said he decided that evening to end Tracy's life," Enns writes.

Enns also concludes that Laura effectively admitted that Tracy's life was not really a life when she testified: "Her birth was way, way sadder than her death."

As for Latimer himself, a psychiatrist pronounced him "a stubborn man with a phobia about medical intervention causing tissue damage."

Because she had difficulty in eating, Tracy was severely malnourished. At the time of her murder, she weighed only 38 pounds.

"Several years earlier," Enns recounts, "the Latimers had refused a gastrostomy, or feeding tube, for Tracy, partly on the advice of Robert's sister, a nurse, who had told them that such tubes are just the first step in prolonging the dying process."

However, many disabled people regard feeding tubes as no more unnatural than colostomies. Both sustain life.

Also, don't forget that Latimer had a fear of such devices. He considered vaccinations cruel and he was so squeamish that he had to turn over the cover of a magazine because it had a picture of a syringe on it.

Can a loving father watch his disabled daughter starve, or is this the sign of a man who is so plagued by his own phobias that he cannot consider others?

In the first trial, the jury pronounced Latimer guilty of second degree murder. The second trial saw him being given the unprecedented, lenient sentence of two years, one year to be spent in jail and the other on his farm.

At no time during either trial did the Crown call disabled people themselves, especially those with cerebral palsy, to show they could lead useful, happy lives. The media blindly followed this disgracefully one-sided presentation.

From the beginning, the story was told in such a way that linked Latimer with euthanasia, and euthanasia with disability.

The following is an entry from the journal Laura Latimer kept for the development centre Tracy attended: "Tracy had a good weekend, sat out on the deck lots. Grandma and grandpa came yesterday, Tracy was so happy to see grandma."

This doesn't sound like a child who was in constant pain as Latimer's defence lawyer claims.

I have cerebral palsy, as do many of my friends. Not one of us feels the unrelenting pain Tracy is supposed to have had. Pain is not an overwhelming issue in the lives of most people with cerebral palsy.

If the Latimers couldn't cope with a disabled child, murder was not Latimer's only option. Tracy could have lived in a group home or other facility where she had already spent considerable respite time.

When I was born, other people asked my Mother: "Aren't you sorry you had Mona? What can she ever accomplish in life?"

My mother replied: "Even if all she does is look up at the stars at night and appreciates their beauty, isn't that better than if she had never existed?"

It wasn't sad that Tracy was born. What was sad was that she was born to Robert and Laura Latimer.

– 19 –

Remarkable achievers

Mona frequently profiled remarkable individuals in "Disabled Today." Some were people without noticeable disabilities themselves who made lasting contributions, and others were pioneering leaders with disabilities whose achievements continue to inspire. All of them, Mona knew as she told their stories, could provide leadership by example.

Introducing Miss Brown

June 9, 2002

"In the tight little cavern that I live in, it is darker than dark and quieter than silence."

These are the poignant words of Mae Brown, the first deaf-blind person in Canada to graduate from the University of Toronto in 1972.

June is Deaf-Blind Awareness Month in Ontario because Helen Keller's birthday is June 27. It is appropriate, therefore, that we become familiar with Mae Brown, whose remarkable story is told in the biography *Bravo! Miss Brown* by Joan Mactavish.

Brown was born in 1935 in Thunder Bay to a poor but proud family. She had hearing and sight, but both steadily deteriorated. It wasn't until her teens, however, that she was diagnosed with neurofibramatosis, a rare disease of the nervous system, movingly portrayed in the 1980 movie *The Elephant Man*.

Neurofibramatosis is manifested by an abnormally large growth on the body that is caused by a big underlying tumour. The disease caused Brown to lose her vision completely and she registered with the Canadian National Institute for the Blind (CNIB), which took a lifelong interest in her and her abilities.

An operation to remove a brain tumour resulted in her becoming totally deaf as well. A strong religious belief and a fierce determination to be independent, plus the love and support of her family, helped to get her through this difficult time.

Brown learned Braille and other alternate methods of communication. The CNIB sent her to Texas for special training. They then engaged a teacher, Peter Saxton, who helped Brown complete her high school education.

High school teacher Joan Mactavish was Brown's tutor throughout the five years it took her to get her BA from Scarborough College. Her graduation attracted worldwide attention.

It was just 16 months later, when Brown was doing well in a challenging career, that she suddenly dropped dead. She was only 38 at the time of her untimely death.

If she had been an American, there would have been scores of books and articles written about her by now. There would also have been at least one TV movie of the week that showed a couple of her romances that went awry.

As it is now, I had never heard of her until I read this book. Mae Brown deserves more.

Activist to receive Order of Canada

July 28, 1996

Beryl Potter will be presented with a most-deserved Order of Canada in an Ottawa ceremony later this year.

She says: "I am very honoured to receive this award, but if it weren't for all the people who have worked with me through the years and the support of the public, it just wouldn't have happened.

"I am particularly grateful to my son, Dennis, who has always believed in and helped me."

Potter is a triple amputee as a result of an accident 31 years ago. One leg was removed above the knee and the other taken off somewhat higher. She also had one arm amputated. Despite all this, the feisty activist for disability rights has accomplished more than many other people without disabilities.

Potter has won 26 awards—including the Order of Ontario and the Ontario Medal for Citizenship. She's also been inducted into the

Terry Fox Hall of Fame and received an honorary law degree from the University of Waterloo.

She very much enjoys giving educational talks to school children and has a great deal of faith in their knowledge and abilities. However, she's dismayed by the apathy of disabled people. "I am wondering if anybody cares enough to carry on with the work we've been doing. The young people of today are losing many services. Why aren't they becoming angry with the way they're being treated?

"If they want to retain the benefits already achieved, they must get involved," she warns.

The outspoken advocate is also critical of the abuse of Wheel-Trans by disabled people and seniors.

"In one seniors' apartment building, if some of them are refused a ride by Wheel-Trans, they hop on the conventional transit," she charges.

Currently, Potter is being faced with one of the biggest challenges of her life. Because her legs were not amputated exactly the same length, this has caused her posture to be uneven when she sits in her wheelchair.

In turn, this has resulted in excruciating pain as swelling caused by her uneven posture presses against internal organs. It's a chronic condition that doctors don't seem to know how to relieve.

People with other disabilities are also facing more problems as they become older that cannot entirely be blamed on the aging process.

What is needed is for the medical and related professions to turn their attention to solutions or, even better, preventative measures so these difficulties, if they arise, will not be so severe.

This will enable us to retain our independence as long as possible.

Mona sent the applause meter rocketing skyward when actors with disabilities appeared on stage, in film, or on television. Her following profile of Geri Jewell showed, though, the barriers that prevent disabled individuals appearing on stage and screen.

Jewell's a gem

November 3, 1991

When Geri Jewell landed a recurring role on the TV comedy show *Facts of Life* in the late 1970s, she became the first person with a disability to be cast in a prime time series.

Jewell has cerebral palsy and she feels that stand-up comedy is a way to make her disability work for her instead of against her. She concentrates on her strengths—primarily her sense of humour—and tries to find a positive or funny aspect in every negative experience.

"The challenge was not in getting on *Facts of Life*. Norman Lear saw my act and then cast me in the series—I was in the right place at the right time. My challenge was in surviving *Facts of Life*," Jewell recalls.

"The years of 1985 and 1986 were probably the most painful ones of my life. The show had ended, my contract was not renewed, and I couldn't find a job. I was struggling—both financially and emotionally.

"I didn't know who I was. I was a role model to millions of people, yet I hadn't become a role model for myself.

"Those years allowed me to embrace who I really was, what I'm here to do, and make my peace with cerebral palsy. I learned that I can love CP, but I don't have to like it. I can love it in the same way that we love our children. We don't always like what they do, but we still love them," she said.

Now, Jewell's career is on a upswing. She's doing a great deal of stand-up comedy and recently finished taping an *Evening at the Improv* program that will air first week of December.

She's also doing training sessions all over the U.S., in connection with the new Americans with Disabilities Act (ADA). She goes into both government and corporations, and advises on how to make ADA work for them.

Workshops on health and humour—how having a sense of humour about yourself results in good mental health—are included in her work too.

Recently, Jewell has begun to wear hearing aids.

We both had a giggle when I asked her about personal relationships and she retorted: "Say, are you from the *Enquirer* or something?"

She's engaged to a writer and trainer in the field of disability. He wrote *Windmills*, an attitudinal program, and is hearing impaired himself as a result of the Vietnam War.

"I think the TV show *Life Goes On* strengthens the message that I started and I'm proud of the producers for taking the challenge. I hope that, if the series lasts another season or two, focus will be taken off Chris Burke and his Down syndrome and concentrate on who he is as a person. It's already gradually happening," Jewell said.

"Much of what you see on TV is influenced by the sponsors. I believe that people with disabilities have to be used regularly in all the media. This is only going to happen when sponsors, network heads, and other people are educated and lose their fear of disability."

Mona celebrated creation of the Terry Fox Hall of Fame as a way to feature disabled Canadians and others whose significant contributions benefited people with disabilities. She recognized the educational and inspirational value of enshrining outstanding achievements in a way that was simultaneously graced with an aura of fame, and lasting. In 1995 Mona was herself inducted into the Terry Fox Hall of Fame.

In 2009, with sadness on the part of all connected with this unique Canadian entity, at the formal behest of Fox family members, it was renamed the "Canadian Disability Hall of Fame"

Their own hall of fame

April 3, 1994

The new Terry Fox Hall of Fame in Toronto recognizes Canadians who have made extraordinary contributions to physically disabled people.

"Extraordinary means more than the usual voluntary accomplishments—it means you have devoted your life to achieving something very concrete for physically disabled people," says Vim Kochhar, chairman of the Canadian Foundation for Physically Disabled Persons.

"This could be establishing homes for physically disabled people, creating employment opportunities, encouraging disabled athletes to participate in sports, or arousing the awareness of the media. It absolutely has to be more than an ordinary effort," he stresses.

The recently opened Hall of Fame is named after the late Terry Fox because, with determination and hope, the one-legged runner raised money for cancer research with his attempt to run across Canada.

Located on the third floor of Metro Hall, the Hall of Fame is a project of the Canadian Foundation. There are pictures of the inductees, along with a summary of what each has accomplished. The first six inductees are:

- Lieutenant-Colonel Edwin Baker, co-founder of the Canadian National Institute for the Blind;
- John Counsell, a founder of the Canadian Paraplegic Association;
- Margaret McLeod, who established Cheshire Homes in Canada;
- Rick Hansen, the "Man in Motion";

- Dr. Robert Jackson, who first helped wheelchair athletes compete in Paralympic Games;
- André Viger, holder of numerous gold Paralympic medals.

Anyone in Canada—disabled or non-disabled—can be nominated for the Terry Fox Hall of Fame. The selection board is chaired by David Crombie, chairman of the Toronto Waterfront Regeneration Trust.

"In future years, we want to make certain that not only famous people are nominated for this award, but also persons who do things quietly and have not been recognized for their efforts," Kochhar says.

"From now on, a limit of three people will be inducted each year into the Terry Fox Hall of Fame."

Occasionally, international figures like Leonard Cheshire, who began Cheshire Homes for disabled people in England and saw the concept spread throughout the world, may be inducted.

Mona also wrote features on the winners of the King Clancy Award, which is given to those who promote public awareness about the potential of people with disabilities.

Gala honours for two King Clancy Award winners
February 9, 1992

David Onley has known what he wants to do since he was 11.

The popular morning news anchor and co-host of City-TV's *Breakfast Television* show chuckled as he recalled writing a school essay saying that he wanted to be a television announcer covering the space program.

Onley is one of the two winners of the 1992 King Clancy Award. It will be presented in Toronto Friday evening at the Great Valentine Gala. The event is sponsored by the Canadian Foundation for Physically Disabled persons and the Don Valley Rotary Club of Toronto.

"I've had a lifelong interest in television. When I was a youngster, I was in hospital a great deal and couldn't get out as other kids did because of my polio and the operations that followed afterwards. Therefore, television was a major source of entertainment and interaction," Onley told me.

In 1981, he wrote a bestselling novel about the space program called *Shuttle*. He also became an authority on the environment.

"Unfortunately, we have never accepted a fundamental obligation to leave the earth in better condition at the end of our generation than it was when we found it," he says.

When Moses Znaimer, City-TV's president and executive producer, offered Onley a job as the weatherman in 1984, he accepted. Then Znaimer said to him: "Now, tell me, what is this problem that you have?"

"In his own way, he was asking, "What is the nature of your disability?"' Onley explains.

"I immediately said to myself: This is a guy I know I'm going to enjoy working with. First, he asked me whether I wanted a job and then about my disability and how it would impact on the job. If all employers had this attitude, there would be fewer problems with disabled people obtaining jobs," he said.

To other disabled people who want to work in television, Onley offers this advice:

"Develop an area of expertise—become knowledgeable in a specific subject that television has a high demand for, such as business or health; enrol in the radio, television and arts courses; and remember that government is putting pressure on television and radio stations to hire minorities."

Dick Loiselle is the second King Clancy Award winner. From Halifax, he's the executive director of the Abilities Foundation of Nova Scotia with an abiding interest in sports for disabled people. Loiselle is the only person ever to serve on all three international governing bodies: International Sports Organization for the Disabled, International Stoke Mandeville Games Federation, and the Pan American Games Federation.

"My greatest satisfaction has been to see these athletes accepted as athletes—not as disabled people who are playing games," he said.

"However, I see two great challenges for the future. One is to overcome the negative aspects of the discovery that some disabled athletes were taking performance-enhancing steroids.

"The other challenge is to convince Sports Canada, the funding body, to have the same funding levels for athletes with disabilities as they do for able-bodied athletes," Loiselle said.

In the same way that the Terry Fox Hall of Fame and the King Clancy Award are inclusive in honouring notable contributors, regardless of their degree of disability, Mona likewise profiled non-disabled people whose actions were improving the lives of people with disabilities.

Legal fund is his legacy

June 27, 1993

Thanks to the life of a remarkable man, people with developmental disabilities have been left a legacy of faith and hope.

Jim Montgomerie began teaching at 17 and was a school principal in North York for many years. He became involved with summer camps for mentally handicapped people because of his experience as director of North York's day camps.

"When he turned 54, he was eligible for retirement," recalls his widow, Ann Rostrup, a professor at Seneca College.

"After serving on the boards of both the provincial and national associations for community living, he felt he could be more effective by becoming a lawyer to make legal changes happen faster for developmentally disabled people," says Rostrup.

But it was not to be. Shortly before he was to begin law school in 1985, Montgomerie died of cancer.

It was Rostrup's idea to set up a trust fund in Montgomerie's memory, to help fight injustices confronting people with mental handicaps.

The Jim Montgomerie Legal Fund is administered by the Ontario Association for Community Living, which recently launched the "A Day in Court" campaign." This money-raising venture is aimed primarily at lawyers.

"The purpose of the fund is to pay disbursements and witness fees in cases where lawyers act free of charge. The issue must be precedent-setting, so that it affects not only the individual involved but also can help other people, explains OACL staff member Linda Sullivan.

An example is the Becky Till case being heard before the Ontario Human Rights Commission, in which the York Region public school board is charged with discrimination on the basis of disability.

"There's a greater awareness among lawyers of the particular needs, such as the value of inclusion, for people with developmental handicaps," declares Rod Walsh, OACL's legal counsel.

"For every one of the lawyers who attended the opening reception of the campaign, there were three others who said they didn't go to this type of event but they would be glad to make a donation or help us with a case," Walsh says.

At the campaign reception, three lawyers—Mary Louise Dickson, Tim Gilbert, and Harry Radomski—and myself were honoured for helping to further human rights for developmentally handicapped people.

Pioneer with a big heart

June 2, 1991

Gus Ryder was more than just a great swimming coach. He also encouraged disabled people to reach their highest potential.

I first met him and his lovely wife, Phyllis, during the Saturday morning swimming lessons he had for handicapped children and adults at Toronto's Oakwood Collegiate. It didn't matter to him how disabled any of us were—if we wanted to learn to swim, he welcomed us into the water.

However, it wasn't always this easy for him to teach us.

"Back in 1930," he used to recall, "we had to hold all-night vigils outside Toronto's Board of Education offices to persuade them to give us a pool that could be used by disabled people.

"Even later on, when we built the Lakeshore Swimming Club, ignorant people would ask if we changed the water in the pool after it was used by persons with disabilities so that able-bodied people could go in it. I would tell them 'no' and suggest that they find another pool to do their swimming in," he said.

When my family moved from the area, I lost track of Ryder for a while. Then, in the late 1970s, we made contact again and began a correspondence that lasted until the middle of last year, when he began to find it tiring to write. I have always treasured his letters because they contain a sensitive understanding of what disabled people can accomplish when they are given a chance.

"Our goal has always been to prove that disabled people are the equal of anybody else," he said.

Nobody was more delighted than Ryder when I began writing this column in 1986. "Always remember that you are speaking for those who can't," he cautioned me. "You have a wonderful opportunity to bring people of various disabilities and abilities closer together."

Increasing health problems gradually prevented him and his wife from being as active as they once were. Nonetheless, he was 81 when he accepted a new challenge: giving swimming lessons to people who had strokes.

Ryder also helped many disabled people financially, through a trust fund that he and his wife set up.

He was warm and generous in his praise. He also seemed instinctively to sense when I needed a few heartening words.

"Keep up your independent spirit. If you allow it to go out, it's hard to ignite again," he wrote in one letter.

Looking back over his letters, my remembrances have been combined with a few tears and an overwhelming feeling of gratitude that I had the privilege of knowing such a fine person.

He would frequently end his letters with the words: "We are on your team. Keep punching."

It was this unequivocal belief in our abilities—sometimes long before anyone else saw them—that marked him as a true pioneer not only in sports for disabled people, but also in bringing out the best in us whatever we did. Because of him, we lead richer, more rewarding lives today.

And sometimes it was simply people in her own daily life who inspired Mona to pause and give thanks for kindnesses received.

Thanks to these special folks
October 13, 1996

In keeping with the spirit of this Thanksgiving weekend, I am going to express gratitude today to people who may sometimes be taken for granted:

All the staff at the Wheel-Trans office who continue to do their job efficiently and courteously, despite the headaches and problems of the current re-registration process. The telephone staff is to be particularly commended. They have shown monumental patience at a time when some riders, frustrated by the lack of rides, react with rudeness and anger when their ride requests are rejected.

Wheel-Trans drivers are also a special breed of people—helpful and considerate. My rides are mainly in taxis and, though there are a few unpleasant taxi drivers, the vast majority of them are cheerful and friendly with a sincere desire to be of assistance.

The Home Care Program of Metropolitan Toronto deserves recognition for its efforts, despite big budget cuts, to keep aid flowing to where it's needed the most. Some elderly neighbours of mine had a series of mishaps several weeks ago that resulted in them both needing help in some of the activities of daily living. A phone call to the Home Care co-ordinator in our area arranged, within a very short time, for them to have a temporary homemaker. This timely intervention not only allowed them to stay in the peace and privacy of their own home but also kept them out of a costly institution.

Most public libraries have an outreach program that delivers books and magazines to people who, either because of disability or age, cannot visit a library to select their own reading material. This is a wonderful service for anyone who loves to read. Their choice of books is uncannily similar to those you would choose for yourself. Thoughtful librarians also widen your horizons by introducing authors and series of books you may not have considered before.

To people involved with Wheel-Trans, Home Care, and public libraries, I wish a special Happy Thanksgiving!

– 20 –
Love and friendship

Love—whether it be the love of friends, family, or romantic partners— is an active ingredient in human life. For many people with disabilities, physical problems and issues such as mobility restrictions can make it difficult to develop and maintain loving relationships, although as Mona herself demonstrated, these hurdles can be surmounted. She devoted many "Disabled Today" columns to discussing the problems and joys of personal and intimate relationships.

Handicap no bar to friends
December 28, 1986

Everyone needs friends. They add a special joy to life that makes our days livelier and more meaningful.

Some of us who are disabled may believe that because of mobility problems and other physical difficulties, we are limited in the friendships we can form. This is only true if we possess a fixed idea of where and how friendships are made.

For example, if we think the best ways to form relationships are by attending parties and by being socially active, then many of us will be doomed to a disappointing lifestyle.

However, if we realize friendships can be made anywhere— going shopping, using transportation, attending meetings—in short, anywhere there is interaction with other people—then life becomes a series of exciting possibilities.

I know a woman with cerebral palsy who was experiencing considerable difficulties finding a clothing style she could manage independently. She wrote to United Cerebral Palsy in United States and The Spastics Society in England—to no avail.

One day she walked into a dress store near where she lived. The saleswoman was very friendly and understanding. After a while, the saleswoman found a solution to her problems: the substitution of a zipper for buttons.

"Not only was a worrisome problem solved that day, but a beautiful friendship was born," says the woman with cerebral palsy. "We have become the best of friends. Each of us gives and learns a great deal from the relationship."

Another important point to keep in mind is that we all need a variety of friends and friends of all ages. Different people make us aware of differences in our own personalities. They also bring a wide variety of perceptions that make life a constantly challenging experience.

No one has more friends than a woman I know by the name of Sarah Binns. I describe her as "Eighty-five, going on Sweet Sixteen!"

Binns became severely disabled in her early twenties as a result of rheumatoid arthritis. Today she lives in Providence Villa in Scarborough. However, until four years ago, she confounded everyone by maintaining her own apartment with a minimum of assistance. She always has visitors—even on Christmas Day. They range from doctors, political activists and horticulturalists to business people, teenagers and teachers. No matter how frequently one visits her, the warmth and enthusiasm of her welcome make her visitors feel like the privileged one.

Despite hearing and vision problems, she is both an excellent listener and keenly interested in current events. Last summer, when Toronto's baseball fever was at its highest pitch, she confided cheerfully to one fan : "I'm rooting for the Blue Jays!"

No matter how many friends we have, we need to keep making new ones. This is wise for two reasons. It not only replaces old friends lost through moving far away, death, or changing interests, but it also injects fresh ideas, thoughts, and concepts into our own lives.

How do we make new friends? Binns has a simple recipe: "Be one," she says succinctly.

Here's to fantastic neighbours: they're friends who rarely intrude

August 18, 1991

I live in the friendliest apartment building in Metro.

My neighbours are kind and considerate. Yet they never intrude, nor does my cerebral palsy cause them to question my ability to live on my own.

A task I find hard is getting my mail because I have difficulty handling keys and also on account of the fact that I have trouble reaching my mailbox, which is in the highest row. If any neighbours are around, they always offer a helping hand. When I thank them, their usual response is: "We all need a little assistance now and then."

A while ago, I woke up one morning not feeling well and decided to stay in bed a little longer. Around 9:30, there was a knock at my door. It was the superintendent, who had been alerted by one of my neighbours. Knowing that I'm normally an early riser, she had become concerned when she noticed that my drapes were still closed and asked the super to check up on me. Such thoughtful caring adds to my feeling of security.

It is Wheel-Trans that has been responsible for me meeting most of my neighbours, for during my waiting time in our front hall I've exchanged greetings with them coming in or going out.

Different neighbours are good to me in different ways. For example, a couple from England will often bring me in hot, homemade soup on the weekend when they know I don't receive Meals on Wheels. I'll never forget their heart-warming response when I told them, in 1986, that this column was commencing.

"We always knew you had it in you, Mona. All you needed was someone to give you a chance," they said with beaming faces.

Their obvious joy and belief in me added immeasurably to my own happiness.

A rule that I made for myself when I first began living on my own was that I would not seek help from neighbours unless it was absolutely necessary. This is why I have resisted some health care professionals who wanted me to ask my neighbours for everything from helping insert my hearing aid to putting drops in my eyes after cataract surgery. I don't mind requesting occasional assistance. However, to do so daily or even more frequently is not my idea of independent living.

A couple of winters ago, I was shopping in our local bakery when a blinding snowstorm blew up. I hadn't booked Wheel-Trans because the day was supposed to be fair and dry. A uniformed policeman was also in the bakery. The next thing I knew, the saleslady, who knew both of us, was asking the policeman to give me a ride home. He graciously consented and away we went.

When we arrived at my building, he helped me and my shopping cart in. Just then, we met one of my neighbours.

"Well, Mona, what was it this time? Drunk and disorderly or creating a public mischief?" the neighbour asked with a twinkle in his eyes.

It took me a long time to live that one down.

I feel that I get the best of both worlds. I observe our Jewish holidays and then, around Christmas, my neighbours bombard me with one of my biggest weaknesses—homemade shortbread.

My wonderful neighbours are one of the reasons I so enjoy living on my own.

Mona made sure her readers knew that people with disabilities could marry and lead happy lives with one another, although at the same time she also emphasized that personal bliss does not exist in a vacuum. For instance, a couple's restricted incomes caused by government rules could be a real impediment.

Anne and Rob want to marry
December 24, 1989

All that Anne Abbott and Rob Warenda really want for Christmas is to be able to get married.

They met almost two years ago through a computer bulletin board system. Though Anne, 31, is a wheelchair user, Rob, 26, is not handicapped. After sending messages back and forth, the two finally arranged to meet face to face.

"Before we met, Anne told me she had cerebral palsy and couldn't talk," remembers Rob.

Anne uses both a voice synthesizer and alphabet board to communicate. On the day that we met, she was only using her alphabet board because the voice synthesizer was being recharged.

As they sat in her cozy Thornhill apartment, it soon became apparent that Rob knew what Anne is going to say before she finished spelling out the words.

"I didn't dream he'd fall in love with me—I didn't even think he would feel comfortable around me," says Anne, exchanging a fond look with Rob. Her vivid paintings decorate the walls. She is also a writer.

Rob feels that he was lucky because he got to know her before he met her and, as a result, her disability hasn't played a major role in their relationship.

They want to marry, but here's the problem: Anne receives a monthly disability allowance of around $520 and out of this amount, she pays $150 each month in subsidized rent.

Though Rob is currently unemployed, when he is working he earns $800 to $1000 per month. If they were married and Rob's wages were $1000 a month, Anne's disability allowance would be cut to a monthly $200 to $300.

If they marry while Rob is still unemployed, however Anne's monthly allowance would be increased to around $1000.

This couple, and others like them, would find it difficult to live on the allowance alone and yet, even if Rob worked, they would be ahead by only $200 to $300 a month. These asinine rules not only penalize anyone for working, they also offer no incentive to the individual who wants to find a job and get off social assistance.

"From a philosophical perspective, one might be saying that disabled people should not be facing a social assistance system in the first place. Their coverage should be taken care of through a pension system," says John Stapleton, who is with the income maintenance branch of the Ministry of Community and Social Services.

Social assistance is based on both need and income, whereas a pension does not give any extra benefits but, on the other hand, it doesn't look at income either.

The new Supports to Employment Program does benefit some individuals but it, too, is subject to regulations and conditions.

If government were to change its short-sighted, Scrooge-like behaviour and encourage disabled people to find jobs and become independent, this Christmas and all of those yet to come would be happier and more promising ones for Anne and Rob and others like them.

Gord and Betty show marriage can work

January 25, 1987

Betty and Gordon McGhie of Richmond Hill have been married 35 years and have two sons. Both Betty and Gordon have cerebral palsy.

In Gordon's case, the disability mainly affects his speech, while Betty does not possess much strength in her fingers.

"What she can't do, I can—and what I can't do she can," Gordon said. They were married when Betty was 21 and Gordon, 31. Betty entered the marriage wanting children, as she had been an only child and knew how lonely life could be.

Tim, their eldest son, is now 33 and a physical education teacher in Pembroke. He is married with three children of his own. Bill, 30, works for Air Canada in Vancouver.

"Before Tim was born, I was a little concerned whether I would be able to handle the safety pins in diapers," Betty recalls. "This was before the days of Velcro! When I became used to them, however, the pins gave me no problem."

Betty, Gordon, and the boys did everything together. Neither Tim nor Bill gave their parents any worry. Many of Betty and Gordon's friends had disabilities, therefore the boys became accustomed to seeing various types of disabled people.

During this time, Gordon was working at several institutions for the mentally handicapped. He was originally employed on their poultry farms, then he moved indoors where he supervised a canteen at Pine Ridge in Aurora, and taught the residents life skills.

Due to worsening arthritis, he was forced to relinquish many of the responsibilities involved in caring for their home. Gordon retired in 1977. He also won the Queen's Jubilee Award that year for his volunteer activities with the residents of Pine Ridge. "Truthfully," Gordon says with twinkle in his eye, "I feel I won the award for having survived 25 years of marriage with Betty!"

Betty and Gordon both drive. Gordon remembers with painful humiliation the infrequent times when, because of the manner in which he speaks he was mistaken for being impaired—both by police and private citizens. Unfortunately, this is not an uncommon experience for people who have cerebral palsy.

Another thing that annoys the couple are able-bodied motorists parking in handicapped parking spaces. Gordon declares, "Disabled people should be deputized to give these motorists tickets!"

They have this advice for other disabled people who wish to marry:

- Never get into debt—pay as you go.
- Remember marriage is a 50/50 proposition.
- Don't have secrets from each other—share your thoughts.

If they could live their lives over again, they would seek more education. Gordon would have become a social worker.

To me, it seems they have made a remarkable successes of their lives the first time around.

Because relationships involve sexual expression and physical desires, Mona opened the lens on the interaction of sex life and disability. She also directed readers to books where they could learn more about this fascinating and essential subject.

Talking about loving
October 23, 1994

"We're a society particularly disturbed with the idea of people who have physical and/or intellectual disabilities making love, expressing their sexual desires, possibly producing children, or even being intimate with one another . . ."

The above is an excerpt from a new book, *Couples With Intellectual Disabilities Talk About Living And Loving,* by Karen Melberg Schwier. The author interviews 15 couples in Canada, the U.S. and New Zealand who talk movingly and honestly about their relationships.

The underlying theme in all of them—including the platonic ones—is a need to be close to someone, a longing to share life's ups and downs with one special person.

No one would willingly choose a life of isolation and loneliness. It's wrong, therefore, to impose that existence—either by action or attitude – on anyone else.

One of the platonic friendships is between Hoppy and Irene of New Zealand. Irene describes a friend of hers with these poignant words: "I got a friend who doesn't have nobody. She gets very sad. She don't have nobody to look after her, nobody to talk to."

Some of the couples, who are a wide variety of ages, are engaged; others are married and are childless by choice, or have one or two children.

Not all the couples remain together and there's one where the wife dies after the interview. In short, this is a slice of real life with people who experience both sadness and joy, not they-all-lived-happily-ever-after stories.

Melberg Schwier's sensitive, journalistic skills are enhanced by the fact that she's the mother of a 20-year-old son with Down syndrome and also the communications co-ordinator of the Saskatchewan Association for Community Living.

This soft cover book is must reading for parents of disabled children of all ages, professionals and caregivers with open minds, and disabled people themselves.

Loving look at sex

April 5, 1992

I never thought it would be possible to read too much about sex.

Yet when I finished *Enabling Romance*, I had the same replete feeling I get after over indulging on chocolates.

The book has a subtitle of "A Guide to Love, Sex, and Relationships for the Disabled."

It was written by the U.S. husband and wife team of Ken Kroll and Erica Levy Klein. He's a wheelchair user as a result of dystonia and she is non-disabled.

The authors mailed hundreds of questionnaires to people with disabilities and to those with disabled partners. Although all the respondents were heterosexual, Kroll and Klein feel that homosexuality and bisexuality deserve the same respect given to heterosexuality.

The first half of the book deals not only with the still prevalent myth that all persons with disabilities are asexual, but also confronts how the very idea of disabled persons having sex is distasteful to some people. These attitudes make it particularly difficult for newly disabled adults to learn what their sexual options are.

It also discusses sex where one or both partners are disabled, and masturbation. As independent living grows increasing popular, another problem is emerging: how do persons with disabilities and their attendants give each other the privacy and space that sex requires?

Some disabled people and their partners choose oral sex as an alternative to intercourse. Their descriptions of this leave very little to the imagination.

The second half of the book zeros in on specific disabilities and the adjustments required to make sex a loving and fulfilling act. A list is given at the end of each chapter of American sources to write for more information. The appendixes at the end of the book also list everything from U.S. videos to dating services. Scattered throughout are eye-catching illustrations.

The book has two conspicuous omissions: nothing is said about the HIV virus. and even AIDS is only fleetingly mentioned. In addition, too much emphasis is placed on sex and not enough on the love and relationships some disabled people find equally difficult to attain.

Despite these shortcomings, this book would be helpful to disabled people themselves and to those working with them.

Children's sexuality, a topic that causes many parents to become concerned, can generate particular anxiety for parents of children with disabilities. Mona addressed this frankly and informatively.

Sexuality concerns

November 21, 1993

More concerns regarding sexuality are faced by disabled young people than their non-disabled peers.

This will be one of the topics discussed when public health nurse Ann Barrett conducts the workshop, "Raising Sexually Healthy Children" at a mini-conference of the Down Syndrome Association of Metropolitan Toronto.

The keynote speaker will be Hamilton lawyer Randy Mazza, an eloquent advocate for people with disabilities.

"Parents must prepare their children for puberty and adolescence," declares Barrett.

"Children with disabilities are like other children—they become excited, confused, and scared about the changes that puberty brings. Boys need information about erections and sperm and young women must be prepared for periods and breast changes.

"A disability that causes bowel and bladder accidents can result in that part of the body becoming associated with many negatives. Individuals may never have been told that their body can give them pleasure," she said.

Children who are raised with a healthy knowledge of their bodies feel more in control. They can cope with the changes of puberty and realize when they are touched inappropriately.

"As parents, we should help our children learn that the sexual parts of our bodies are not dirty or bad. We also need to recognize children have many questions and a natural curiosity about how babies are made and why boys and girls are different," Barrett said.

Parents can learn to talk about these things in a matter-of-fact way. It may be very simple statements at first and then become more detailed.

With developmentally handicapped children, the language should be easy to understand and repetitious and accompanied by story books.

"Parents should be a little more explicit and clear about what they teach disabled children—even regarding such everyday functions as cleanliness—because they may not have had as much chance to pick up this knowledge from other sources," Barrett advises.

They must learn about masturbation and where it's acceptable and where it's not. Good information, sensitively provided, is essential and shows the child that the parent cares for him or her.

– 21 –
Favourite things

Yes, there were always important issues to be addressed. But like everyone else, Mona sometimes felt the urge to just relax and enjoy things. And being a columnist, she enjoyed sharing some of her particular joys with readers.

My favourite things
April 24, 1994

I'm sharing with you today some of the things I enjoy:

The look of astonishment on some politicians' faces when they meet me for the first time and discover that "Disabled Today" is actually written by a disabled person!

Curling up in the evening with an engrossing murder mystery in one hand and a hard apple in the other.

The first Friday morning of each month. That's when my local library delivers a fresh selection of books and I can't wait to see the new worlds of stimulation, entertainment and knowledge they will open to me.

Making new friends. They expand both my mind and horizons by offering interesting concepts and ideas.

Keeping old friends. They know most of my shortcomings but care for me just the same.

The company of my nephew Michael and his wife, Allyne. Their affection and encouragement have taught me that relatives can also be friends.

The phone calls and letters from my other nieces and nephews, because it's not something they are told to do but something they choose to do.

The first warm days of spring that set me free from the imprisonment of winter's heavy coats, boots and scarves.

Being a good listener. Everyone has a story to tell and maintaining an interest in other people keeps my own mind alert and informed.

Talking to people who have a well-developed sense of humour. Shared laughter is the best way of breaking barriers and can benefit any relationship.

Serving on boards of directors that welcome questions about how they provide services and are willing to be challenged on any preconceived ideas about disabled people.

Expressing my love, admiration, or gratitude to people now. They cannot appreciate these sentiments when they are dead.

Working with disabled people and parents of special needs children who do not expect government or agencies to address all their needs, but are willing to contribute some of their own energy and time to achieve what they want.

Walking barefoot on a warm, sandy beach and feeling the water lap gently at my toes.

Being greeted in the early hours of the day by one of my favourite Wheel-Trans taxi drivers saying, "Good morning, sweetheart!"

The ongoing challenge of living on my own. Despite its headaches and difficulties, the many rewards make the effort worthwhile.

PART III

The Lessons of
Mona Winberg

1

A timeless relevance

The lessons that Mona Winberg once taught and still imparts through her enduring body of work are wise and far-reaching. Her newspaper columns from the 1980s and 1990s remain relevant in three ways.

First, no other Canadian so consistently, for such an extended period, gave such close scrutiny to so many issues affecting people with disabilities as Mona Winberg did in her *Sunday Sun* columns. As a result, her writing preserves a unique record of our recent past. It even dips back into issues and ideas of the 1970s, interestingly, because Mona culled her best writing of that decade from the cerebral palsy publications *Contact* and *Partici-Paper* and recycled it in a number of her early *Toronto Sun* columns.

This archival record means that what were "current events" then are social history now, just as these columns document a record of public policy in late twentieth century Canada. The lives of people featured in Mona's columns a decade or more ago have certainly changed, but her printed words about them endure, fixed in time, the reality of a newspaper columnist's efforts to crystallize significance from the passing parade.

Today, when Ontario's Lieutenant Governor David Onley speaks about disability issues – as he is often called upon to do, rolling up to the podium in his vice-regal scooter – he likes first to consult her columns. "It's all there, the real source," he says. "Over the years, Mona Winberg dealt with everything."

The second relevance of Mona's body of written work is how it sheds light on the current disabilities front by comparison and contrast with earlier developments she reported. Because the passage of time gives an illuminating perspective to issues Mona raised, we can see where progress has been made, and where not.

Topics such as integrating children with disabilities into the educational mainstream, or creating barrier-free accessibility to buildings and transportation systems, boast substantial progress. Other issues, however, seem immutably resistant to change.

Her hard-line positions on cut-backs in government spending that affect society's most vulnerable members, the problems she identified facing individuals trying to achieve independent living, and the connection she emphasized between disability and poverty, all endure as current realities, with very little change, even in many of their particulars.

Lieutenant Governor Onley has observed that the bleak statistics Mona reported years ago have, too often, not improved in all the time since. In short, Mona's columns provide a baseline for comparing conditions and programs over time.

Third, Mona Winberg's character, presented in the Part I portrait of her solitary courage and triumph over disabilities, and preserved in Part II through her own written legacy, can ideally inspire others to pick up her torch today. A newspaper writer now covering disability issues, Helen Henderson of the *Toronto Star*, told me in July 2010, "Mona Winberg has always been my inspiration."

Helen Henderson and others were fortunate to know Mona Winberg. Perhaps someone now encountering Mona for the first time through this book will also value her life and character. She certainly inspired me by being high-minded, bright, and selfless; offering her voice to the voiceless; becoming a goad to government and a conscience for the Canadian public; showing intelligent humour, clear thinking, and devotion to family and friends; and, by no means least, having the determination to put personal discomfort and limitations aside in order to persevere in a higher calling.

Mona Winberg's kind of leadership shows how a person can take charge of her or his own life while contributing to the larger community in ways beneficial to both. Mona's pioneering ways offer an enduring example of how to live in unkind times.

Among the many lessons she imparted, six recurrent concepts in her writing are truly timeless:

- respecting human dignity by seeing people as they are,
- the radicalization of individuals suddenly disabled by illness or accident,
- the muting of advocates who slip into comfortable organizational roles,
- upholding the social compact that binds all people as one,
- accountability to ensure programs and services benefit those intended, and
- the transformative power of tough love.

Mona's own voice, and a voice for silent others

If writers are encouraged to write about something they know and teachers to stick with subjects they understand, it is because those on the receiving end are entitled to authenticity and authoritative accuracy.

Mona Winberg's life and writing were utterly entwined. She not only knew her subject, she lived and breathed it. Her views and analysis were a direct extension of her intelligent sensitivity. Her advocacy was that of a clear-eyed fighter with years of front-line experience. The authenticity of voice in "Disabled Today" was truly her own.

At the same time, however, as a solitary columnist publicizing a disabilities agenda, Mona accepted a solemn responsibility to Canada's scattered and diverse community of disabled people to be *their voice* as well.

When she first began writing for the *Toronto Sun* in 1986, renowned swimming coach Gus Ryder was delighted his long-time friend Mona would have a column. He emphasized: "You have a wonderful opportunity to bring people of various disabilities and abilities closer together." Then, like the instinctive coach that he was, Ryder helped stiffen her resolve: "Always remember that you are speaking for those who can't."

After she'd learned to speak at age six, it was still a big effort to get her words out before her listeners' patience ran out. With writing, however, no matter how long it took behind the scenes, she was able to say concisely what she wanted others to know, in a printed form that was quick and easy to read, and in a format that was reassuringly familiar.

To write was, for Mona, a ticket to ride. She first experienced how far she could go when editing and writing the newsletters for the cerebral palsy organizations, and then took a quantum leap forward when her readership became that of a major urban newspaper. Because her life-long desire to write dovetailed with the *Sunday Sun's* resolve to publicize disability issues, the "Disabled Today" column served Mona and the paper as a consistent voice in speaking truths to the powerful on behalf of those who could not.

Mona's lessons in context

This third and final part of *Solitary Courage* draws on Mona Winberg's columns in Part II to offer some overview and synthesis of the "lessons" she left behind. To do so, it is important to be clear about the context and focus of her writing.

"Disabled Today" examined government policies according to fundamental principles of justice, especially the equality guarantees of the *Charter* that give individuals equal benefit and equal protection of the law, without discrimination on the basis of mental or physical disability. "Disabled Today" publicized the operation of government on community programs when they worked well, and exposed their adverse impacts when they did not. It presented personal issues encountered by people with disabilities and their families and caregivers. It incorporated highly personal stories, both Mona's and those of people she encountered.

Such stories of individual experience with disability can be deeply moving and widely appealing. Recent books such as *The Boy in the Moon: A Father's Search for His Disabled Son* by Ian Brown and Jean-Dominique Bauby's *The Diving Bell and the Butterfly* heighten public mindfulness about citizens with disabilities. Those memoirs and many other such books, as well as similarly inspired movies, are very important for the way they touch human emotions which, in turn, can trigger constructive thoughts and actions.

However, while Mona included personal experiences to engage readers with substance and captivate them with the moving realities of people's lives, her *primary* work was to engage the larger framework of policies, the deeper operation of programs, and the very fundamentals of social and economic conditions.

Mixing criticism and praise

In doing this work, Mona followed the news and how stories got covered, how they were ignored, or how, in her view, they were distorted.

She would decry the absence of news media coverage for paraplegic sports events, and how star Canadian athletes in the arena of international disabled competitors were aggressively ignored – the kind of article on the front page of the *Globe and Mail* about the state of mind in Vancouver "now that the 2010 Winter Olympic Games are over," when the Special Olympics had not yet even taken place. She would call for more mainstreaming of people with disabilities in television programming, but also joyfully publicize breakthroughs when they did occur – a character with Down Syndrome having a major role in a television series, or a fashion model in a wheelchair appearing on CTV.

Mona did not impart her lessons by pedantic lecturing but in a more engaging mixture that added a little encouragement or cajoling to her criticism. She was forever hopeful that the misguided or misinformed could be brought around, whether to play a more constructive role as journalists and broadcasters or to perform more effectively as public officials in order to improve conditions in society for disabled Canadians.

She did not hesitate to take other columnists to task when she believed they were shallow in their understanding of what it took to live with disabilities.

For example, in her September 24, 1989 column entitled "Segregation is no solution--columnist off base," Mona challenged point-by-point *Sun* education columnist Christina Blizzard's take on the cost of integrating students with disabilities in the school system. Then she ended, "The final thing I would like to say to you, Chris, is integration needs bright people like you."

Likewise, Mona's December 18, 1994 column "Life is precious for all" took strong exception to *Globe and Mail* columnist Margaret Wente's humanistic justification for euthanasia when it involved the murder of Tracy Latimer, yet ended by cajoling the writer: "But you, Ms. Wente, are in a unique position. You can either help as we strive for greater acceptance, or place obstacles in our way—all in the language you choose to use."

These examples were typical Mona – trenchant engagement of a true cause with serious consequences, ending not with disparaging dismissal as is so easy to do, but rather with a hopeful appeal to the other columnist's higher instincts and intelligence.

Mona Winberg never ducked hard issues, and did not want others to duck them, either. In her columns about the murder of Tracy Latimer, Mona spared nothing against commentators and religious leaders who justified the killing. Indeed, when Tracy was asphyxiated by her father, Mona's became something of a minority voice, speaking out for vulnerable dependants and in favour of even-handed justice, pitting herself against a rising tide of public opinion that sought to rationalize the murder as a "mercy killing" in humanistic terms.

Nor did she avoid awkward topics, such as the sex life of people with disabilities. "Some people think that because you have a particular disability," said Mona, "you do not have the same sexual instincts everybody else does. Or they cannot come to terms with the physical challenges two people with restricted movement have embracing one another. Some people question the propriety of a person who is disabled making love with someone who is able bodied, or vice versa. Some people even think that it is wrong, or improper, for people who are disabled to make love at all, or even talk or think about it. The act seems somehow improper to them."

— 5 —

Tricking expectations to make a point

In an April 24, 1994 column Mona described how she enjoyed "the look of astonishment on some politicians' faces when they meet me for the first time and discover that 'Disabled Today' is actually written by a disabled person! I felt it was a good education for them."

From this follows a larger lesson about tricking peoples' expectations. At what point does a disability become an advantage? The phenomenon at play here is nowhere better personified, perhaps, than in the case of professor Stephen Hawking. Asked if his work in theoretical physics attracted more attention than it would have if he had not become so utterly disabled, Hawking acknowledged that the astonishment factor played a real role. Hawking, whose pioneering work in quantum physics is leavened by his sense of humour, displayed both in July 2010 at the Innovation Centre in Cambridge, Ontario, delivering lectures through an automated voice device.

Making the same point Mona did many times about her condition being "not socially acceptable," Hawking notes on his website: "One's voice is very important. If you have a slurred voice, people are likely to treat you as mentally deficient. 'Does he take sugar?'"

– 6 –

The independent living philosophy

The concept of "independent living" as pioneered by Sarah Winberg and her daughter Mona from the early 1930s into the early twenty-first century is described in Part I and detailed in Part II. Now, a few final observations help tie things together.

The idea of this independent living concept is maximum self-reliance for people with disabilities. It is clear that while independent living requires support by human services and technical wizardry in the form of assistive devices, its most important component is the integrating philosophy that organized and propelled this approach to education, housing, transportation, employment, and daily living.

Sarah Winberg, as described in chapter 5 of Part I, probably meant "self-reliance" more than "independence," but the term "independent living" carried more appeal and caught on across North America.

This concept is one of general application, not something for just a select minority. Mona stressed, at every opportunity, "The disabled must become more independent." The path she and her mother blazed was to become, Mona hoped, not a narrow trail walked by few but a wide avenue open to many thousands with disabilities.

As Mona preached its meaning, when still president of the Ontario Federation for Cerebral Palsy, "independent living" is a popular phrase among disabled persons themselves and those working with them to describe "a lifestyle where the individual takes responsibility for his or her own decisions and actions."

An essential aspect of this philosophy for independent living was its positive nature. It affirmed the dignity of an individual living with disabilities. It was courageous, not negative, about risk-taking. It certainly meant more than the bleak solitude experienced by a disabled individual who, unable to deal with the emotional pain of "fitting in," becomes isolated.

Mona emphasized that independent living "is in no way related to the degree of physical disability." That is why she valued Ann Shearer's "excellent" book *Living Independently,* because it showed how even severely physically disabled individuals can achieve the goal of independent living, provided two fundamentals exist. The first is the presence, either in the community or on a more organized formal level, of the necessary network of support systems on which a disabled individual can rely to assist with physical needs. The second is the desire on the part of the disabled person to achieve the emotional and mental strength to cope with all the challenges this lifestyle inevitably brings. This made sense to Mona, because her mother and the community had done a great deal to create "the necessary network of support systems," but she herself needed the spark provided by her sister Barbara to kick-start her into action. Unless there is a will, there is no way.

But even where systems exist, and motivation is strong, there could still be further hurdles, as Mona pointed out, such as outright opposition to independent living. Mona dealt with this in many columns. One example, to illustrate the problem, pertained to opposition within a family.

A 26-year-old man with cerebral palsy, after living three years in a residence for disabled people, "decided he would like the fulfillment of living in an apartment building where there existed a 24-hour system of support services for disabled persons." Those most reluctant for him to make this move were his own parents. "We thought that you were settled for life in the residence," they kept protesting. "Why do you want to give up that security for the risk-taking of this new lifestyle?"

Mona acknowledged that it is "natural and understandable" for parents to have such concerns. She could remember how the mother of her childhood friend with cerebral palsy expressed deep concern about the dangers of letting her daughter do things that, for the Winbergs, were part and parcel of their pioneering "independent living."

The 26-year-old man craving more independence was warned by those who "cared" about him that he was making a grave error in judgement. "I have often wondered why it is that when able-bodied people make a mistake, it is regarded as part of life," said Mona pointedly. "However, if disabled people make an error, it is treated as a catastrophe!"

Examples like that were instructive to Mona. In turn, she wanted to make the point to others that the support of one's family required a spirit that went beyond risk aversion and protective impulses. This is the idea of "tough love."

Mona credited her mother for her own independent nature and her ability to cope. "My mother called herself 'the Last Angry Woman'," she told Sandra Naiman in a 1981 interview for the *Toronto Sun's* column "Women on the Move," a half-decade before Mona herself would be writing her column in the same newspaper. "She called herself that because she always got excited about the injustices done to the underdog." One way to overcome those injustices was to ensure that a person could fend for herself, as much as possible.

To Mona, independent living was a trade off: giving up security and dependence for responsibility, effort, and freedom. This choice, she added, "may seem totally unreasonable to a casual onlooker" when it comes to practicalities. Why accept a part-time job when one's humble earnings are eaten up by transportation costs and greater wear and tear on clothes? Why choose to live on one's own, with the great amount of energy and effort this requires, when there are lifestyles that offer more ease?

"The answer to such questions," she explained, "is that no way of life is ever entirely ideal. The individual has to choose what is important to *him*, or to *her*." It was key only that this be done with the individual understanding that there was, in fact, a trade-off, and that the price for independence and freedom would be greater responsibility and effort.

– 7 –

Practicalities of independent living

After Mona moved into her own place following her mother's death in 1968, Joan Hobson, a graduate of Toronto's Wellesley Hospital school of nursing and a staff nurse with the Victorian Order of Nurses in Metro Toronto, became Mona's visiting nurse. Joan was soon inspired by how Mona was "living independently in her own little apartment," and together the two of them decided to draw up a guide for what a nurse in the community can do to help those with cerebral palsy manage on their own. It had three points.

First, it is important for the community nurse to realize she is not just dispensing medical treatment or counselling in health concerns. During her visits to the residence, "the nurse should listen, encourage, support, and share – both in the laughter and the disappointments."

Second, the nurse can assist by discussing the available community services, but should always remember that a person with cerebral palsy "is as much an individual with her own preferred lifestyle as any other person" and "allow her patient the dignity and freedom of choosing her own way of life."

Third, because the community nurse may be the only person her cerebral palsied client sees all day, "it is of inestimable value if the nurse patiently takes the time to make herself aware of any other services that she could perform." These could be just little things that a cerebral palsy person, because of her disability, cannot do for herself. "A nurse has to be realistic and understand that many persons with cerebral palsy, no matter how much they may wish to be independent, cannot manage without some supportive care or service."

Joan Hobson wound up the guide with a summation of her own philosophy about independent living, a combination of her training and Mona's influence: "It is essential for the community nurse to look upon the person with cerebral palsy not as a helpless individual but as a human being of worth and dignity, struggling to make a life for herself in the community."

From Mona, Joan had learned how the visiting nurse "is in a unique position because she has the potential to make this road a great deal easier and freer of obstacles."

Since she'd first become president of the Ontario Federation for Cerebral Palsy in the 1970s, Mona had unrelentingly carried her campaign for independent living forward with all her determined vigour. This included the practical dimensions of establishing accommodation with special support services for disabled adults.

Now that she was herself walking the talk, her advocacy became even more informed and authoritative. "I believe it is essential that we be able to provide handicapped people with their own choice of living accommodation," Mona wrote in the *Canadian Nurses' Journal*, at the editor's invitation, "whether it be residence, group home, or apartment."

Suddenly, anyone can be disabled

One of the sobering lessons here is posed by the question: When will *I* become disabled?

Many able-bodied individuals go through life thinking, thankfully, that the plight of people with disabilities is not their own. That is, until an action or an illness suddenly changes everything. The prospect that mental or physical disability is potentially in every person's future makes many lessons Mona imparted more universal than might at first seem the case.

In her April 1992 column "A Loving Look at Sex," after dealing with how the very idea of disabled people having sex was distasteful to some, Mona went on to say "these attitudes make it particularly difficult for newly disabled adults to learn what their sexual options are."

Reference to "newly disabled adults," people not born with mental or physical defects but who acquired them through accident or disease, was commonplace in Mona's writings, because she was encountering such individuals all the time.

For example, among many "newly disabled adults" mentioned in Mona's columns, she described:

The leadership of Beryl Potter as an advocate for people with disabilities. Beryl had given little thought to disability issues because she did not need to until an accident in 1965 resulted in amputation of one arm and most of her two legs. The triple amputee then founded the Ontario Active Awareness Foundation to break down attitudinal barriers to full participation and integration of those with disabilities into the community. Potter's tireless efforts, noted Mona, were enhancing the quality of life for disabled people in education, recreation, housing, and transportation.

The altered life and mature courage of Barbara Turnbull. Barbara was a teenager happily attending school while working part-time in a variety store, until suddenly one day in the 1980s she was shot in a hold-up and became a quadriplegic. Her life changed utterly, including having to go to a different community in the United States to continue her education and avoid the issues with friends and others "readjusting" to her in her Canadian locale.

The accomplishments of André Viger, Canada's most successful wheelchair athlete. André, a successful Quebec businessman, suffered spinal cord damage in a 1972 car crash when his friend, driving the car, fell asleep at the wheel. Then he became a record-breaking marathon "wheeler" with numerous gold paralympic medals and marathon awards, created the André Viger Foundation, and began making frequent motivational presentations to groups of all ages.

Ronald Satok, whose star was in the ascendant as an international artist. In 1978, Ronald suddenly became blind due to glaucoma. An artist, musician, dancer, athlete, and inspirational public speaker who'd shared the lectern in the United States with Andy Warhol, Pearl S. Buck, and Senator Hugh Scott, Satok found that when he became blind, the lights went off outside, but came on inside him. He started a school to help people with disabilities creatively express themselves.

Montreal's Nechama Werner, another accomplished artist. Nechama had reached age 36 in full flight when suddenly a massive stroke left her in a wheelchair with her left arm paralysed and just partial use of her right hand.

Randy Firth's heroic efforts to overcome blindness. Randy became blind in 1980 at the age of 20, the result of a car accident that changed the course of his life as it robbed him of his sight.

Bob Rae, sometime New Democrat premier of Ontario. Bob, today a leading Liberal member of parliament, told Mona that one of the most important things he'd learned is that disability can happen to anyone, regardless of income or background. "This was really brought home to me," he said, "when my younger brother, who in addition to having cancer, was struck by a syndrome that causes temporary paralysis. Here was somebody who, until he was 31, never thought he would be disabled."

Mona implicitly understood and had fully accepted that each of us is disabled in some way, or likely will be.

– 9 –

Seeing people for who they are

One of Mona's best lessons is the importance of seeing people for who they are.

Her writing reflects her perspective that saw the common attributes of all people, not their place on one side or the other of a community divided between "them" and "us" – those with disabilities and those without disabilities. Such social apartheid was frequently dispelled by her writings about individuals such as those just mentioned who had suddenly suffered an accident or illness that left them with a major disability.

Another illustration of "seeing people as they are" is how she emphasized the common connection, yet important distinction, between people with disabilities and senior citizens. She observed in a number of columns how each relied upon social services and special supports, caregivers, and accessible or adapted housing. She also acknowledged the mixture of contradictions when someone needs support yet craves independence, a complex state of being shared by many individuals with disabilities and by those in advancing years alike. Yet she was outspoken about the folly of lumping both groups together, whether in housing projects or under social service programs, as if their requirements were sufficiently similar to have no significant differences. Insistence on this distinction, both for practicalities in daily living and to respect the human dignity of all concerned, recurred increasingly in Mona Winberg's columns as she herself encountered new limitations with the wear of advancing years.

Seeing people for who they are is important in other ways, too, such as preventing programs for "the disabled" from wrongly lumping together individuals with dramatically different needs and wholly incompatible interests. One of the early "myths" Mona demolished in "Disabled Today" was that people with disabilities enjoy one another's company, which would be as true as all people in Manitoba wearing green shirts being joyfully compatible.

– 10 –

Teaching by the example of people's lives

In educating readers about issues relating to people with disabilities, Mona kept the focus always on the human dimension – the people living lives, not issues in the abstract. She wisely understood that integration of people with disabilities into all aspects of life would only be achieved if they were treated as individuals, not as issues.

Using the forum provided by "Disability Today," Mona introduced herself, and others, to readers. Some were people with disabilities who achieved great things; others were non-disabled people who contributed significantly to improving the lives of those coping with disabilities. A number of these lives are presented in the selection of columns in Part II under the heading Remarkable Achievers, such as Mae Brown, Beryl Potter, Geri Jewell, Edwin Baker, John Counsell, Margaret McLeod, Rick Hansen, Dr. Robert Jackson, André Viger, David Onley, Jim Montgomerie, and Gus Ryder. Friends and neighbours also frequently found their way into her columns. So, too, did her family.

Like parables, Mona told the stories of people with disabilities who were accomplishing something special in order to teach larger lessons. Examples engaged readers by their human interest. In the telling, Mona was not only publicizing progress on the disabilities agenda, but emphasizing the resourcefulness of people with disabilities.

Because Mona saw little to applaud in the political arena, and indeed boasted how she criticised all governments of every partisan hue, it is interesting to note the fate of two men she wrote about, in relation to their ability to connect disabilities and the world of Canadian politics.

Gary Malkowski was featured in a 1990 "Disabled Today" column, when he became the first deaf person elected to Ontario's legislature. Malkowski never did become the cabinet minister Mona hoped for. Yet this MPP who represented York East riding for the New Democrats did become the first deaf parliamentarian in the world to address a legislature in sign language. He did serve as parliamentary assistant to the minister of citizenship from 1990 to 1993, and to the minister of education and training from 1993 to 1995. And in 1994, when he introduced *The Ontarians with Disabilities* bill to improve service accessibility for disabled people, Malkowski became the first politician in the world to introduce a piece of legislation in sign language.

Mona tracked in other columns how *The Ontarians with Disabilities* bill introduced by Malkowski never did get passed into law, and how he was defeated in the 1995 general election. This advocate for disabled people, a pioneer in terms of deaf citizens, moved on to become an activist vice-president with the Canadian Hearing Society, his adventures recounted both in Richard Medugno's biography *Deaf Politician: The Gary Malkowski Story* and Medugno's stage play *Bigger Dreams*, as well as in more of Mona's columns.

Another individual Mona wrote about frequently was Vim Kochhar, and no wonder. Kochhar, an immigrant from India who became a whirlwind of accomplishments for people with disabilities, started up the Canadian Foundation for Physically Disabled Persons, the Great Valentine Galas to benefit people with disabilities, the Canadian Helen Keller Centre, Rotary Cheshire Homes for the Deaf-Blind, "Rolling Rampage" for wheelchair athletes, the "Why Not?" marathon for the Paralympics, and the Terry Fox Hall of Fame.

Mona and Vim were in one another's company frequently at disabled community events, including award ceremonies of several of these organizations when she was recipient of one honour or another. All the while, the progress being accomplished for people with disabilities by these many organizations in which Vim Kochhar had a guiding hand were frequently featured in "Disabled Today."

Mona never witnessed Vim Kochhar's appointment to the Senate of Canada by Prime Minister Harper on January 29, 2010, coming as it did a year after she died. Mona would surely have cheered the new role for Senator Kochhar, as she celebrated when Gary Malkowski became a member of the provincial parliament. She knew clearly how important it is to have representatives in our legislative assemblies who are inspired to speak up forcefully for those unable to do so themselves.

– 11 –

Many lessons about organizations

Mona devoted on-going attention to organizations and programs. There are observable changes in the nature of a number since she wrote about them, again the benefit of having her earlier body of work as a base-line to draw out lessons about continuity and change in structures and operations.

For example, Mona celebrated creation of the Terry Fox Hall of Fame. It would be a permanent institution to honour the Canadian youth who became a hero as he hop-ran across our vast country to raise money for cancer research, and then became a national legend when he died in his quest. The Terry Fox Hall of Fame would uphold his inspiring memory while honouring others named to it for their own significant contributions to the advancement of people with disabilities. Mona was extremely proud to be admitted herself to the Terry Fox Hall of Fame in 1995. She would not live to be surprised and disappointed when, in October 2009 as the result of legal initiatives by the Fox family, this unique Canadian centre was forced to drop his name and become re-designated the more impersonal "Canadian Disabilities Hall of Fame."

If an unfortunate change like that could touch a prominent entity like the Terry Fox Hall of Fame, it is hardly surprising that changes also touched smaller operations Mona featured in "Disabled Today," such as The Jim Montgomerie Legal Fund, Bill Alcock's Handicapped Charter & Tour Services of Metropolitan Toronto, and blind artist Ronald Satok's non-profit Satok School of the Arts, to name but three. Many philanthropic and social projects get their start from an individual who is highly motivated by personal experience. Yet unless the project grows to become more than a founder-organization dependent on that one individual's energy, time, and financial resources, it may fade away when the driving force dissipates and lack of funding exerts a terminal stranglehold.

One lesson from Mona's writing about these organizations is that, while one might lament the demise of initiatives that ride out with the life of their initial sponsor, we might also appreciate the vitality of a society where people want to make improvements in the lives of others, believe they can do so, and are free to try. Seen from this perspective, an enduring value of these columns is the documented case studies they provide of this phenomenon. Each one celebrates a vibrant and even defiant human spirit, notwithstanding disability's constraints and time's eventual toll.

Another lesson emerging here is that, sometimes, these individualistic initiatives spark a wider program or a more comprehensive policy on the part of government. This can be seen, for example, with the advances in transportation services for people with disabilities since the time Mona first publicized Bill Alcock's leadership in developing special-needs bus tours.

A third lesson may be more cautionary. Many Canadians turn instinctively to government for solutions, but it would probably be a misjudgement to think that, *if only* such projects as the ones started by Jim Montgomerie's friends, Bill Alcock, or Ronald Satok had been "taken over" by a government agency, they would have been guaranteed perpetual existence. The fact is that government programs themselves change, and even disappear, with the passage of time, something equally evident when looking over Mona's columns. While a coordinating body such as the Atlantic Provinces Special Education Authority continues to function much the same way today as when Mona described it in August 1994, other major government programs about which she wrote extensively – for example, the Canada Assistance Plan and Ontario's advocacy regime – came to an end in 1995 and 1996, respectively.

In the case of Ontario's Advocacy Act, Mona initially celebrated the concept of government-based social advocacy on behalf of vulnerable people in the community. Yet as this new advocacy regime became surrounded by controversy of its own making, which Mona detailed in several further columns during this entity's troubled and controversial life, it highlights the dynamic nature of government projects.

Not only was this self-aggrandizing public body in Ontario an operational challenge to non-governmental advocacy groups such as People First and the Advocacy Resource Centre for the Handicapped (ARCH) founded by dedicated lawyer David Baker, but the failures of Ontario's Advocacy Commission raised a deeper philosophical question about whether government-based advocacy is itself inherently flawed as a concept. Who makes the most effective champion for the vulnerable people in society?

Whatever the answer, there is no question about the on-going need for advocacy, quite apart from whether or not a governmental entity is seeking to be a player, especially in the face of further government spending cuts that hurt people with disabilities, as Mona pointed out in a number of columns. Repeal of the NDP's ill-fated Advocacy Act by the incoming government of Premier Mike Harris certainly did not remove from society those whose vulnerability calls for protectors and advocates. In time, more limited replacement legislative measures at Queen's Park readdressed this advocacy need, demonstrating in the process how government policies and programs are in constant evolution.

In the second example, the end of the Canada Assistance Plan in 1996, a much larger pattern of change was in play with the revamping of a program begun in 1966 as part of the social welfare agenda of Prime Minister Lester Pearson's government. The Canada Assistance Plan had been the funding mechanism for Ottawa's financial contributions to costs incurred by provinces and territories for their social services and social assistance programs, a number of which touched the lives of citizens with disabilities. Starting in April 1996, the new vehicle for federal transfers, which replaced the Canada Assistance Plan, was called the "Canada Health and Social Transfer."

Where the previous formula provided federal-provincial cost-sharing on a 50-50 basis for specific programs, the new plan gave a general transfer of money, called "block funding," which rolled together a wide variety of provincial and territorial programs in such fields as health, social services, and education – pretty much everything from health insurance to costs of post-secondary education. The reason for changing this system was to give provinces and territories more freedom and flexibility while maintaining a significant national level of support.

However, after this new system operated for just eight years, another change was made in April 2004 when federal transfer payments for health became channelled instead through a new vehicle called the "Canada Health Transfer," and money from Ottawa for post-secondary education and social assistance and services began to flow to provinces and territories through a newly named "Canada Social Transfer." By fiscal year 2010-2011, the total amount being transferred to provincial and territorial programs in this fashion reached a record high of $54.4 billion. Public sector programs, like private initiatives, alter with the march of time.

If a number of the foregoing lessons about programs and organizations emerge implicitly from Mona's writing about them, she also had some explicit things to say about organizations and their role in the field of disabilities. The spring 2003 edition of Community Living Ontario's publication Directions, featuring Mona's views as the lead story, noted how, within the disability community, she saw three levels of need: (i) people who live with disabilities need to have a voice, (ii) organizations that support them need to respond to that voice and work together toward a common goal, and (iii) governments need to be held accountable for how they fund supports and services for people living with disabilities.

In 2003 Community Living Ontario, the organization that began life called the Ontario Association for the Mentally Retarded until forced by those it served to change its controversial "labelling" name, was entering its fiftieth year, describing itself as "a facilitator, advocate, and leader." Mona cautioned, however, that organizations "have an average life span of about forty years. After that, there is a tendency for them to deteriorate because the original people who started the organization are tired and getting old, and somehow the people who replace them don't have the same fervour or idealism."

Mona warned that an aging organization must strive to reinvent and renew itself if it is going to push the movement forward. "One way to ensure renewal is to listen to the voice of the people, and then act. There is strength in numbers." A collective voice of all people living with disabilities will be heard more loudly than individual voices, she stated, even though lamenting "every time a unification of disability groups has been attempted, it has failed. Most groups are jealously guarding their own turf."

To what extent could a half-century old organization like Community Living Ontario be vocal about the collective needs identified by disabled people, push government for accountability in its spending, and expose all levels of government for cuts in services to people with disabilities? To do all these things required, stated Mona, that the organization reinvent itself. "If it does not, Community Living Ontario may become entrenched in what it is doing and won't see the obstacles to be faced in the future. The organization needs to look at the gains over its fifty-year history, examine what has *not* been accomplished, determine which way to go forward, and find creative ways to get there."

– 12 –

Love and reaching out

Did Mona have any lessons, either learned or to impart, about love?

She told Sandra Naiman in a 1981 interview that she'd been in love, but that to the best of her knowledge this love had never been reciprocated. "Marriage wouldn't be sensible for me," she explained, echoing the view of her late mother. "I've never dated, never gone through the whole boy-meets-girl thing. Yet I've begun to find that some men find me attractive. I can't come to terms with that."

A little later in the 1980s, when Mona was admitted to St. John's Rehab Hospital in Toronto for two weeks, she said afterwards, "Despite all the physical discomfort and mental anguish, I felt my time in hospital was a most worthwhile learning experience. It taught me that even though disabled people may have to work a little harder at gaining acceptance, the understanding and warmth that one receives in return makes any effort well rewarded."

She told reporter Enzo Di Matteo in a 1988 interview, "It has only been in the last few years that I feel I've been reasonably accepted. I find in any new situation, I'm the one who has to break the ice. And when you're naturally shy it's not easy, but you have to do it otherwise you may be left entirely alone."

As for friendship, Mona advocated the cultivation of an open mind to new possibilities. Writing on December 28, 1989, she said, "Some of us who are disabled may believe that because of mobility problems and other physical difficulties, we are limited in the friendships we can form. This is only true if we possess a fixed idea of where and how friendships are made." Mona then proceeded, in that column [republished in full in Part II], just as she did in so many others, to proffer sage advice for all, whether or not a reader was disabled, reflecting the holistic way she saw the human community.

A columnist cannot know how her subject and its treatment might alter a reader's life, any more than a singer can be aware of the special and timely ways his song might touch someone who hears it. "Little did I expect that a world would open up to me three years ago," wrote Susan Satok on a website, "when I responded to Mona Winberg's article in the *Sun* describing Ronald Satok's school and requesting volunteers."

A decade earlier, Satok, who had worked hard to make it in the international art world, had lost his sight. As a blind artist with a clear vision, he became inspired to launch the Satok School of the Arts. It was a school to "energize people's creativity" with the goal of "changing society's perception of people with disabilities by enriching the existing educational system with its emphasis on the rational side of people to the impoverishment of their creative side." Mona understandably promoted the Satok School in "Disabled Today," pitching for volunteers to help at the school. Three years later a woman who responded to that appeal had become not only Ronald Satok's assistant, but also his wife.

If there is a lesson here, beyond living life with an expectation to be surprised, perhaps it is that by seeking to do good in this world, as was Mona's purpose in writing her columns, good comes into being in inexplicable ways. Forces beyond an individual's control can abet the spirit, so fully manifested by Mona Winberg, to uphold the noble and encourage people's better selves.

Mona's take on politicians and Canada's welfare state

A fighter for people with disabilities in Canada has to come to grips with government.

Politicians of all stripes received Mona's praise if they earned it, her condemnation if that was their due.

She became acquainted with many senior political leaders and public officials personally, but that connection never prevented "Disabled Today" from excoriating them when government came up short in programs or services for people with disabilities. "There were five different governments in office during the years I wrote my column," said Mona, "three in Ontario and two nationally, representing Progressive Conservatives, Liberals, and New Democrats. I criticized them all."

Rather than overlooking problems when they involved those with whom Mona had a personal connection, she remained true to her mission. Sentiment never obstructed Mona's view when dealing with the reality of disabilities.

In addition to focusing on individual politicians, many columns dealt with the enduring structure of the Canadian state itself – the institutions, culture, programs and administrators that sail on regardless of which elected representatives may be standing on the upper deck at any given moment.

Whether she was challenging government spending cutbacks affecting people with disabilities, or "the asinine" policies that financially penalize disabled people trying to get ahead with some gainful employment (by reducing their benefits in relation to their slightly higher income), her focus was on the larger workings of government that seem beyond any levers that politicians can pull or push.

What emerges from this is that grappling with the facets of contemporary government, a major enterprise for many Canadians much of the time, is not an easy thing to do, whether one is Mona Winberg or the prime minister. It is worth remembering why the scale of Canada's governmental operation of social benefits is vast, its entrenchment deep, and its moving parts hard to change.

The development of Canada's welfare state after the Great Depression and World War II began in a quest for social justice, propelled by the visceral anger that "never again" would poor and unemployed people suffer the way they had in the "Dirty Thirties." Instead of the original specific measures to address poverty, sickness, and unemployment in a direct and focused way, however, programs designed to support vulnerable and needy Canadians were increasingly promoted to the post-war electorate by political leaders offering the financial benefits to everyone, under the guise of a "universality" principle that essentially was to ensure support at the ballot box in elections while dealing with this agenda.

This critical early shift, from specific need to generalized benefits, came about because post-war political leaders, wanting to retain public office while doing good, feared the wrath of the country's large electorate of hard-working middle-class voters. They suspected that, despite caring sentiments nobly expressed in public, many voters did not really want their tax money going to poor and marginalized people. They also feared a backlash from low-income voters if they were subject to a financial means test – called by its opponents "the meanest test of all" because of its humiliating invasion of privacy – which would have to be part of a regime of payments directed only to individuals really needing state support.

The path of least resistance was to just pay everybody, to give benefits universally, without regard to real financial need. Thus, beginning with "universality" of the so-called Baby Bonus in the late 1940s, rich mothers as well as impoverished ones got cheques in equal amounts for each baby they had, money unneeded by the former, inadequate to the latter. This was just the beginning. The universality principle was then extended to more coverages and additional benefits as election cycles came and went. Unemployment insurance was stretched into a universally available and costly support program for seasonal workers who were not unemployed. Middle-class Canadians expressed themselves "proud" of our country's social support system, ignoring the reality that poor people, including many of the country's two million people with disabilities, still remained locked below in poverty's cellar.

This soft approach to the hard problems of poverty and groups at society's margins meant that because most of the population, not just those in need, received funding, after several decades they became dependent upon it. Mona was not alone in noting how the spreading of available dollars for social spending over the entire population meant not enough money was ever focused where it was truly needed to break the cycle of poverty itself.

After many years and untold billions of dollars spent on welfare, Canada's middle-class had developed a viscerally entrenched attitude of entitlement toward benefits, government *over*spending had become structured and statutory, and Canada still was home to a large number of poor and marginalized people.

In tandem, a similar lack of long-term hard focus saw a parallel phenomenon emerge on Canada's corporate and commercial front with what were called "economic development policies" but which to many seemed little more than a welfare system for unhealthy corporations and economically stagnant regions. Whatever one's view, the dependency upon subsidies and grants, a solid sense of entitlement on the part of those receiving public funding, and ineffectual spending in government support programs for businesses and regional economic development all further added to government overspending.

Taken together, these decades-long patterns made deficit spending by governments a Canadian norm, which resulted in mounting public debt and its companion silent killer, the upward-spiralling interest payments on that growing debt that consumed billions of dollars each year. When cutbacks came, as inevitably they had to, the perversity of Canada's benefits-for-everybody welfare state came full circle. The impact of the spending cuts hurt those vulnerable citizens most needing support – the poor and marginalized citizens for whose benefit the system had ostensibly been invented in the first place.

Hundreds of times, Mona bewailed government spending cuts in her columns. Significantly, during these years when cut-backs began, a majority public opinion in Canada consistently held firm that welfare and social benefits should go to weak and vulnerable citizens who could not fend for themselves, and always people with disabilities were cited as an example of those who deserved this helping hand from government.

As a beneficiary of the welfare state, Mona understood the role of social assistance programs and financial support for those with little or no income. Her dependence on public funding, social assistance programs, adapted public transit, homecare and healthcare, accessible housing, and adaptive devices did not mean Mona uncritically embraced everything about Canada's welfare state. Interspersed among her constant alarms about how cutbacks were hurting vulnerable Canadians with disabilities, for instance, were sharp criticisms about Big Brother government, data collection programs, loss of privacy, and the patronizing attitudes of public officials.

By the early 1980s, when Mona was in her early 50s, she was paid a disability allowance by the government, and was entitled to earn only $125 above that, with anything more in earnings being deducted from the disability allowance, leaving her always with $500 a month to live on, or $6,000 a year.

"It's so vexing the way the financial system is set up," she often pointed out.

As long as the disability allowance was not seen as an equalizer for someone lacking the advantages of an able-bodied person in the marketplace, where both were competing to earn a livelihood, but was seen instead as a benefit that could be reduced even though the disability remained, disabled Canadians faced a built-in disincentive to ever get ahead. Initiative to build up a personal launching pad was undermined by the perverse workings of the welfare state. Just what lessons needed to be learned seemed clear, especially when Mona pointed out the fact that "if a disabled person is placed in hospital, the government will subsidize him more than if he is in a residence on his own."

She was upset by "the hypocrisy in the system" which penalized a disabled person for working to earn income that could help them get out of the poverty endemic to most disabled Canadian citizens.

In an April 1989 interview for *The Ryersonian,* Mona said, "I want to make clear that I'm not just asking for more money from the government. What I want the government to do is make it possible for more disabled people to become employed and get off social assistance. People who don't know much about disability think we are all taken care of by the government. They think we all live in subsidized housing and that we have no financial worries. Well, the opposite is true."

"Dollars must be found to make things happen," said Mona in 2003. "Provincial and federal governments are not spending taxpayers' money wisely, so it is important to push for accountability in government spending. Why hasn't the Ontario government been challenged on the amount of money wasted on unnecessary consulting fees while cutting vital services to people with disabilities? Our federal government should be queried on the amount earmarked for nebulous 'foundations' as opposed to the amount of money spent on people with disabilities. Then there's the waste on the gun registry. I think we've all been brainwashed into believing government doesn't have the money. I certainly don't buy that."

– 14 –
The work hard philosophy

If Mona Winberg had a philosophy of life, she said, it would be similar to that of a Canadian pioneer: *work hard*.

"All my life I've worked hard, but I feel that when a person works extra hard the rewards are extra sweet. By rewards, I don't necessarily mean that other people have to know, as long as you know you did the best you could."

"Everyone has a talent," said Mona, "disability or not. Find out what your talent is and then go for it. Don't let other people discourage you, even though they may be well meaning. No one is a better judge of your capabilities or limitations than yourself."

"Every disabled person is his or her best advocate," said Mona, almost like a mantra.

– 15 –
Human rights become real in small places

Mona Winberg's life became entwined with the quest to make equality rights real in the places people live their daily lives. Her columns championed the right of Canadians to legal equality – as guaranteed to individuals with mental and physical disabilities by article 15 of the *Charter of Rights and Freedoms* – when and where it matters.

The lesson she taught was that the principles of equality may find legal expression in constitutions and charters of rights, but they only become real if they have meaning in peoples' daily lives where they live, work, play, and travel. Where, after all, do universal rights begin? In small places, close to home, so close and so small that they cannot be seen on any maps of the world.

As Eleanor Roosevelt understood, and as this book portrays through the life of Mona Winberg, those small places *are* the "world" of the individual person: the neighbourhood she lives in; the school or college he attends; the factory, farm or office where she works. "Such are the places where every man, woman and child seeks equal justice, equal opportunity, equal dignity without discrimination," said Roosevelt. "Unless these rights have meaning here, they have little meaning anywhere."

— 16 —

Optimism and realism

A newspaper column mirrors the one who writes it.

"Disabled Today" was infused with intelligence and humour, but other qualities of Mona Winberg were equally on display. She focused on the all-important details, yet without becoming lost in personal issues to the exclusion of a wider view of the community in which we all live. She expressed a kindly humanistic view of those around her that was counter-balanced by her well-aimed criticism of those, whether government officials or members of the disabled community itself, who failed to acquit themselves responsibly.

Many of Mona's suggestions were radical, in the sense she understood the need to dig down to the often unseen root of a condition in order to really deal with problems in housing, transportation, employment, education, income, social services, and accessibility for people with disabilities to facilities and services.

When asked by the *North York Mirror* in May 1988 if she had a secret ambition, Mona replied without hesitation: "To ice skate. It looks so graceful." Then she paused for reflection. "But I don't think I have the balance. I already practically skate when walking."

She knew where ambitions must dovetail with abilities. So instead of following Kurt Browning around the rink, she continued to do what she knew she did best. Mona wrote and remained active in the community, determined to make government and the public aware of the concerns of the disabled. "I will fight for the right of all disabled people to have lives of dignity, privacy, and self-determination."

Mona experienced frustration and anger, but sought to offset those emotions by a sense of hope and her sense of humour. She seemed to have an innate balance. Her optimism was tempered by realism, her clear-eyed view of reality uplifted by an optimistic spirit.

In the end, Mona Winberg ended where she began in her very first "Disabled Today" column: "Disabled people are neither larger than life heroes nor pathetic objects of pity. We possess strengths and weaknesses, hopes and fears, capabilities and limitations, just like everyone else."

Credits

Mona Winberg co-operated fully in the preparation of this book, through many personal interviews and discussions, providing copies of documents, loan of photographs, and contact with family members and close friends for interviews. Members of the Winberg family helping round out a portrait of their aunt include her nephew Michael Winberg and his wife, Allyne Winberg, of Toronto; her niece Debbie and husband Sidney Troister of Toronto; her nephew Harold Winberg of Richmond, British Columbia; her niece Deena Baltman of Toronto, and nephew David Winberg of Delta, B.C.

The *Toronto Sun* has been indispensable in making this book possible. In particular, Mona's *Sunday Sun* editor, Michael-Burke Gaffney, offered information and insights; *Toronto Sun* director of electronic information, Julie Kirsh, assisted with professionalism and enthusiasm in providing copies of Mona's "Disabled Today" newspaper columns for republication here in book form; and Glenna Tapscott in the *Sun* library provided information.

Mona's helper Sue Skinner photocopied many clippings from her nine scrapbooks. Nicola Carty helped with an initial sorting of Mona's hundreds of columns according to themes. Dominic Farrell helped refine and organize the collected columns further.

Among those interviewed were Anne Golden, president of Toronto's United Way at the time Mona was a member of its board of trustees; Barbara Hickey, executive assistant to the United Way president, who became a close companion of Mona's; Jill Keenleyside, who met Mona when working for CBC and became a special friend for life; Orville Endicott, lawyer with the Canadian Association for Community Living, who worked with Mona on numerous issues affecting citizens with disabilities; Sheila and Harry Edgar, who first met Mona as counselors at the Woodeden summer camp and remained such devoted friends that Harry first read Mona's column before turning to see the newspaper's "other Sunshine girl."

Hon. Lincoln Alexander, who knew Mona as a friend and loved her as an inspiring human being, shared information and has graced *Solitary Courage* with his Foreword, a message from one pioneer along the frontiers of Canadian human rights about another.

Elsa Franklin helped shape the material. Sonia Holiad and Cheryl Cooper edited it. Jennifer Yiu provided communications. Heidi-Melissa Hopper oversaw production.

I am indebted to them all.

Index

About the Authors

Mona Fleur Winberg was born in Toronto, Ontario on January 27, 1932 with severe cerebral palsy. Supported by her mother's tough love, she grew up, learned to communicate, got an education, joined the workforce, enjoyed the dignity of "independent living" with support from family and service providers, and became a resilient public advocate for people with disabilities.

In the 1970s Mona Winberg overcame her innate shyness, not to mention personal reluctance to address audiences because of her speech difficulties, in order to advance the interests of people with disabilities.

In the 1980s, her forceful and intelligent efforts to make governments and the general public aware of the needs, achievements, problems, and capabilities of disabled people began reaching an even wider audience. She worked for community development on the boards of many agencies and organizations, became president of the Ontario Federation for Cerebral Palsy, and became an editor and a writer.

As columnist for Toronto's *Sunday Sun*, she won many journalism and community awards for the high calibre of her work in addressing the disabilities agenda. Recognition of Mona Winberg's contributions to Canadians included induction into the Terry Fox Hall of Fame, and her investiture into the Order of Canada.

She died in Toronto on January 19, 2009.

J. Patrick Boyer was born in Bracebridge, Ontario on March 4, 1945 and since then has been a printer, journalist, lawyer, parliamentarian, television host, and university teacher. He is author of some twenty books of biography, law, politics and history, holds a number of university degrees, and has worked as a journalist in Saskatchewan, Ontario and Quebec.

A Queen's Council, Boyer was partner in a major Toronto law firm before his election to Parliament in 1984. He chaired three parliamentary committees, and was parliamentary secretary for external affairs, and later national defense. As a faculty member in the political science department at University of Guelph, he created and taught a number of popular courses on ethics and political accountability. He has been a strong advocate for equality rights of Canadians with mental or physical disabilities.

Mona Winberg and Patrick Boyer knew each other and worked together for more than two decades, first when she was writing for the *Toronto Sun* and he was chairing the parliamentary committee on equality rights, later when he was chair of parliament's committee on the status of disabled persons, and finally as friends working on this book.

About this Book

Solitary Courage is the story of a mother's tough-love determination, her severely disabled daughter's astonishing triumphs, and a documentary record of the political battles, organizational conflicts, and human struggles that citizens with disabilities face and fight every day of their lives.

Mona Winberg became a pioneer of independent living, and emerged a leading advocate for citizens with mental and physical disabilities. Her courageous causes erupted from her deep reservoir of compassion and concern. Her unflinching challenges to the *status quo* expressed both optimism and realism about life and society. Her life is testament to the power of solitary courage.

Between 1986 and 1999 she was the only newspaper columnist in North America regularly writing about disability issues. Through her award-winning column "Disabled Today" in Toronto's *Sunday Sun*, Mona Winberg painstakingly built up a body of work of more than 600 articles chronicling front-line battles for equality. She was a realist, a wise person with a no-nonsense approach, kind but clear-eyed.

Solitary Courage begins with the story of Mona Winberg's life, followed by a representative selection of 156 of her columns organized into 20 thematic chapters, the best of Mona in her own words. The last part of the book reflects upon Mona Winberg's legacy of lessons that still connect to programs and policies touching the lives of Canadians with disabilities today.

The subjects are wide-ranging and engaging because Mona used personal examples of individuals with disabilities and news-making issues raised by their plight. She also reported on the street-level outcomes of government policies. This variety and approach to disability issues provides real education and genuine human interest, whatever a reader's background or experience.